P9-DEC-267

WHAT THE BIBLE SAYS ABOUT MONEY

WHAT THE BIBLE SAYS ABOUT MONEY

by Larry Burkett

Wolgemuth & Hyatt, Publishers, Inc.
Brentwood, Tennessee

The mission of Wolgemuth & Hyatt, Publishers, Inc. is to publish and distribute books that lead individuals toward:

- A personal faith in the one true God: Father, Son, and Holy Spirit;

- A lifestyle of practical discipleship; and

- A worldview that is consistent with the historic, Christian faith.

Moreover, the company endeavors to accomplish this mission at a reasonable profit and in a manner which glorifies God and serves His Kingdom.

© 1989 by Larry Burkett

Wolgemuth & Hyatt, Publishers, Inc.
P.O. Box 1941, Brentwood, Tennessee 37027.

All rights reserved. Published September, 1989. First Edition.

No part of this publication may be reproduced, stored in a retrieval system, or transmitted in any form by any means, electronic, mechanical, photocopy, recording, or otherwise, without the prior written permission of the publisher, except for brief quotations in critical reviews or articles.

Unless otherwise noted, all scripture quotations are from the New American Standard Bible, copyright © 1960, 1962, 1963, 1968, 1971, 1972, 1973, 1975, 1977 The Lockman Foundation.

Library of Congress Cataloging-in-Publication Data

Burkett, Larry.
    What the Bible says about money / by Larry Burkett. — 1st ed.
      p.   cm.
    ISBN 0-943497-75-2 : $11.95
    1. Money—Biblical teaching—Indexes. 2. Finance, Personal-
-Biblical teaching—Indexes. 3. Bible—Indexes. I. Title.
BS680.M57B87   1989
241'.68—dc20   89-27861
                                         CIP

Printed in the United States of America.
      1 2 3 4 5 6 7 8 — 94 93 92 91 90 89

Dedication

To the many men and women around the country
who teach and counsel on a nonprofit basis so that
others may know God's principles of finance.

Contents

Introduction / 9

Part I—Topical Index

Topic 1: Right Attitudes / 13
1.A. Positive Attitudes / 13
1.B. Honesty / 13
1.C. Humility / 14
1.D. Forgiveness / 14
1.E. Thankfulness / 14
1.F. Obedience / 15
1.G. Contentment / 15
1.H. Trust / 16
1.I. Fairness / 17
1.J. Counsel of Men / 17
1.K. Paying Vows / 17
1.L. Wisdom / 18

Topic 2: Wrong Attitudes / 19
2.A. Love of Money / 19
2.B. Bribe / 19
2.C. Pride / 20
2.D. Covetousness / 21
2.E. Greed / 21
2.F. Dishonesty / 22
2.G. Envy / 24
2.H. Partiality / 24
2.I. Disobedient / 24
2.J. Injustice / 25
2.K. Ego / 26
2.L. Futility of Riches / 26
2.M. Fear / 27
2.N. Bad Counsel / 27
2.O. Indulgence / 28
2.P. Suing / 28

Topic 3: Credit / 29
3.A. Borrowing / 29
3.B. Lending / 29
3.C. Interest / 30
3.D. Usury / 30
3.E. Surety / 30
3.F. Paying Debts / 30

Topic 4: Giving / 31
4.A. Storehouse / 31
4.B. Giving to Men / 31
4.C. Tithe / 32
4.D. Offerings / 33
4.E. First Fruits / 34
4.F. Gifts / 34
4.G. Worthless Gifts / 35
4.H. Helping Needy / 35
4.I. Giving to Get / 37

Topic 5: Family / 38
5.A. Inheritance / 38
5.B. Counsel and Discipline / 39
5.C. Provision / 40

Topic 6: God's Blessings / 41
6.A. God's Promises / 41
6.B. Counsel of God / 42
6.C. Blessings / 43
6.D. Provision / 43
6.E. Discipline / 45
6.F. Justice / 45
6.G. Wealth / 46

Topic 7: God's Curses / 48
7.A. To Wicked / 48
7.B. False Gods / 49

Topic 8: Government / 50
8.A. Church Tax / 50
8.B. Administrative Tax / 50

Topic 9: Investing / 52
  9.A.   Multiplication / 52
  9.B.   Savings / 52
  9.C.   Get Rich / 52
  9.D.   Selling / 52

  9.E.   Buying / 53
  9.F.   Profit / 55
  9.G.   Loss / 55

Topic 10: Planning / 56

Topic 11: Restitution / 57

Topic 12: Work And Wages / 59
  12.A. Work / 59
  12.B. Wages / 60
  12.C. Employee/Employer / 61
  12.D. Quality / 61

  12.E. Slothful / 61
  12.F. Diligent / 61
  12.G. Yoke / 62

Part II—Scriptural Index
  Genesis / 65
  Exodus / 77
  Leviticus / 88
  Numbers / 93
  Deuteronomy / 99
  Joshua / 109
  Judges / 112
  Ruth / 114
  I Samuel / 115
  II Samuel / 118
  I Kings / 120
  II Kings / 124
  I Chronicles / 130
  II Chronicles / 133
  Ezra / 140
  Nehemiah / 143
  Esther / 146
  Job / 148
  Psalms / 153
  Proverbs / 162
  Ecclesiastes / 183
  Song of Solomon / 188
  Isaiah / 189
  Jeremiah / 192
  Lamentations / 195
  Ezekiel / 196
  Daniel / 202
  Hosea / 205
  Joel / 206
  Amos / 207
  Obadiah / 209
  Jonah / 210
  Micah / 211

  Nahum / 212
  Habakkuk / 213
  Zephaniah / 214
  Haggai / 215
  Zechariah / 216
  Malachi / 218
  Matthew / 219
  Mark / 231
  Luke / 235
  John / 246
  Acts / 248
  Romans / 252
  I Corinthians / 254
  II Corinthians / 256
  Galatians / 258
  Ephesians / 259
  Philippians / 260
  Colossians / 261
  I Thessalonians / 262
  II Thessalonians / 263
  I Timothy / 264
  II Timothy / 266
  Titus / 267
  Philemon / 268
  Hebrews / 269
  James / 270
  I Peter / 273
  II Peter / 274
  I John / 275
  III John / 276
  Jude / 277
  Revelation / 278

About the Author / 281

Introduction

This guide references virtually every scripture on finances in God's Word, the Bible. The number of scripture verses dealing with the subject of finances should tell us what an important topic this is. But even more, our Lord tells us that unless this area of our lives is under God's authority, no other area can or will be (see Luke 16:10–12).

The guide is divided into two parts:

- **Part One** is a topical index listing every Scriptural reference by topic.

  There are twelve topics arranged alphabetically within the index and several subtopics within each topic. Example: Topic 3—Credit has subtopics dealing with borrowing, lending, interest, usury, surety, and paying debts.

  The topical index is intended for quick reference of Scripture by topic. Since many Scripture verses contain multiple topics, they may appear in more than one category.

  For each subtopic the Scripture references are found in the middle column of the page, and a brief comment is found in the right column.

  The topic and subtopic assignments have been selected by Larry Burkett based on the most common usage of each verse.

- **Part Two** is a listing of all Bible verses dealing with the subject of finances or material assets. They are listed as they occur in the books of the Bible.

  Each verse has a notation of where it is referenced in the topical index. For example, the first Scripture reference, Genesis 2:12, appears in the topical index Topic 6 (God's Blessings), subtopic D (Provision). The highlighted portion of most Scripture references is added to assist the user in locating a specific Scripture without having to read each one in its entirety.

This work is meant to be a tool to aid the users in a study of God's Word as it deals with the material area of our lives. It is not presented as an exhaustive concordance on finances, but rather a topical reference on the subject of stewardship—the management of another's property.

Part I—Topical Index

Right Attitudes

"You shall have just balances, a just ephah, and a just bath."
— Ezekiel 45:10

This topic references the Scriptures dealing with God's principles as they apply to material possessions. For instance, God requires that Christians be **honest** in their dealings with others. By referencing subtopic 1.B., Honesty, the user will find several Scriptures dealing with this subject. Similarly, if you desire to locate Scriptures dealing with fairness, they can be found by referencing subtopic 1.I., Fairness. (There are twelve subtopics.) In reality the material aspect of a Christian's life should be governed to a high degree by the "Right Attitudes."

Subtopic:	Scripture:	Comments:
1.A. Positive Attitudes	Proverbs 16:2	God weighs all motives
What God desires from	Proverbs 21:3	Justice
believers	Matthew 12:11–12	Do good to men
	Luke 9:26	Don't be ashamed
	John 21:15–17	Love God
	I John 2:15–16	Don't love the world
1.B. Honesty	Genesis 30:33	Jacob's sheep
Being honest with money in	Exodus 18:21	Honest leaders
thoughts and deeds	Exodus 19:12	Obedience
	Leviticus 19:12	Perjury
	Leviticus 19:35	Honest judgment
	Leviticus 19:36	Just weights
	Deuteronomy 17:15–17	Honest king
	I Samuel 12:3	Samuel's honesty
	Job 2:3	Job blameless
	Proverbs 3:3	Kindness, truth
	Proverbs 3:4	Good favor
	Proverbs 10:9	Integrity
	Proverbs 10:31	Wisdom
	Proverbs 10:32	Truthful
	Proverbs 11:3	Integrity
	Proverbs 12:5	Thoughts
	Proverbs 12:17	Truthful
	Proverbs 14:2	Upright fear God
	Proverbs 16:11	Honest scales
	Proverbs 19:1	Better poor than dishonest

Subtopic:	Scripture:	Comments:
1.B. Honesty—*cont'd*	Proverbs 21:29	Wicked
	Proverbs 22:1	A good name is first
	Proverbs 28:6	Better to be poor and honest
	Proverbs 28:12	Righteous triumph
	Proverbs 28:13	Confess wrongs
	Isaiah 33:15	Honesty
	Ezekiel 45:10	Just balance
	Ezekiel 45:11–12	Honest weight
	Matthew 12:35	Treasure
	Mark 10:19	Ten Commandments
	Luke 3:12–13	Collecting taxes
	Romans 13:9	Shall not steal
	II Corinthians 2:17	Don't peddle the word
	I Timothy 3:8	Deacons—honesty
	Titus 1:7	Pastor—honesty
	Titus 2:10	Pastor—honesty
1.C. Humility *Not egotistical about riches*	II Chronicles 7:14	Call for humility
	Psalms 37:11	Humble will inherit land
	Psalms 131:1–2	Heart is not proud
	Proverbs 12:9	Better to be humble
	Proverbs 15:33	Humility
	Proverbs 16:8	Little with righteousness
	Proverbs 22:4	Reward of humility
	Proverbs 29:23	Pride will bring low
	Matthew 5:25–26	Humble yourself before opponent
	Matthew 5:38–40	Turn other cheek
	Matthew 5:43–46	Love your enemies
	Matthew 6:1	Beware of practicing righteousness
	Matthew 20:25–27	First shall be last
	Matthew 23:12	Humble will be exalted
	Luke 14:11	Humble will be exalted
	Luke 18:10–14	Sinner in temple
	Acts 8:27	Ethiopian eunuch worships
	Romans 12:16–17	Associate with lowly
	Philippians 2:3	Do nothing from selfishness
	Revelation 2:9	Poor
1.D. Forgiveness *Forgiving wrongs by others*	Proverbs 24:17–18	Rejoicing when enemy falls
	Proverbs 25:21–22	Care for enemy
	Matthew 18:23–35	Forgive debts
	Luke 7:41–42	Forgive debts
	Luke 17:3	Forgive brothers
1.E. Thankfulness *An attitude of gratefulness*	Psalms 119:14	For God's word
	Psalms 119:72	For God's law
	Psalms 119:127	For God's commandments
	Psalms 119:162	For God's word
	Proverbs 18:23	Poor give thanks
	Luke 15:8–9	Found lost coin

Subtopic:	Scripture:	Comments:
1.E. Thankfulness—*cont'd*	II Corinthians 6:10	Poor but rich
	I Thessalonians 5:18	In everything give thanks
	I Timothy 6:5–8	Food and clothing
	James 1:1–2	For trials
	James 1:3	For testing
1.F. Obedience	Numbers 3:51	Moses obeyed
Willing to follow God's	Numbers 22:17–18	Balaam obeyed
directions	Numbers 24:13	Balaam honored
	Deuteronomy 5:32	Do not turn aside
	Deuteronomy 28:13	You shall be the head
	Deuteronomy 30:14–15	Choice of Jews
	Joshua 24:15	Choose whom you serve
	I Samuel 2:35–36	Faithful priest
	Nehemiah 5:11–13	Jews return property
	Psalms 101:6	God's eye on faithful
	Proverbs 1:10	Avoid sin
	Proverbs 14:34	Exalts
	Matthew 6:24	Can't serve two masters
	Matthew 7:20	Fruit
	Matthew 8:21–22	Father died
	Matthew 13:24	Sower of good seed
	Matthew 16:24	Deny self
	Matthew 19:27	Apostles' reward
	Matthew 19:29	Left family
	Matthew 24:46–47	Obedient slave
	Luke 5:11	Disciples followed Jesus
	Luke 5:28	Matthew followed Jesus
	Luke 8:18	Whoever has, will give more
	Luke 9:23	Pick up cross
	Luke 9:61–62	Don't look back
	Luke 16:10	Faithful in little
	Luke 17:31	Peril in last day
	John 21:16–17	Obedience
	Acts 5:29	Obey God rather than men
	Acts 19:19	Burned magic books
	Hebrews 11:26	Christ vs. riches
	James 1:22	Be doers of word
1.G. Contentment	Job 1:21	Lord gives, Lord takes
Accepting what God	Job 2:10	Accept good and bad
provides	Psalms 37:16	Little, but with righteousness
	Psalms 119:57	God is portion
	Proverbs 15:16	Little with peace
	Proverbs 27:7	Hungry content with food
	Proverbs 30:7–9	Neither poverty nor riches
	Ecclesiastes 5:12	Working man sleeps well
	Matthew 8:20	Without homes
	Luke 3:14	Be content with wages
	Acts 20:33–35	Paul's work
	Philippians 4:11	Be content in any circumstances

Subtopic:	Scripture:	Comments:
1.G. Contentment—*cont'd*	Philippians 4:12	Good times or bad
	Philippians 4:13	I can do all things
	Philippians 4:14	Share in Paul's affliction
	I Timothy 3:3	Free from love of money
	I Timothy 6:5–8	Nothing from world
	Hebrews 13:5	Be content
	I Peter 5:2	Shepherd without gain
	II Peter 1:5–6	Self-control
1.H. Trust	II Kings 22:6–7	Temple builders trusted
Placing confidence in God's	II Chronicles 25:6–9	Amaziah's troops
power	Job 5:24	Fear no loss
	Job 23:12	God's word
	Psalms 32:10	Trust in God
	Psalms 37:7	Wait on God
	Psalms 37:8–9	Do not fret
	Psalms 112:1	Fear God
	Proverbs 3:5–6	Trust God
	Proverbs 10:27	Fear of the Lord
	Proverbs 28:25	Those who trust prosper
	Ecclesiastes 8:12	Fear God
	Ecclesiastes 12:13	Fear God
	Lamentations 3:24	Hope in God
	Micah 6:8	Walk humbly with God
	Matthew 6:25–32	Do not be anxious
	Matthew 6:33–34	Seek God
	Matthew 7:9–11	God gives to those who trust
	Matthew 10:29–30	Even hairs are counted
	Matthew 10:37	God before family
	Matthew 21:21	Have faith
	Matthew 21:22	Believe and receive
	Mark 6:8	Take no provision
	Mark 11:24	Ask and believe
	Luke 9:3	Take no provision
	Luke 10:4	Take no provision
	Luke 12:25	Worry
	Luke 12:29–31	Do not be anxious
	Luke 12:34	Where your treasure is
	Luke 14:33	Give up possession
	Luke 18:28	Gave up homes
	Luke 18:29–30	Reward in kingdom
	Luke 22:36	Now carry sword
	John 6:27	Work for Christ
	John 12:25	Christ before life
	John 12:26	Serve Christ
	Acts 14:9–10	Faith made well
	Romans 6:16	Slaves for obedience
	Philippians 4:6	Do not be anxious
	Colossians 3:2–3	Mind on God
	II Timothy 3:16–17	Scripture for teaching
	I Peter 1:7	Proof of faith

Subtopic:	Scripture:	Comments:
1.I. Fairness *Treating others as God* *would*	Genesis 12:16	Abram treated well
	Genesis 31:39	Jacob bore losses
	Genesis 36:6–7	Esau leaves Jacob
	Genesis 45:4	Joseph forgives
	Exodus 23:3	Do not be partial
	Leviticus 19:10	Leave some for needy
	Deuteronomy 1:17	Do not be partial
	Deuteronomy 16:19	Don't distort justice
	Deuteronomy 22:1–2	Return lost goods
	Deuteronomy 22:4	Help neighbor
	Deuteronomy 24:17	Justice for alien, orphan, widow
	Psalms 19:9–10	Judgments of Lord are true
	Psalms 140:12	Lord protects afflicted
	Psalms 146:9	Lord thwarts wicked
	Proverbs 2:9	Righteousness and justice
	Proverbs 19:22	God desires kindness
	Jeremiah 22:3	Do not mistreat strangers
	Daniel 4:27	Show mercy
	Zechariah 7:9	Dispense true justice
	Zechariah 7:10	Do not oppress widows
	Matthew 18:23–35	Parable of talents
	Mark 4:24	Be careful how you judge
1.J. Counsel of Men *Willingness to learn from* *others*	Psalms 1:1–2	Avoid ungodly counsel
	Proverbs 1:5	Seek wise counsel
	Proverbs 9:9	Give a wise man instruction
	Proverbs 11:14	Abundance of counselors
	Proverbs 12:1	Love discipline
	Proverbs 12:15	Wise man listens
	Proverbs 12:17	Honesty
	Proverbs 12:25	Anxiety weighs you down
	Proverbs 13:10	Counsel is wisdom
	Proverbs 13:18	Don't neglect discipline
	Proverbs 13:20	Fools walk with fools
	Proverbs 14:15	Naive believe everything
	Proverbs 15:22	Plans fail without counsel
	Proverbs 19:20	Listen to counsel
	Proverbs 20:18	Plan by counsel
	Proverbs 24:6	Abundance of counselors
	Proverbs 27:9	Counsel is good
	Proverbs 27:10	Be loyal to a friend
	Ecclesiastes 4:13	A fool rejects counsel
	Matthew 18:15–17	Confront a Christian
	Romans 14:12	Give account to God
1.K. Paying Vows *Keeping verbal or written* *commitments*	Genesis 26:28	Isaac's covenant
	Leviticus 27:1–9	Payment for vow
	Numbers 30:2	Do what you vow
	Deuteronomy 23:21	Not to fulfill a vow is sin
	Deuteronomy 23:23	Do what you vow
	Psalms 22:25	Pay vows

Subtopic:	Scripture:	Comments:
1.K. Paying Vows—*cont'd*	Psalms 50:14–15	Pay your vows and call on God
	Ecclesiastes 5:4	Do not be late in paying vows
	Ecclesiastes 5:5	Better not to vow than not pay
	Hebrews 9:16–17	A will is for the dead
1.L. Wisdom *Seeking the wisdom of God and man*	I Kings 10:7	Solomon's wisdom
	Proverbs 1:7	Fear of God
	Proverbs 3:13–19	Wisdom discussed
	Proverbs 14:18	Prudent have knowledge
	Proverbs 14:35	Wise servant
	Proverbs 15:20	Wise son
	Proverbs 16:16	Wisdom better than gold
	Proverbs 18:15	Prudent seek knowledge
	Proverbs 20:15	Knowledge precious
	Proverbs 24:3–4	Wisdom builds home
	Proverbs 29:3	Son's wisdom
	Proverbs 30:7–9	Neither poverty nor riches
	Ecclesiastes 4:13	Poor but wise
	Ecclesiastes 6:8	Wise vs. fool
	Ecclesiastes 7:12	Wisdom vs. riches
	Ecclesiastes 9:15	Poor but wise
	Ecclesiastes 9:16	Wisdom vs. strength
	Revelation 5:12	Lamb slain receives wisdom

Wrong Attitudes

Pride goes before destruction, and a haughty spirit before stumbling. —Proverbs 16:18

Topic 2 covers the wrong attitudes regarding finances. These attitudes include "The Love of Money," meaning those whose actions reflect a greater commitment to materialism than to serving God, "Bribe," taking money to pervert justice, "Pride," an elevated self-worth because of wealth, and more.

In this topic virtually every wrong attitude relating to money has been listed. It is truly unfortunate that in our generation we see the demonstration of many, if not most, of these characteristics being presented as "normal." A Christian seeking to serve God would do well to plan a devotional series around the contrast between Topic 1 and 2. The **normal** Christian life should be found in Topic 1.

Subtopic:	Scripture:	Comments:
2.A. Love of Money *Money is more important than God*	Ecclesiastes 2:23	Vanity
	Ecclesiastes 5:10	Never satisfied
	Haggai 1:4	Self-indulgence
	Haggai 1:9	Self-indulgence
	Matthew 6:24	Two masters
	Mark 10:21–22	Rich young ruler
	Mark 10:23–26	Hard for rich
	Luke 9:25	Gain the world
	Luke 9:59–60	Bury father
	Luke 16:13	Two masters
	Luke 16:14	Pharisees—lovers of money
	I Timothy 6:9	Get rich
	I Timothy 6:10	Love of money
	II Timothy 3:1–2	Men—lovers of money
2.B. Bribe *Use of money to pervert justice*	Exodus 23:8	Don't take bribes
	Numbers 22:7	Balak's bribe
	Numbers 35:31–32	Murderer's ransom
	Deuteronomy 10:17	God cannot be bribed
	Deuteronomy 16:19–20	Don't take bribes
	Deuteronomy 27:25	Cursed takes bribes
	Judges 9:4	Abimelech bribed followers
	Judges 16:5	Delilah's bribe
	Judges 16:18	Delilah's bribe
	I Samuel 8:3	Samuel's sons' bribes

Subtopic:	Scripture:	Comments:
2.B. Bribe—*cont'd*	I Samuel 17:25	Saul's bribe
	II Samuel 18:11–12	Joab's bribe
	I Kings 13:7	Jeroboam's bribe
	I Kings 13:8	Prophet's refusal
	II Kings 16:8	Bribe
	II Chronicles 16:2–3	Bribe
	II Chronicles 19:7	God detests bribes
	II Chronicles 28:21	Bribe
	Esther 3:9	Haman's bribe
	Esther 5:11	Haman's bribe
	Job 6:22	Don't take bribes
	Psalms 15:5	Refused bribe
	Psalms 26:10	Wicked bribes
	Proverbs 17:8	Bribe is a charm
	Proverbs 17:23	Wicked receives bribe
	Proverbs 21:14	Bribe subdues wrath
	Proverbs 29:4	Bribe perverts justice
	Ecclesiastes 7:7	Bribe corrupts
	Isaiah 1:23	Rulers take bribes
	Isaiah 5:23	Justify wicked
	Ezekiel 16:33	Israel's bribe
	Ezekiel 16:34	Worse than harlot
	Ezekiel 22:12–13	Bribes for blood
	Amos 5:12	Bribes
	Micah 3:11	Leader's bribe
	Micah 7:3	Bribe
	Matthew 28:12–15	Pharisees' bribe to soldiers
	Mark 14:10–11	Pharisees' bribe to Judas
	Luke 16:1–9	Unrighteous steward
	Luke 22:4–5	Judas' bribe
	Acts 8:18–21	Simon's bribe for Holy Spirit
	Acts 24:26	Felix's bribe
2.C. Pride	Deuteronomy 8:13–14	Pride over riches
Desire to display riches	Deuteronomy 8:17	Pride over riches
	II Kings 20:13	Hezekiah's pride
	II Chronicles 32:25	Pride
	Esther 5:13	Haman's pride
	Job 3:15	Pride over riches
	Job 31:24–25	Pride over riches
	Job 31:28	This pride denies God
	Job 36:19	Riches will not save
	Psalms 10:5	Wicked are prideful
	Psalms 30:6	Pride of prosperity
	Psalms 75:4	Do not boast
	Proverbs 11:2	Pride gets dishonor
	Proverbs 12:9	Better to be lightly esteemed
	Proverbs 15:25	Lord tears down proud
	Proverbs 16:5	Proud are abomination
	Proverbs 16:18	Pride before destruction
	Proverbs 16:19	Better humble than proud
	Proverbs 18:12	Destruction for proud

Subtopic:	Scripture:	Comments:
2.C. Pride—*cont'd*	Proverbs 18:23	Rich are gruff
	Proverbs 24:17–18	Rejoicing when enemy falls
	Proverbs 29:23	Pride brings a man low
	Ezekiel 28:4–5	Pride over riches
	Daniel 5:23	Self-exultation
	Luke 18:10–14	Pharisee in temple
	I Timothy 6:17	Conceited rich
	I Peter 3:3–4	Let adornment be internal
	I John 2:16	Pride of life
	Revelation 3:17–18	Pride of riches
2.D. Covetousness	Exodus 20:17	Don't covet
Desire for what others have	I Corinthians 5:11	Covetous in church
	I Corinthians 6:10	Thieves and covetous
	Ephesians 5:5	Idolater of things
2.E. Greed	Genesis 31:30–32	Rachel stole idols
Overwhelming desire for	Numbers 11:4	Greedy
more	Numbers 11:34	Buried greedy
	Deuteronomy 7:25	Covet golden idols
	Joshua 6:18	Covet banned goods
	Joshua 6:19	Goods belong to God
	Joshua 7:1	Stole banned goods
	Joshua 7:21–22	Stole banned goods
	I Samuel 25:2	Rich Nabal
	I Samuel 25:3	Nabal's greed
	II Samuel 12:1–3	Nathan's parable to David
	I Kings 20:3	Ben-hadad's greed
	I Kings 20:7	Ben-hadad's greed
	I Kings 21:2	Ahab's greed
	II Kings 5:25	Gehazi's greed
	II Kings 5:26	Elisha's response
	II Kings 5:27	Leprosy
	Job 5:5	Schemer
	Psalms 10:3	Greedy curse God
	Proverbs 11:6	Caught by greed
	Proverbs 11:16	Woman's honor
	Proverbs 12:12	Greed causes strife
	Proverbs 23:17	Don't envy sinners
	Proverbs 25:16	Take what is needed
	Ecclesiastes 5:13	Hoarded riches
	Isaiah 56:11	Wicked—greedy
	Jeremiah 6:13	Everyone is greedy
	Jeremiah 8:10	Everyone is greedy
	Lamentations 4:2	Sons of Zion
	Ezekiel 33:31	Heart after gain
	Ezekiel 38:13	Greed of Gog
	Micah 2:2	Covet and rob
	Micah 2:9	Eviction of Jews
	Matthew 10:37	Greed makes unworthy
	Matthew 21:33–41	Parable of vineyard
	Matthew 26:15	Judas' greed

Subtopic:	Scripture:	Comments:
2.E. Greed—*cont'd*	Matthew 27:3–10	Judas' greed
	Mark 4:18–19	Parable of sower
	Mark 12:1–9	Parable of vineyard
	Mark 14:10–11	Judas' betrayal
	Luke 12:15	Beware of greed
	Luke 12:16–20	Parable of rich fool
	Luke 12:21	Lay up treasures
	Luke 16:14	Pharisees loved money
	Acts 16:16	Greed—slave girl
	Acts 16:19	Profit gone
	Acts 19:24–26	Demetrius' greed
	Romans 1:29	Filled with greed
	Romans 2:22	Rob temples?
	Ephesians 5:3	Avoid greed
	I Thessalonians 2:5	Pretext of greed
	I Timothy 6:5–8	Gain from teaching
	Titus 1:11	Teach for sordid gain
	James 4:1–2	Lust, greed
	James 4:3	Wrong motives
	II Peter 2:3	Greed will exploit
	II Peter 2:14	Trained in greed
	Jude 11	Balaam's error
	Revelation 18:3	Greed of merchants
2.F. Dishonesty	Genesis 27:35–36	Jacob's deceit
Perverted in heart	Genesis 29:25	Laban's deceit
	Genesis 31:7	Laban's deceit
	Genesis 31:11–12	Laban's deceit
	Genesis 31:19	Rachel's deceit
	Genesis 31:20	Jacob's deceit
	Exodus 20:15	Shall not steal
	Leviticus 19:11	Do not steal
	Deuteronomy 25:13–15	Differing weight
	Deuteronomy 27:17	Move boundary
	Deuteronomy 27:18	Mislead blind
	Deuteronomy 27:19	Cheats widows, orphans
	Joshua 7:11	Jews' deceit
	II Kings 5:25–27	Gehazi's dishonesty
	Job 5:5	Schemer
	Job 20:18–20	Illegal riches
	Psalms 101:7	Lies separate us from God
	Psalms 119:36	Dishonest gain
	Psalms 119:113	Double-minded
	Psalms 120:2	Lying tongue
	Proverbs 2:12	Perverse ways
	Proverbs 2:15	Crooked paths, devious
	Proverbs 3:32	Crooked
	Proverbs 4:24	Deceitful mouth
	Proverbs 6:12	False mouth
	Proverbs 6:13	Winks eye
	Proverbs 6:16–19	Six things God hates
	Proverbs 10:2	Ill-gotten gain

Subtopic:	Scripture:	Comments:
2.F. Dishonesty—*cont'd*	Proverbs 10:10	He who winks
	Proverbs 10:31	Lying tongue
	Proverbs 11:1	False balance
	Proverbs 11:20	Perverse
	Proverbs 12:22	Lying lips
	Proverbs 13:11	Fraud
	Proverbs 15:27	Illicit gain
	Proverbs 16:30	Winks eye
	Proverbs 18:8	Words of whisper
	Proverbs 19:9	False witness
	Proverbs 20:10	Differing weight
	Proverbs 20:14	Double-tongued
	Proverbs 20:17	Lying to gain
	Proverbs 20:23	Differing weights
	Proverbs 21:6	Gain by lying
	Proverbs 21:29	Wicked are bold
	Proverbs 22:28	Move boundaries
	Proverbs 24:8	A schemer
	Proverbs 26:18–19	Deceit
	Proverbs 26:28	Lying tongue
	Proverbs 28:6	Rich crook
	Proverbs 28:9	Prayers are abomination
	Proverbs 28:12	Wicked rise—men hide
	Proverbs 28:13	Deception
	Isaiah 59:4	Deceit
	Jeremiah 8:10	Priest's deceit
	Jeremiah 9:4	Craftiness
	Jeremiah 17:9	Heart is deceitful
	Jeremiah 22:17	Dishonest gain
	Ezekiel 28:18	Deceit in trade
	Daniel 11:24	Schemes against stronghold
	Daniel 11:28	King's heart against Holy covenant
	Hosea 12:7	False balance
	Hosea 12:8	No dishonesty
	Amos 8:5–6	Dishonest scales
	Obadiah 1:5	Thieves
	Obadiah 1:16	Wealth
	Micah 2:9	Evict widow
	Micah 6:10–12	False scales
	Habakkuk 2:9	Evil gain
	Habakkuk 2:19	No life in idols
	Matthew 12:35	Evil men bring evil
	Matthew 15:19	Thieves, liars
	Luke 16:1–9	Parable of unrighteous steward
	Acts 5:1–10	Ananias and Sapphira
	Romans 2:21	Do you steal?
	I Corinthians 6:10	Thieves won't enter
	Ephesians 4:14	Avoid deceitfulness
	Ephesians 4:28	Steal no more
	Colossians 2:23	Appearance of wisdom

Subtopic:	Scripture:	Comments:
2.F. Dishonesty—*cont'd*	I Timothy 3:8	Deacons
	I Peter 4:15	Thief
	II Peter 2:15	Followed Balaam
2.G. Envy	Genesis 27:41	Esau's envy
Jealousy over what others	Genesis 31:1	Laban's sons
have	Psalms 37:1	Envy of wrongdoers
	Psalms 73:2–3	Envy of arrogant
	Proverbs 23:17	Don't envy sinners
	Proverbs 24:1	Don't envy evil
	Proverbs 24:19–20	Don't envy wicked
	Ecclesiastes 4:4	Rivalry—envy
	Matthew 20:1–16	Parable of the vineyard
	Luke 7:25	Luxury
	Acts 7:9	Joseph's brothers
	James 4:1–2	Lust
	James 4:3	Wrong motives
	I Peter 2:1	Put aside all guile
2.H. Partiality	Psalms 82:2	Judge unjustly
Giving unreasonable favor to	Psalms 82:3	Justice to poor
someone	Psalms 82:4	Rescue needy
	Proverbs 14:20	Many love rich
	Proverbs 19:4	Wealth adds friends
	Proverbs 19:7	Brothers hate poor
	Proverbs 24:23	Partiality is wrong
	Proverbs 28:21	Partiality is wrong
	Matthew 12:7	Don't condemn innocent
	Luke 6:41	Speck vs. log
	Luke 7:25	Luxury
	Colossians 2:16	Let no one be judged
2.I. Disobedient	Exodus 17:2–3	Jews test God
Ignoring God's direction	Numbers 11:20	Jews reject God
	Deuteronomy 8:20	Would not listen to God
	Joshua 18:3	Israel's disobedience
	Judges 4:9	Barak's timidity
	Judges 8:27	Gideon's ephod
	Judges 17:2–4	Micah's theft
	I Samuel 15:21	Israel took spoil
	I Kings 12:28	Jeroboam's idols
	II Kings 17:7–9	Israel sinned against God
	II Kings 17:17	Evil in sight of God
	II Chronicles 13:8	Israel's rebellion
	II Chronicles 16:9	The eyes of the Lord
	Ezra 10:8	Disobey elders—forfeit goods
	Job 21:15	Challenge to God's authority
	Job 21:16	Wicked's counsel
	Psalms 66:18	God will not fear
	Proverbs 15:10	Hates reproof
	Isaiah 43:23–24	Israel's lack of offerings
	Jeremiah 22:21	Disobey God

Subtopic:	Scripture:	Comments:
2.I. Disobedient—*cont'd*	Luke 16:11	Unfaithful with money
	Luke 16:12	Unfaithful with borrowed money
	Revelation 9:20	Unrepentant
2.J. Injustice	Genesis 37:26–28	Joseph sold
Taking unfair advantage	Leviticus 19:15	Injustice in judgment
	Deuteronomy 24:17	No justice for widows
	II Samuel 12:4–6	Parable to David
	Esther 3:11, 13	Haman oppresses Jews
	Esther 4:7	Haman oppresses Jews
	Job 6:27	Cast lots for orphans
	Job 12:6	Destroyers prosper
	Job 20:18–22	Persecutor will not prosper
	Job 24:3–4	Rob needy
	Job 24:9–10	Afflict, rob poor
	Job 24:14	Poor, needy
	Psalms 10:2	Wicked
	Psalms 14:1	No one does good
	Psalms 82:2	Judge unjustly
	Psalms 82:3–4	Rescue poor
	Psalms 109:16	Persecute needy
	Proverbs 1:13–14	Deceptive profits
	Proverbs 1:19	Gain by violence
	Proverbs 13:23	Injustice to poor
	Proverbs 14:20	Poor is hated
	Proverbs 16:8	Injustice
	Proverbs 17:5	Mock poor
	Proverbs 19:7	Brothers hate poor
	Proverbs 22:16	Oppressor of poor
	Proverbs 22:22	Do not rob poor
	Proverbs 22:23	Lord intercedes for poor
	Proverbs 23:10–11	Move boundaries
	Proverbs 28:3	Poor oppressing poor
	Proverbs 28:16	Oppressive leader
	Proverbs 31:7	Poverty
	Ecclesiastes 5:8	Oppression of the poor
	Ecclesiastes 7:7	Oppression makes wise angry
	Ecclesiastes 10:6	Fools are exalted
	Isaiah 3:15	Oppression of poor
	Isaiah 10:1–2	Unjust decisions
	Isaiah 57:17	Unjust gain
	Jeremiah 5:28	Oppress poor
	Jeremiah 17:11	Unjust is a fool
	Lamentations 3:35–36	Defraud in lawsuit
	Ezekiel 22:25	Prophets conspire
	Ezekiel 22:29	People wrong poor
	Daniel 11:20	Oppressor through jewel of kingdom
	Amos 2:6–7	Sell righteous for money
	Amos 4:1	Bashan's oppression of poor
	Amos 5:11	Excessive rent on poor

Subtopic:	Scripture:	Comments:
2.J. Injustice—*cont'd*	Obadiah 1:13	Do not loot Jews
	Micah 2:2	Covet and rob
	Habakkuk 3:14	Devour oppressed
	Zechariah 8:17	Do not love perjury
	Matthew 10:17	Beware of men
	Mark 3:27	Bind the strong man
	Luke 20:46–47	Beware of scribes
	James 2:1–16	Dishonor poor
2.K. Ego	Esther 1:4	Ahasuerus' pride
Self-elevating attitude	Psalms 127:2	Vain to work long hours
	Proverbs 27:1	Don't boast about tomorrow
	Proverbs 28:11	Rich think they're wise
	Proverbs 28:25	Arrogant stir strife
	Isaiah 39:4	Hezekiah's pride
	Jeremiah 9:23	Rich shouldn't boast
	Matthew 6:2	Hypocrites in synagogues
	Matthew 6:3–4	Giving alms
	Matthew 23:12	Whoever exalts himself
	Luke 14:11	Proud will be humbled
	I Corinthians 4:8	Proud Corinthians
	I Timothy 6:17	Conceited rich
2.L. Futility of Riches	Job 15:31	Do not trust in emptiness
Recognition that riches are	Job 28:15–19	Wisdom more precious than gold
temporary	Job 30:15	Prosperity passes
	Psalms 17:13–15	Riches are not life
	Psalms 22:29	Prosperous will bow
	Psalms 39:6	Riches left to others
	Psalms 49:6	Boast in riches
	Psalms 49:7	No ransom for soul
	Psalms 49:10	Rich and poor both die
	Psalms 49:11–12	Man in pomp will perish
	Psalms 49:16	Do not be afraid
	Psalms 49:17	Nothing material endures
	Psalms 52:7	Trust in wealth
	Psalms 62:10	Don't trust in riches
	Psalms 73:12	Wealthy at ease
	Proverbs 7:20	Money vs. family
	Proverbs 10:15	Money is everything
	Proverbs 11:4	Riches in day of wrath
	Proverbs 11:28	He who trusts riches will fall
	Proverbs 14:12	End is death
	Proverbs 18:11	Money is protection
	Ecclesiastes 1:14	All is vanity
	Ecclesiastes 2:1	Pleasure is futile
	Ecclesiastes 2:8–11	Solomon's vanity with pleasures
	Ecclesiastes 2:20	Despair with riches
	Ecclesiastes 2:22	Vanity from riches
	Ecclesiastes 4:7–8	Vanity of labor

Subtopic:	Scripture:	Comments:
2.L. Futility of Riches— *cont'd*	Ecclesiastes 5:15	Naked he will return
	Ecclesiastes 6:1–2	Hoarded riches
	Ecclesiastes 6:7	Appetite never satisfied
	Ecclesiastes 7:14	God makes prosperity and adversity
	Ecclesiastes 8:10	Wicked soon forgotten
	Ecclesiastes 10:19	Futility of money
	Isaiah 2:7	Wicked prosper
	Isaiah 30:6	Riches of Negev
	Isaiah 55:1–2	Futility of pleasures
	Jeremiah 17:5	Trust in man
	Jeremiah 17:6	Won't see prosperity
	Lamentations 1:7	Precious things
	Lamentations 4:1	Pure gold changed
	Lamentations 4:5	Ash pits
	Ezekiel 16:17	Idols from God's provision
	Daniel 11:43	Control over treasure
	Amos 6:1–7	Woe to Zion
	Nahum 3:16	Riches of Nineveh
	Matthew 6:19–20	Do not lay up on earth
	Matthew 6:21	Heart and treasures
	Matthew 13:7	Seed among thorns
	Matthew 13:22	Seed among thorns
	Matthew 16:26	Gain world, lose soul
	Matthew 19:23	Hard for rich
	Mark 8:36–37	Gain world, lose soul
	Luke 6:24	Woe to rich
	Luke 8:14–15	Seed among thorns
	Luke 9:25	Gain world, lose soul
	Luke 12:25	Worry
	Luke 16:19–25	Rich man and Lazarus
	Luke 18:22–25	Rich young ruler
	John 12:25	Christ before life
	I Corinthians 15:32	Eat, drink, be merry
	I Timothy 6:9	Temptation of riches
	I Timothy 6:17	Rich not to be conceited
	James 1:10	Rich in humiliation
	James 1:11	Rich will die too
	James 5:1–5	Warning to rich
	I Peter 1:18	Not redeemed with gold
	Revelation 17:4	Harlot's riches
	Revelation 18:12–13	Babylon's riches
2.M. Fear *Lack of trust regarding money*	Genesis 50:15	Joseph's brothers' guilt
	Proverbs 12:25	Anxiety weighs heart down
2.N. Bad Counsel *Listening to wrong advice*	Proverbs 13:20	Don't listen to fools
	Proverbs 14:7	Leave a fool
	Proverbs 22:24–25	Associate with angry men
	I Corinthians 15:33	Bad company corrupts
	II Thessalonians 3:6	Brother leads unruly life

Subtopic:	Scripture:	Comments:
2.O. Indulgence *Surplus to the point of waste*	Proverbs 21:17 Proverbs 25:28 Proverbs 27:7	Don't love pleasure No self-control Too much is bad
2.P. Suing *Taking another to court*	I Corinthians 6:1	Don't sue Christians

Credit

My son, if you have become surety for your neighbor, have given a pledge for a stranger, if you have been snared with the words of your mouth, have been caught with the words of your mouth, do this then, my son, and deliver yourself; since you have come into the hand of your neighbor, go, humble yourself, and importune your neighbor. —Proverbs 6:1–3

No single principle from God's Word has been more commonly violated than that of credit. Few Christians understand the **balance** that the Bible requires in borrowing, lending, charging, and interest.

Even a quick review of the Scriptures referenced under this topic will reflect that, as in any other area of life, this area must be placed under **God's** authority. Of special interest should be a study of lending to "brothers," charging "interest" on loans to brothers, and signing "surety" for debts.

Subtopic:	Scripture:	Comments:
3.A. Borrowing *Use of another's money*	Exodus 22:14	Restitution for borrowed property
	Exodus 22:15	No restitution for rented property
	Deuteronomy 28:43–45	Disobey God and become borrower
	Nehemiah 5:2–5	Jews borrowing from Jews
	Psalms 37:21	Wicked does not repay
	Proverbs 22:7	Borrower is lender's slave
	Isaiah 24:2	Borrower will be like lender
3.B. Lending *Allowing another to use your money*	Exodus 22:25	Lend to brothers without interest
	Deuteronomy 15:6	Lend but not borrow
	Deuteronomy 28:12	Obey God and lend
	Psalms 37:26	Godly man lends
	Psalms 112:5	God blesses lender
	Isaiah 24:2	Buyer like seller
	Jeremiah 15:10	I have not lent
	Ezekiel 18:7	Restore pledge to borrower
	Ezekiel 18:8	Does not lend at interest
	Ezekiel 18:12	Evil retains pledge
	Ezekiel 18:13	Lends at interest
	Ezekiel 18:16–17	Does not keep pledge
	Habakkuk 2:6–7	Woe to those who lend at interest

Subtopic:	Scripture:	Comments:
3.B. Lending—*cont'd*	Luke 6:34–35	Lend, expecting nothing
3.C. Interest *Premium for the use of money*	Deuteronomy 23:19	Do not charge interest to a brother
	Deuteronomy 23:20	May charge foreigner interest
	Psalms 15:5	Do not charge interest
	Proverbs 22:26–27	Don't sign pledges
	Proverbs 28:8	Wrong to lend at interest
	Ezekiel 18:7	Godly returns pledge
	Ezekiel 18:8	Godly does not charge interest
	Ezekiel 18:12	Wicked keeps pledge
	Ezekiel 18:13	Wicked charges interest
	Ezekiel 18:16–17	Godly does not charge interest
	Ezekiel 18:18	Ungodly extort from poor
3.D. Usury *Excessive interest*	Leviticus 25:35–37	Do not charge a brother usury
	Nehemiah 5:7–10	Charging a brother usury
	Proverbs 28:8	Usury will revert to God
3.E. Surety *Personal liability for a loan*	Genesis 43:9	Surety for Benjamin
	Genesis 44:32	Surety for Benjamin
	Exodus 22:26	Return a pledge
	Deuteronomy 24:10–13	Do not keep poor man's pledge
	Job 22:6	Has taken a pledge from brothers
	Psalms 109:11	Seize all a debtor has
	Proverbs 6:1–5	Beg to be released from surety
	Proverbs 11:15	Surety for a stranger
	Proverbs 17:18	Ignorant becomes surety
	Proverbs 20:16	Ignorant pledges cloak as surety
	Proverbs 21:27	Sacrifice of wicked
	Proverbs 22:26–27	Do not become surety
	Proverbs 27:13	Take his garment
3.F. Paying Debts *Returning borrowed money*	Genesis 38:20	Judah paid harlot
	Deuteronomy 15:1–5	Seven-year remission of debts
	Deuteronomy 31:10	Year of remission of debts
	II Kings 4:1	Widow's children for debts
	II Kings 4:7	Elisha pays widow's debt
	Proverbs 3:27–28	Pay when debt is due
	Matthew 5:25–26	Make friends of lenders
	Luke 12:58–59	Make friends of lenders
	Romans 13:8	Do not be left owing
	Colossians 2:14	Cancel debts
	Philemon 18–19	Paul offers to pay debts

Giving

"Who has given to Me that I should repay him? Whatever is under the whole heaven is Mine."   —Job 41:11

The topic "Giving" runs all the way from the least, a tithe, to giving everything, as God asked the disciples to do in Acts 4. Quite often it is difficult to separate the various levels of giving such as tithes, first fruits, offerings, etc. Therefore, no attempt has been made to do so.

If the New American Standard Bible translators used the term "Storehouse," all such references will be found in subtopic 4.A. "Tithes" will be found in subtopic 4.C. "First Fruits" in subtopic 4.E. etc. Other general subtopics have been referenced to help users locate additional topics. For instance, under subtopic 4.G., Worthless Gifts, you would find the gifts from a harlot's wages, sick sheep, etc. A thorough review of each subtopic and the comments given will provide an insight when looking for a needed passage.

Subtopic:	Scripture:	Comments:
4.A. Storehouse *Storage of tithes and offerings*	I Chronicles 26:20	Levites over treasure
	I Chronicles 26:22	Levites over treasure
	I Chronicles 26:24	Levites over treasure
	Nehemiah 12:44	Storehouse overseers
	Nehemiah 13:5	Storage rooms
	Nehemiah 13:12–13	Priest in charge of storehouse
	Malachi 3:10	Tithes to storehouse
4.B. Giving to Men *Men giving to other men*	Genesis 24:22	Rebekah paid
	Genesis 24:53	Gifts to Rebekah's family
	Genesis 32:17–20	Jacob's gifts to Esau
	Genesis 33:10–11	Jacob's gifts to Esau
	Genesis 42:25–28	Joseph's gifts to his family
	Genesis 42:35	Joseph's gifts to his family
	Genesis 43:18	Joseph's gifts to his family
	Genesis 43:26	Joseph's gifts to his family
	Genesis 44:1–2	Joseph's gifts to his family
	Genesis 45:17	Joseph's gifts to his family
	Genesis 45:20	Joseph's gifts to his family
	Genesis 45:22	Joseph's gifts to his family
	Genesis 47:11	Joseph's gifts to his family
	Numbers 3:45–49	Ransom for Aaron
	Deuteronomy 12:19	Don't forsake Levite
	I Samuel 9:8	Saul pays prophet

Subtopic:	Scripture:	Comments:
4.B. Giving to Men—*cont'd*	I Samuel 25:27	Abigail's gift to David
	II Samuel 8:10–11	Gifts to King David
	I Kings 5:10–11	Hiram's gifts to Solomon
	I Kings 9:14	Gifts to Solomon
	I Kings 9:28	Gifts to Solomon
	I Kings 10:2	Gifts to Solomon
	I Kings 10:10	Gifts to Solomon
	I Kings 10:14	Gifts to Solomon
	II Kings 5:5	Aram's gift for Naaman
	II Kings 5:15–24	Naaman's gift to Elisha
	II Kings 16:8	Ahaz's gift to Assyria
	II Kings 25:30	Allowance for Jehoiachin
	II Chronicles 8:18	Solomon's gifts
	II Chronicles 9:1	Solomon's gifts
	II Chronicles 9:9–10	Solomon's gifts
	II Chronicles 9:13	Solomon's gifts
	II Chronicles 9:24	Solomon's gifts
	II Chronicles 16:2	Asa's gifts to Ben-hadad
	II Chronicles 17:11	Philistine's gifts to Jehosha-phat
	Proverbs 18:16	Gifts bring us before great men
	Daniel 2:6	Gifts for Daniel
	Daniel 5:17	Gifts for Daniel
	Daniel 5:29	Gifts for Daniel
	Zechariah 6:11	Crown for Joshua
	Luke 11:13	Fathers' gifts to children
	Galatians 6:6	Share with teacher
4.C. Tithe *First part of earnings*	Genesis 14:20	First tithe to God
	Genesis 28:22	Tenth to God
	Leviticus 27:30–33	Tithe to God
	Numbers 18:26	Tithe to Levites
	Numbers 18:28–29	Tithe of tithes
	Deuteronomy 12:6	Bring tithes
	Deuteronomy 12:7	Eat of tithes
	Deuteronomy 12:11	Tithe of God's house
	Deuteronomy 12:17	Do not eat of tithes
	Deuteronomy 14:22–23	Tithe to eat
	Deuteronomy 14:24–26	Sell tithe and buy food
	Deuteronomy 14:27–28	Tithe for Levite
	Deuteronomy 14:29	Tithe to widows and orphans
	Deuteronomy 26:10–12	Third-year tithe
	Deuteronomy 26:13	Tithe to widows and orphans
	Nehemiah 10:37	Tithe for Levites
	Nehemiah 10:38–39	Tithe to storehouse
	Nehemiah 12:44	Overseers of tithe
	Nehemiah 13:5	Room for tithes
	Nehemiah 13:12–13	Tithes for workers
	Amos 4:4	False tithes
	Malachi 3:7–9	Rob God of tithes
	Malachi 3:10	Bring tithes to storehouse

Subtopic:	Scripture:	Comments:
4.C. Tithe—*cont'd*	Malachi 3:11	Keep devourer away
	Matthew 23:23	Pharisees' tithes
	Luke 11:42	Pharisees' tithes
	Hebrews 7:1–9	Abraham's tithe
4.D. Offerings	Genesis 4:3	Cain's offering
Additional giving for needs	Genesis 4:4	Abel's offering
	Exodus 22:29	Offering of harvest
	Exodus 25:2–3	Offering to build sanctuary
	Exodus 30:12–16	Offering to build sanctuary
	Exodus 35:5	Offering to God
	Exodus 35:21–22	Offering to God
	Exodus 35:24	Offering for sanctuary
	Exodus 36:3	Offering for sanctuary
	Exodus 36:5–6	Offering for sanctuary
	Leviticus 14:21–22	Poor man's offering
	Leviticus 14:30–31	Poor man's offering
	Leviticus 22:21	Peace offering
	Leviticus 23:10–11	Peace offering
	Leviticus 27:13	Redeem offering
	Leviticus 27:15–28	Redeem offering
	Numbers 7:13–14	Offering for sanctuary
	Numbers 15:6–7	Offering to God
	Numbers 15:18–21	Offering to God
	Numbers 18:8–9	Offering to God
	Numbers 31:50–54	Offering to God
	Deuteronomy 12:6–7	Offerings
	Deuteronomy 12:11	Offerings
	Deuteronomy 16:17	Every man give as he is able
	Deuteronomy 17:1	No defective offerings
	II Samuel 24:24	David's offering
	I Kings 5:17	Offerings for temple
	I Kings 6:20–22	Offerings for temple
	I Kings 6:28	Offerings for temple
	I Kings 7:51	Offerings for temple
	I Kings 10:16–18	Offerings for temple
	I Kings 15:15	Offerings for temple
	II Kings 12:4–7	Offerings for temple work-men
	II Kings 12:9–16	Offerings for temple work-men
	II Kings 22:4–5	Offerings for temple work-men
	II Kings 22:8–9	Offerings for temple work-men
	I Chronicles 21:23	Ornan's offerings to David
	I Chronicles 26:26–27	Offerings for temple
	I Chronicles 29:7	Offerings for temple
	II Chronicles 24:11–12	Offerings for temple
	II Chronicles 24:14	Offerings for temple
	II Chronicles 31:14–15	Free will offerings
	Ezra 1:4	Free will offerings

Subtopic:	Scripture:	Comments:
4.D. Offerings—*cont'd*	Ezra 8:25–27	Free will offerings
	Ezra 8:30	Free will offerings
	Nehemiah 10:34–35	Offerings for priests
	Ezekiel 20:28	Offerings
	Ezekiel 20:39–40	Contributions of Israel
	Ezekiel 42:13	Offerings
	Amos 4:5	Thank offerings
	Malachi 3:3	Levites—and offering to God
	Mark 12:42–44	Widow's mite
	Mark 14:3–7	Mary's oil for Jesus
	Luke 21:1–4	Widow's mite
	Acts 4:36–37	Barnabas' offering
	Acts 21:24	Paul's offering
	Acts 24:17	Paul's offering
	II Corinthians 9:6	Sowing and reaping
	I Timothy 5:3	Honor widows
	III John 8	Support evangelists
4.E. First Fruits *Another term for the first part of earnings*	Genesis 4:3	Cain's offering
	Genesis 4:4	Abel's offering
	Exodus 22:29–30	First animals
	Exodus 34:19	First animals
	Exodus 34:26	First fruits to God
	Leviticus 23:10–11	First of harvests
	Numbers 3:13	All first-born
	Numbers 15:18–21	First of food
	Numbers 18:12–13	First of food
	Deuteronomy 12:17	Cannot eat first fruits
	Deuteronomy 18:4	Give first fruits
	Deuteronomy 26:2	Give first fruits
	Deuteronomy 26:10	First fruits to God
	Joshua 6:24	First fruits to God's house
	Nehemiah 10:34–35	First fruits to God's house
	Nehemiah 10:37–39	First fruits to priests
	Nehemiah 12:44	Men over distribution
	Proverbs 3:9–10	Honor God from first fruits
	Ezekiel 44:30	First fruits for priests
	Romans 8:23	Christians are God's first fruits
	James 1:18	Christians are God's first fruits
	Revelation 14:4	First fruit among men
4.F. Gifts *Special giving*	Numbers 5:9–10	Gifts to priest
	Joshua 6:24	Silver, gold
	I Chronicles 29:2–5	David's gift for the temple
	II Chronicles 15:18	Asa's gift to the temple
	II Chronicles 34:9	Gifts to repair temple
	II Chronicles 34:14	Gifts to repair temple
	Ezra 1:6	Freewill gift
	Ezra 2:69	Gifts for rebuilding temple
	Ezra 7:15–18	Artaxerxes' gift to temple

Subtopic:	Scripture:	Comments:
4.F. Gifts—*cont'd*	Nehemiah 7:70–72	Gift to temple
	Proverbs 11:24	Scatter and increase
	Proverbs 11:25	Generous will prosper
	Proverbs 19:6	Generous man
	Proverbs 22:9	Generous will be blessed
	Proverbs 28:27	Givers will not want
	Matthew 2:11	Wise men's gifts
	Matthew 5:42	Give to those who ask
	Mark 12:41	Widow's offering
	Luke 6:29–30	Give to those who ask
	Luke 6:38	Give and it shall be given
	John 12:3–7	Mary's gift of oil to Jesus
	Romans 12:8	Gift of giving
	II Corinthians 9:7	Cheerful giving
	Revelation 21:6–7	God gives water of life
	Revelation 22:17	God gives water of life
4.G. Worthless Gifts *Unacceptable to God*	Deuteronomy 23:6	No peace from idols
	Deuteronomy 23:18	Wages of a harlot
	I Samuel 2:29	Taking the best parts
	Malachi 1:13	Stolen, sick, lame
	Malachi 2:12	Israel's gift
	Acts 5:1–10	Ananias and Sapphira's gift
4.H. Helping Needy *Care of widows, orphans, poor, etc.*	Exodus 23:11	Seventh year gleaning
	Leviticus 19:10	Gleaning of vineyard
	Leviticus 23:22	Gleaning of fields for poor
	Leviticus 25:35–37	Care for poor
	Deuteronomy 10:18–19	Show love for foreigners
	Deuteronomy 15:7–11	Freely give to poor
	Deuteronomy 24:14–15	Pay poor promptly
	Deuteronomy 24:19–21	Leave gleaning for poor
	I Samuel 18:23	David's poverty
	I Samuel 22:2	David's army of poor
	Esther 9:22	Gifts to poor
	Job 20:10	Sons favor poor
	Job 29:12	Sons favor poor
	Job 29:16	Father to needy
	Job 30:25	Grieved for needy
	Job 31:16–19	Cared for needy
	Psalms 9:18	Needy not forgotten
	Psalms 12:5	God hears the needy
	Psalms 34:6	Poor cried out, God heard
	Psalms 40:17	God is the deliverer of needy
	Psalms 41:1	Blessed is he who considers needy
	Psalms 68:6	God makes a home for lonely
	Psalms 68:10	God provides for poor
	Psalms 69:33	God hears needy
	Psalms 72:4	God saves children of needy
	Psalms 72:12–14	Compassion on poor
	Psalms 107:40–41	God sets needy securely

Subtopic:	Scripture:	Comments:
4.H. Helping Needy— *cont'd*	Psalms 109:31	God is at right hand of needy
	Psalms 112:9	Freely given to poor
	Psalms 113:7–8	Lifts needy
	Psalms 138:6	God hears needy
	Psalms 140:12	God aids needy
	Proverbs 14:21	Be gracious to poor
	Proverbs 14:31	Being gracious to poor honors God
	Proverbs 19:17	Helping poor is lending to God
	Proverbs 21:13	Ignore poor and God will ignore you
	Proverbs 28:27	Those who give to poor
	Proverbs 29:7	Righteous care about poor
	Proverbs 31:9	Helping needy
	Proverbs 31:20	God aids needy
	Isaiah 25:4	She helps poor
	Isaiah 41:17	God is defense for helpless
	Isaiah 58:7	Divide bread with hungry
	Jeremiah 22:16	Plead case for needy
	Jeremiah 39:10	Poor left to tend Israel
	Ezekiel 16:49	Sodom ignored poor
	Matthew 10:42	Give even water
	Matthew 11:5	Poor have Gospel preached
	Matthew 15:5–6	Helping parents
	Matthew 19:21	Sell possessions, give to poor
	Matthew 25:35–41	Did you help poor?
	Matthew 25:42–44	Care for poor
	Matthew 25:45	Helping poor
	Matthew 26:7–12	Mary's gift of oil
	Mark 7:11–12	Helping parents
	Mark 10:21–26	Rich young ruler
	Mark 14:3–7	Mary's gift of oil
	Luke 3:11	Two tunics, share one
	Luke 4:18	Poor have Gospel preached
	Luke 6:20	Blessed are poor
	Luke 7:22	Poor have Gospel preached
	Luke 9:48	Receive children
	Luke 10:35	Good Samaritan
	Luke 12:33	Sell possessions, give to charity
	Luke 14:12–14	Invite poor in
	Luke 18:22–25	Rich young ruler
	Acts 2:44–45	Believers shared property
	Acts 3:2–6	Peter: no silver or gold
	Acts 4:32–35	Believers shared property
	Acts 4:36–37	Barnabas' gift
	Acts 6:1–2	Disciples serving widows
	Acts 10:2	Cornelius shared with Jews
	Acts 10:4	God blessed him
	Acts 10:31	God blessed him

Subtopic:	Scripture:	Comments:
4.H. Helping Needy— *cont'd*	Acts 11:29	Disciples shared with Judeans
	Acts 24:17	Paul's offerings
	Romans 15:26–27	Gifts to Jerusalem church
	I Corinthians 16:1–2	Collection for church in Jerusalem
	II Corinthians 6:10	Giving to others
	II Corinthians 8:2–5	Giving from Philippians
	II Corinthians 8:9	Christ's gifts
	II Corinthians 8:11–12	Give according to what you have
	II Corinthians 8:13–15	Share in your plenty
	II Corinthians 9:8–12	Sowing and reaping
	II Corinthians 9:13	Proof of obedience
	Galatians 2:10	Remember the poor
	Philippians 4:15–18	Philippians' gift to Paul
	I Timothy 5:3	Care for widows within family
	I Timothy 5:5	Care for widows within family
	I Timothy 5:16	Honor widows
	I Timothy 6:18–19	Be generous and ready to share
	Hebrews 10:34	Giving up property
	James 1:27	Helping widows and orphans
	James 2:1–16	Helping brother or sister in need
	I John 3:17–18	Do not pass by needy
	III John 6–7	Sending saints on their way
	Revelation 7:16	They shall hunger no more
4.I. Giving To Get *Self-centered giving*	Job 41:11	Who gives to God?
	Romans 11:34–36	Who gives to God?
	I Corinthians 13:3	Giving, but without love

Family

An inheritance gained hurriedly at the beginning, will not be blessed in the end.   —Proverbs 20:21

Obviously God's Word has a great deal to say about families—spiritually, emotionally, **and materially**. This topic references those passages dealing with inheritance (subtopic 5.A.), counsel and discipline (subtopic 5.B.), and provision (subtopic 5.C.).

Subtopic:	Scripture:	Comments:
5.A. Inheritance *Distribution of assets of others*	Genesis 15:2–4	Abram's heir
	Genesis 25:5	Abraham left everything to Isaac
	Genesis 25:6	Gave to other sons while living
	Genesis 25:8	Abraham dies
	Genesis 25:31–34	Esau sells birthright
	Genesis 27:30	Isaac blesses Jacob
	Genesis 31:14–16	Rachel and Leah's inheritance
	Numbers 18:20	Aaron's inheritance
	Numbers 18:21	Levi's inheritance
	Numbers 18:24	Levi's inheritance
	Numbers 26:54–56	Israel's inheritance
	Numbers 27:7	Daughters of Zelophehad's inheritance
	Numbers 27:8	No son, daughter inherits
	Numbers 27:9	No daughters, brothers inherit
	Numbers 27:10	No brothers, father's brothers inherit
	Numbers 27:11	No uncles, nearest heir inherits
	Numbers 33:54	Israel's inheritance
	Numbers 35:2	Levite's inheritance
	Numbers 35:8	Israel's inheritance
	Numbers 36:3–4, 6–7, 9	Rules of inheritance for Israel
	Deuteronomy 18:1–2	Levitical priests—no inheritance

Subtopic:	Scripture:	Comments:
5.A. Inheritance—*cont'd*	Deuteronomy 18:8	Sale of fathers' estates
	Deuteronomy 21:17	First-born receives double
	Joshua 11:23	Land divided as inheritance
	Joshua 13:14	Levites received no inheritance
	Joshua 13:33	Levites received no inheritance
	Joshua 14:1	Land divided as inheritance
	Joshua 14:4	Levites received no inheritance
	Joshua 14:14	Caleb's inheritance
	Joshua 17:6	Daughters of Manasseh
	Joshua 24:32	Joseph's sons' inheritance
	Judges 11:2	Gilead's sons' inheritance
	Judges 18:1	Danites' inheritance
	Ruth 4:3–7	Naomi's inheritance
	I Chronicles 23:27–28	Levites' inherited responsibility
	II Chronicles 21:3	First-born's rights
	Ezra 9:12	Leave land as inheritance
	Psalms 17:13–15	Unrighteous leaves an inheritance
	Proverbs 13:22	Good man's inheritance
	Proverbs 19:14	House and wealth are inheritance
	Proverbs 20:21	Hasty inheritance
	Ecclesiastes 2:18	Riches left to sons
	Ecclesiastes 2:21	Foolish heir
	Ecclesiastes 6:3–4	Those who die broke
	Lamentations 5:2	Inheritance given away
	Joel 2:17	Israel—God's inheritance
	Matthew 21:33–41	Parable of vineyard
	Matthew 25:34	Inherited the kingdom
	Mark 12:1–9	Parable of vineyard
	Luke 15:11–24	Parable of prodigal son
	Luke 20:9–16	Parable of vineyard
	Acts 13:19	Israel's inheritance
	II Corinthians 12:14	Parents save for children
	Galatians 4:1	Child cannot control inheritance
	Galatians 4:7	Heir of God
	Hebrews 12:16–17	Esau's birthright
	Revelation 21:6–7	Gives water of life
5.B. Counsel and Discipline *Father and mother's instructions*	Proverbs 1:8	Father and mother's teaching
	Proverbs 6:20	Father and mother's teaching
	Proverbs 10:1	Wise son
	Proverbs 13:1	Father's discipline
	Proverbs 15:5	Father's discipline
	Proverbs 17:25	Foolish son
	Proverbs 19:18	Discipline son
	Proverbs 22:6	Train up a child

Subtopic:	Scripture:	Comments:
5.B. Counsel and Discipline *—cont'd*	Proverbs 23:13–14	Discipline child
	Proverbs 23:22	Listen to father and mother
	Proverbs 29:15	Rod gives discipline
	Proverbs 29:17	Correct son
	Proverbs 31:10	An excellent wife
	Proverbs 31:11	No lack of gain
	Ephesians 6:4	Fathers don't provoke children
5.C. Provision *Caring for family needs*	Deuteronomy 20:5	Dedicate new home
	Matthew 13:52	Head of household
	I Timothy 5:8	Provide for your family
	I Timothy 6:5–8	Godliness gain

God's Blessings

It is the blessing of the LORD that makes rich, and He adds no sorrow to it. —Proverbs 10:22

This topic actually covers God's blessings to those who obey and serve Him, as well as God's discipline and justice toward those who turn away from His path. The two attributes of God cannot be separated. God promises both mercy and justice for those who serve Him.

As a review of this topic, it will show God provides **discipline** in an effort to correct a situation that might later require **punishment**.

Subtopic:	Scripture:	Comments:
6.A. God's Promises	Genesis 49:20	Asher yields riches
Rewards to faithful followers	Exodus 17:12	Israel's victory
	Deuteronomy 10:17	God is not partial
	I Samuel 2:3	God honors those who honor Him
	I Samuel 2:7	God makes poor and rich
	I Kings 3:11–13	God's promise to Solomon
	I Kings 10:23	Solomon's great riches
	II Chronicles 1:11–12	God's promise to Solomon
	II Chronicles 1:15	Silver and gold like stones
	II Chronicles 9:20	Eating utensils were of gold
	II Chronicles 9:22	Solomon's riches
	II Chronicles 15:1–2	God's promise to Judah
	II Chronicles 17:5	Jehoshaphat's riches
	II Chronicles 26:5	Uzziah's riches
	II Chronicles 32:27–29	Hezekiah's riches
	Nehemiah 2:8	God's provision for Jerusalem
	Nehemiah 2:20	Israel's portion
	Job 5:17–20	God's deliverance
	Job 22:24–25	God is our riches
	Job 23:10	God is our riches
	Job 34:19	God is not partial
	Job 36:11	Serve God, have prosperity
	Job 42:10	God restored Job's wealth
	Psalms 15:1–2	The honest walk with God
	Psalms 34:19	The Lord delivers righteous

Subtopic:	Scripture:	Comments:
6.A. God's Promises—*cont'd*	Psalms 37:28–29	God preserves the godly
	Psalms 50:14–15	Honor God and He will rescue
	Psalms 105:37	Gold for Israel
	Psalms 113:7–8	God helps needy
	Psalms 115:14	God's increase
	Psalms 122:7	Prosperity
	Psalms 128:5	Prosperity
	Proverbs 2:6	The Lord gives wisdom
	Proverbs 3:2–4	The Lord gives years, peace
	Proverbs 8:10–12	Knowledge
	Proverbs 8:35	Obtaining favor from God
	Proverbs 10:16	Righteous have life
	Proverbs 10:22	Riches, but no sorrow
	Proverbs 11:16	Gracious woman attains honor
	Proverbs 20:22	God repays evil
	Proverbs 22:2	God made rich and poor
	Song of Solomon 8:7	Riches can't buy love
	Isaiah 11:4	God will judge poor justly
	Isaiah 60:5	God's promise to Israel
	Isaiah 60:17	God's promise to Israel
	Ezekiel 39:25	God will restore Israel
	Hosea 2:8	God provided for Israel
	Zephaniah 2:7	God will restore Israel
	Haggai 2:7–8	God will restore Israel
	Zechariah 1:17	God's future promise to Jews
	Zechariah 2:12	God's future promise to Judah
	Zechariah 13:9	God will restore Israel
	Zechariah 14:14	God's future promise to Jews
	Matthew 5:12	Reward in heaven
	Matthew 16:25	Lose life to save it
	Mark 4:25	Whoever has, to him more will be given
	Mark 10:29–30	Promises for giving up homes
	Luke 12:42	Good steward
	Luke 12:44	Good steward is in charge
	John 16:26–27	Ask in Jesus' name
	Romans 10:11–12	Riches for all
6.B. Counsel of God *God's directions to men*	Genesis 29:15	Jacob's wages
	Joshua 9:14–15	Israel ignores God
	Psalms 32:8–9	God will instruct
	Proverbs 1:29–33	Listen to God and prosper
	Proverbs 5:10	Ignore God and suffer
	Proverbs 8:10–11	God's counsel, not riches
	Proverbs 19:21	Man's plans, God's counsel
	John 15:19	Be not of world

Subtopic:	Scripture:	Comments:
6.C. Blessings *Special blessings* *for obedience*	Genesis 15:14	Israel's provision from Egypt
	Genesis 24:35–36	Abram's riches
	Genesis 26:3	God's promise to Israel
	Genesis 26:12–14	God blessed Isaac
	Genesis 31:9	Jacob's provision
	Genesis 39:2–3	Joseph's riches
	Genesis 39:4–6	God blesses Joseph's master
	Genesis 39:8	Joseph prospers
	Genesis 39:23	Joseph prospers in prison
	Exodus 35:31–32	God gifted temple craftsman
	Deuteronomy 28:8	God's promise to Israel
	Deuteronomy 28:11	God's promise to Israel
	Deuteronomy 29:9	Keep God's Word and prosper
	Deuteronomy 30:8–11	God's promises to Jews if they obey
	Joshua 1:8	Obey law and prosper
	Ruth 3:10	God blesses Ruth
	Ruth 4:11	Ruth's blessing
	I Samuel 2:30	God honors those who honor Him
	I Chronicles 29:28	David's riches
	II Chronicles 9:20–22	Solomon's riches
	II Chronicles 18:1	Jehoshaphat's wealth
	Job 36:11	Prosperity
	Psalms 37:28–29	God's protection
	Psalms 127:3	Children are a gift from God
	Proverbs 31:10	An excellent wife
6.D. Provision *Demonstration that God* *supplies needs*	Genesis 2:12	Promised land
	Genesis 12:5	Abram's riches
	Genesis 13:2	Abram's riches
	Genesis 13:6	Abram's riches
	Genesis 14:11–12	Lot's riches
	Genesis 14:16	Lot's riches
	Genesis 14:23	Abram's riches
	Genesis 28:4	Promised land
	Genesis 30:20	Leah's children
	Genesis 30:43	Jacob's riches
	Genesis 41:52	Joseph's children
	Genesis 45:4	Joseph in Egypt
	Genesis 45:5	God's will
	Genesis 46:6	Jacob moves to Egypt
	Exodus 3:21–22	Egyptians give to Jews
	Exodus 6:8	Promised land
	Exodus 9:4	God protects Jews' livestock
	Exodus 11:2–3	Egyptians give to Jews
	Exodus 12:35–36	Jews plundered Egyptians
	Exodus 16:4	Manna in the desert
	Exodus 16:16	Manna in the desert
	Exodus 16:18–21	Manna in the desert
	Exodus 16:32	Manna in the desert

Subtopic:	Scripture:	Comments:
6.D. Provision—*cont'd*	Exodus 17:6	Water from rock
	Leviticus 25:19	Land will produce
	Numbers 31:50–54	Offering
	Deuteronomy 2:7	God's provision in desert
	Deuteronomy 8:18	God gives wealth
	Deuteronomy 10:18	God provides for foreigner
	Deuteronomy 10:19	Care for foreigners
	Joshua 22:8	Spoils of war
	Joshua 24:13	God provided land
	I Kings 17:13–14, 16	Elijah's barrel
	II Kings 7:16	Jews plunder Arameans
	I Chronicles 29:12–14	Riches and honor are from God
	II Chronicles 3:4–17	Wealth of the temple
	II Chronicles 4:19–22	Wealth of the temple
	II Chronicles 5:1	Wealth of the temple
	Ezra 1:9–11	Provision to rebuild temple
	Ezra 5:14	Wealth from the temple
	Ezra 5:17	Decree from King Cyrus
	Ezra 6:1	Decree from King Cyrus
	Ezra 6:4–5	Wealth of the temple
	Nehemiah 2:8	God's provision for walls
	Nehemiah 9:21	Clothes in the desert
	Job 1:21	Lord gives and takes away
	Job 2:10	Accept good and bad
	Job 42:11	Job's new wealth
	Psalms 8:6	Men over God's works
	Psalms 24:1	The earth is the Lord's
	Psalms 25:12–13	Fear God and prosper
	Psalms 33:18–19	Fear God and prosper
	Psalms 34:9	Fear God and prosper
	Psalms 35:1	Contend with enemies
	Psalms 37:4	Delight yourself in the Lord
	Psalms 37:7–8	Rest in the Lord
	Psalms 37:9	Those who wait will inherit
	Psalms 37:18–19	Provision for blameless
	Psalms 37:25	Righteous will not be forsaken
	Psalms 37:34	Wait for the Lord
	Psalms 50:12	The world is God's
	Psalms 62:11–12	God repays our work
	Psalms 106:5	Chosen ones prosper
	Psalms 112:3	Wealth and riches
	Psalms 118:25	Send prosperity
	Psalms 124:1–3	Lord on our side
	Psalms 132:15	God provides for needy
	Proverbs 8:18–21	Riches and honor
	Proverbs 10:22	God's blessings make rich
	Proverbs 29:13	God provides to rich and poor
	Isaiah 10:14	God's riches
	Isaiah 30:23	Riches and plenty

Subtopic:	Scripture:	Comments:
6.D. Provision—*cont'd*	Isaiah 45:3	Hidden wealth
	Isaiah 45:13	God's control of kings
	Isaiah 61:6	Acquire riches
	Jeremiah 32:44	God restores Israel
	Ezekiel 16:10–13	God's provision for Israel
	Ezekiel 28:13	Satan's riches
	Haggai 2:7–8	Silver and gold is God's
	Mark 6:41	Jesus multiplies fish
	I Corinthians 3:21–23	All things belong to God
	Philippians 4:19	God shall supply needs
6.E. Discipline	Genesis 34:29	Shechem's punishment
To correct wrong actions	I Kings 15:18	Asa paid tribute
	II Kings 14:14	Temple looted
	II Kings 24:13	Temple looted
	II Kings 24:14	People enslaved
	II Kings 25:15	Temple looted
	II Chronicles 12:9	Temple looted
	II Chronicles 28:21	Ahaz's attempted bribe
	Ezra 7:26	Discipline for disobeying law
	Proverbs 13:1	Son accepts father's discipline
	Proverbs 15:5	Fool rejects
	Proverbs 16:2	Lord weighs motives
	Proverbs 19:18	Discipline your son
	Proverbs 22:6	Train up a child
	Proverbs 23:13	Don't hold discipline
	Proverbs 29:15	Rod and reproof give wisdom
	Proverbs 29:17	Correct your son
	Ecclesiastes 12:14	Every act will be judged
	Isaiah 39:6	Israel's punishment by Babylon
	Jeremiah 10:21	Shepherds stupid
	Jeremiah 15:13	Consequence of sin
	Jeremiah 17:3	Treasures given for booty
	Jeremiah 51:13	Treasures
	Ezekiel 18:12–13	Punishment for oppression, usury, etc.
	Ezekiel 26:12	Riches
	Ezekiel 28:16	Satan's punishment
	Ezekiel 28:18	Satan's punishment
	Ezekiel 29:14	Egypt will become lowly
	Zephaniah 1:12–13	Stagnant in spirit will be plundered
	Haggai 1:9	Israel's discipline
	Malachi 3:5	God punishes those who cheat, lie, etc.
	Matthew 13:12	Use it, or lose it
	Revelation 18:14–19	Punishment of Babylon
6.F. Justice	Joshua 9:20	Israel honors
To punish wrong actions	II Kings 7:8–9	Arameans routed by God
	Esther 8:15	Mordecai's honor

Subtopic:	Scripture:	Comments:
6.F. Justice—*cont'd*	Esther 9:16	Jews' revenge
	Job 5:15	God saves poor from mighty
	Job 15:29	Wicked will not endure
	Job 20:15	Riches taken by God
	Job 20:26, 28–29	Wicked punished
	Job 21:13	Wicked in Sheol
	Job 31:12	Wicked punished
	Job 42:11	Job's new riches
	Psalms 73:17–18	The destruction of the wicked
	Ecclesiastes 12:14	Every act judged
	Isaiah 13:17	Medes' used by God
	Isaiah 16:4	Oppressors punished
	Jeremiah 20:5	Israel plundered
	Jeremiah 51:13	End of wicked
	Ezekiel 7:11	No wicked will survive
	Ezekiel 7:19	Wealth will be useless
	Ezekiel 18:18	Extortioners punished
	Ezekiel 26:12	Israel's punishment
	Daniel 10:5–6	Daniel's vision
	Hosea 9:6	Israel's punishment
	Hosea 13:15	Israel's punishment
	Joel 1:17	Israel's crops fail
	Joel 3:5–8	Punishment of those who mistreat Israel
	Amos 3:11	Israel's punishment
	Micah 1:7	Punishment for idols
	Micah 4:13	Punishment of unjust nations
	Nahum 2:9	Nineveh's punishment
	Zephaniah 1:18	Day of wrath
	Zechariah 5:3–4	Thieves, liars punished
	Zechariah 9:3–4	Tyre's punishment
	Matthew 7:2	Judge and be judged
	Luke 1:53	God feeds hungry, ignores rich
	Luke 16:19–25	Rich man and Lazarus
	Revelation 6:15	Kings and rich will hide
	Revelation 18:14–19	Babylon's punishment
6.G. Wealth *General wealth from God*	Exodus 9:29	The earth is God's
	Exodus 25:11	Riches of the ark
	Exodus 25:17–18	Riches of the ark
	Exodus 25:24–26	Riches of the ark
	Exodus 25:28–29	Riches of the ark
	Exodus 25:31	Riches of the temple
	Exodus 25:36	Riches of the temple
	Exodus 25:38–39	Riches of the temple
	Exodus 26:6	Riches of the temple
	Exodus 26:11	Riches of the temple
	Exodus 26:21	Riches of the temple
	Exodus 26:25	Riches of the temple
	Exodus 26:29, 32, 37	Riches of the temple

Subtopic:	Scripture:	Comments:
6.G. Wealth—*cont'd*	Exodus 27:10–11, 17	Riches of the temple
	Exodus 28:5–6	Riches of the temple
	Exodus 30:3–5	Riches of the temple
	Exodus 31:4, 8	Riches of the temple
	Exodus 36:13	Riches of the temple
	Exodus 36:24	Riches of the temple
	Exodus 36:26	Riches of the temple
	Exodus 37:6–7	Riches of the temple
	Exodus 37:16–17	Riches of the temple
	Exodus 37:22–24	Riches of the temple
	Exodus 38:10–12	Riches of the temple
	Exodus 38:17	Riches of the temple
	Exodus 38:19	Riches of the temple
	Exodus 38:24–25	Riches of the temple
	Exodus 39:2–3	Riches of the temple
	Exodus 40:26	Riches of the temple
	Numbers 31:21–22	War booty
	I Kings 10:21, 23	Solomon's riches
	I Kings 10:27	Solomon's riches
	I Chronicles 18:7	David's wealth
	I Chronicles 18:10–11	David's wealth
	I Chronicles 20:2	David's wealth
	I Chronicles 28:14–18	Riches of the temple
	II Chronicles 4:7–8	Building temple
	II Chronicles 9:15–18	Solomon's riches
	II Chronicles 9:27	Solomon's riches
	Esther 1:6–7	Ahasuerus' riches
	Job 1:3	Job's initial wealth
	Job 28:1	Earth's riches
	Job 28:6	Earth's riches
	Psalms 33:6	By God's Word
	Isaiah 2:7	No end to treasures
	John 1:1–3	All things come through Christ
	I Corinthians 10:26	The earth is the Lord's
	I Corinthians 15:20–23	Christ is first fruits

God's Curses

Adversity pursues sinners, but the righteous will be rewarded with prosperity.
—Proverbs 13:21

G od punishes willful disobedience and worship of false gods. The difference between discipline and a curse from God is that discipline is applied in love to redirect, while a curse is to make a clear example of those so afflicted.

Subtopic:	Scripture:	Comments:
7.A. To Wicked *For doing evil to others*	Deuteronomy 7:10	God repays those who hate Him
	Deuteronomy 11:17	God shut up heavens
	Deuteronomy 28:15–20	Disobedience
	Deuteronomy 28:68	Slavery
	Joshua 9:22–23	Hivite slaves
	Judges 3:8–9	Israel slaves to Cushan
	Judges 4:1–2	Israel slaves to Jabin
	Judges 10:7	Israel slaves to Philistines
	I Samuel 3:13	Eli's sons
	I Samuel 12:9	Israel slaves to Sisera
	I Kings 14:25–26	Shishak loots temple
	I Kings 21:20	Ahab's curse
	I Kings 21:25	Ahab's curse
	II Kings 7:19–20	Royal officer trampled
	II Chronicles 20:25	Judah routs enemies
	II Chronicles 25:24	Joash loots temple
	II Chronicles 36:18	Babylonians loot temple
	Job 5:12–13	God frustrates wicked
	Job 6:4	Arrows of Almighty
	Job 27:13–17	The just will inherit wicked's riches
	Job 27:19–20	Wicked's end
	Psalms 37:37–38	Evil will be cut off
	Psalms 146:9	God thwarts wicked
	Proverbs 4:14	Avoid wicked
	Proverbs 10:3	God ignores wicked
	Proverbs 10:27	Wicked die young
	Proverbs 11:18	Wicked can recieve only money
	Proverbs 13:21	Adversity pursues sinners

Subtopic:	Scripture:	Comments:
7.A. To Wicked—*cont'd*	Proverbs 13:25	Wicked is hungry
	Proverbs 15:6	Wicked has trouble
	Proverbs 21:27	Sacrifices of wicked
	Proverbs 29:2	Wicked rule—people groan
	Ecclesiastes 2:26	Sinner collects for righteous
	Lamentations 1:5	Punishment of Judah
	Ezekiel 16:41	Judgment of harlot
	Ezekiel 22:18–20	God's wrath on Israel
	Ezekiel 27:12	Sin of Tyre
	Ezekiel 27:35–36	Fall of Tyre
	Ezekiel 30:4	Egypt's punishment
	Ezekiel 44:13	Levites' punishment
	Daniel 1:2	Oppresses through jewels of His kingdom
	Amos 3:15	Houses of ivory perish
	Amos 6:1–7	Woe to Zion
	Haggai 1:6	Economic consequences of sin
	Zechariah 9:3–4	Punishment of Tyre
	Matthew 20:1–16	Parable of the workers in the vineyard
	I Peter 2:14	Governors' punishment of evildoers
7.B. False Gods *For following false Gods*	Exodus 20:5	False gods
	Exodus 20:23	False gods
	Exodus 32:2–3, 24, 31	Aaron's idol
	Numbers 16:32	Korah dies
	Daniel 1:2	Treasures of Judah in Babylon
	Daniel 5:3–4	Praising gods of gold
	Daniel 5:23	Gods of silver
	Daniel 11:2	Riches of the fourth king
	Daniel 11:8	Gods taken into captivity
	Daniel 11:20	Oppressor through jewel of His kingdom
	Daniel 11:38	Gods honored with gold
	Hosea 8:4	Making idols
	Hosea 13:2	Making idols
	Hosea 13:15	Punishment of Israel
	Matthew 23:16–17	Gold of the temple
	Acts 17:29	God is not an idol
	Colossians 3:5	Idolatry
	Revelation 9:20	Worship of demons
	Revelation 13:16	Worship of the beast
	Revelation 18:3	City of great riches

Government

And Jesus said to them, "Render to Caesar the things that are Caesar's, and to God the things that are God's." —Mark 12:17

G overnment as used in this topic refers to **taxes**. It includes both taxes charged by the political authority and the religious authority.

Subtopic:	Scripture:	Comments:
8.A. Church Tax	Numbers 31:26–29	Tax on booty from war
Jewish temple taxes	II Chronicles 24:5	Tax to repair temple
	II Chronicles 24:9	Levy fixed by Moses
	II Chronicles 24:11–12	Tax to repair temple
	Luke 5:27	Matthew's position
8.B. Administrative Tax	Genesis 47:26	Joseph's tax for Pharaoh
Government taxes	1 Samuel 8:14–19	Tax for Israel's king
	II Samuel 8:6–7	Aramean tax for David
	II Kings 3:4	Moab's tax for Israel
	II Kings 15:19–20	Tax of Israel by Menahem
	II Kings 17:3–4	Assyria's tax on Hoshea
	II Kings 18:14–16	Assyria's tax on Hezekiah
	II Kings 23:33, 35	Pharaoh's tax on Jehoiakim
	II Chronicles 17:5	Jehoshaphat's tax on Israel
	II Chronicles 26:8	Uzziah's tax on Ammonites
	II Chronicles 27:5	Jotham's tax on Ammonites
	II Chronicles 34:17	Tax to rebuild temple
	II Chronicles 36:3	Egypt's tax on Israel
	Ezra 4:13	Reference to Israel's tax to Persia
	Ezra 4:20–21	Israel's tax to Persia
	Ezra 6:8	Persia's tax for the temple
	Ezra 7:21–22	Tax to rebuild temple
	Ezra 7:24	Cannot tax priests
	Nehemiah 5:2–5	Persia's tax on Israel
	Esther 10:1	Xerxes' tax
	Matthew 17:24–27	Christ pays temple tax
	Matthew 22:17–21	Christ's reference to Caesar's tax

Subtopic:	Scripture:	Comments:
8.B. Administrative Tax— *cont'd*	Mark 12:14–17	Christ's reference to Caesar's tax
	Luke 3:12–13	Collect no more tax than due
	Luke 20:22, 25	Render unto Caesar
	Luke 23:2	Taxes to Caesar
	Romans 13:1	Be subject to authority
	Romans 13:6	Pay taxes
	Romans 13:7	Tax to whom tax is due

Investing

Do not weary yourself to gain wealth, cease from your consideration of it. When you set your eyes on it, it is gone. For wealth certainly makes itself wings, like an eagle that flies toward the heavens. —Proverbs 23:4–5

Under the topic of investing is included saving, buying, selling, etc. Investing here really applies to the management of funds to generate a potential profit. Remarkably God's Word has a great deal to say about investing, both positive and negative. As you read through the referenced Scriptures, you will become aware of the balance the Bible always promotes. For example, under subtopic—9.B. Savings, Proverbs 21:20 says, *"There is precious treasure and oil in the dwelling of the wise,"* while in Luke 12 the rich fool is condemned for his obvious hoarding. Somewhere between, there must be the correct balance that aligns with God's Word.

Subtopic:	Scripture:	Comments:
9.A. Multiplication *Maximizing surplus funds*	Ecclesiastes 11:1 Matthew 25:14–30	Cast your bread Parable of the talents
9.B. Savings *Having an available reserve*	Proverbs 6:6–8 Proverbs 21:20 Ecclesiastes 11:2	Parable of the ant Surplus in a wise man's home . Divide and diversify
9.C. Get Rich *Obsession with riches*	Proverbs 19:19 Proverbs 23:4–5 Proverbs 28:20 Proverbs 28:22 I Timothy 6:9	Angry and in need Wealth has wings Hasty to get rich will be punished Evil man hastens after wealth Desire for riches
9.D. Selling *Offering goods to others*	Genesis 37:36 Genesis 41:56–57 Exodus 21:7 Exodus 21:8 Exodus 21:11	Joseph sold to Egyptian Joseph's grain sale Sale of daughter Cannot sell daughter to foreigner Daughter released without payment

Subtopic:	Scripture:	Comments:
9.D. Selling—*cont'd*	Leviticus 25:23	Jews not to sell land permanently
	Leviticus 25:24	Redemption of land
	Leviticus 25:25	Repurchase of kinsman's property
	Leviticus 25:42	Jews not to be sold as slaves
	Leviticus 25:47–50	Repurchase of kinsman
	Deuteronomy 2:28	Sell Jews food
	Deuteronomy 14:21	Sell dead animals to foreigners
	Deuteronomy 21:14	Cannot sell wife
	Deuteronomy 24:7	Cannot sell kinsman
	Deuteronomy 28:68	Cannot sell kinsman
	II Kings 6:25	Donkey head sold for food
	I Chronicles 21:22	David pays for threshing floor
	Psalms 44:12	Israelites sold
	Proverbs 11:26	He who sells grain is blessed
	Proverbs 31:24	Good wife sells garments
	Ezekiel 7:12–13	Sold goods are lost
	Joel 3:5–8	Children of Tyre sold
	Zechariah 11:5	Buying and selling sheep
	Matthew 19:21	Sell all and follow me
	Matthew 21:12–13	Jesus cast out temple merchants
	Matthew 26:9	Mary's perfume
	Mark 11:15	Cast out temple merchants
	Mark 14:5	Mary's perfume
	Luke 12:6	Five sparrows sold for two cents
	Luke 19:45–46	Cast out temple merchants
	John 2:14–16	Temple merchants
	Acts 5:1–10	Ananias and Sapphira
	Revelation 6:6	Wheat, barley a day's wages
9.E. Buying *Purchasing goods from others*	Genesis 17:12–13	Buying servants
	Genesis 17:23	Abraham's purchased servants
	Genesis 17:27	Abraham's servants
	Genesis 20:16	Sarah's purchase
	Genesis 23:9	Abraham's grave
	Genesis 23:15–16	Abraham's grave
	Genesis 23:17–18, 20	Abraham's grave
	Genesis 25:10	Abraham's grave
	Genesis 29:18	Jacob buys Rachel
	Genesis 33:19	Jacob's purchase
	Genesis 34:10	Land ownership
	Genesis 34:12	Dowry
	Genesis 41:57	Joseph and the famine
	Genesis 42:2–3, 5–7, 10	Jacob's sons buy food

Subtopic:	Scripture:	Comments:
9.E. Buying—*cont'd*	Genesis 43:4, 12, 15, 21–23	Israel's sons buy food
	Genesis 43:20	Israel's sons buy food
	Genesis 44:8	Israel's sons buy food
	Genesis 47:18–20	Joseph and the famine
	Genesis 47:22	Did not buy priest's land
	Exodus 12:44	Purchased slave
	Exodus 21:2	Purchased slave
	Leviticus 22:11	Purchased slave
	Leviticus 25:13	Year of Jubilee, return purchased property
	Leviticus 25:14–17	Do not cheat one another
	Leviticus 25:25–28	Rules of property redemption
	Numbers 20:19	Purchase of water from Edom
	Deuteronomy 2:6	Purchase food
	Ruth 4:3–5	Purchase of Naomi's land
	II Samuel 24:24	King David's purchase of threshing floor
	I Kings 10:29	Purchase of chariots
	I Chronicles 19:7	Hired soldiers
	I Chronicles 21:24	Purchase of threshing floor
	II Chronicles 1:17	Purchase of chariots
	II Chronicles 34:11	Purchase of materials
	Nehemiah 10:31–32	No buying on Sabbath
	Jeremiah 32:7–14	Jeremiah buys land
	Jeremiah 32:25	Jeremiah buys land
	Jeremiah 32:44	Israel buys land
	Ezekiel 7:12–13	Buyers in last days
	Ezekiel 27:12–34	Reference to buying in Tyre
	Ezekiel 28:16	Reference to Satan's trade
	Hosea 3:2	Hosea buys his wife
	Jonah 1:3	Jonah pays fare
	Zechariah 11:5	Buying and selling sheep
	Matthew 13:44–46	Pearl of great value
	Matthew 14:15	Multitude to buy food
	Matthew 25:9–10	Purchase of oil by bridesmaids
	Mark 6:37	Multitude to buy food
	Luke 9:13	Multitude to buy food
	John 6:5–7	Multitude to buy food
	John 13:29	Judas in charge of money box
	Acts 22:28	Roman soldier paying for citizenship
	Acts 28:30	Paul's rented quarters
	I Corinthians 6:20	Bought with a price
	I Corinthians 7:23	Bought with a price
	Revelation 13:17	No one can buy or sell without mark
	Revelation 18:11	No one buys from Babylon

Subtopic:	Scripture:	Comments:

9.F. Profit
Selling above costs
	Genesis 47:14–17
	Proverbs 31:16
	Ecclesiastes 4:9
	
	Matthew 25:14–30
	Luke 12:48
	
	Luke 19:13–26
	Acts 2:44–45
	Acts 4:36–37
	James 4:13–14
		Joseph sells grain
		The good wife buys a field
		Two generate a greater
		    return
		Parable of the talents
		From those who have, much
		    is expected
		Parable of the ten minas
		Believers sell property
		Barnabas sells property
		Travel to a city, make a
		    profit

9.G. Loss *Selling below costs*	Ecclesiastes 5:14	Bad investment

Planning

The ants are not a strong folk, but they prepare their food in the summer.   —Proverbs 30:25

T here are no subtopics under planning, but that does not minimize this area of God's Word. Many books could be written on God's directive to **plan** rather than "drift" through life.

Again, it's **balance** that God's Word teaches. Too little planning will result in slothfulness (see subtopic 12.E.). Too much planning will result in a lack of trust in God (see subtopic 2.L.).

Planning is a part of a Christian's walk with God. It is literally committing spiritual goals to written form.

Subtopic:	Scripture:	Comments:
10. Planning	Genesis 41:34–36	Joseph's grain storage
God's principles of preparing	Genesis 47:24	Joseph's grain storage
for the future	I Chronicles 22:5	David's plan for temple
	I Chronicles 22:14	David's plan for temple
	Proverbs 16:1	Man plans, God answers
	Proverbs 16:3	Plans established
	Proverbs 16:9	Man plans, God directs
	Proverbs 19:21	Man plans, God counsels
	Proverbs 20:5	A plan in the heart
	Proverbs 21:5	Diligent vs. hasty
	Proverbs 22:3	Prudent looks ahead
	Proverbs 24:27	Plan, then build
	Proverbs 27:12	Prudent plans, naive doesn't
	Proverbs 27:23–24	Know condition of herds
	Proverbs 30:25	Ants plan
	Luke 14:28–30	Parable of tower

Restitution

"If therefore you are presenting your offering at the altar, and there remember that your brother has something against you, leave your offering there before the altar, and go your way; first be reconciled to your brother, and then come and present your offering."
　　　　　　　　　　　　　　　　　　　　　　—Matthew 5:23–24

Restitution literally means to "restore." In the area of finances this normally refers to replacing the material possessions of another. An example of this would be Zaccheus in Luke 19:8, when he said, *". . . if I have defrauded anyone of anything, I will give back four times as much."*

Subtopic:	Scripture:	Comments:
11. Restitution	Exodus 21:16	Pay for kidnapping
God's principles of correcting	Exodus 21:19	Pay for loss of work
wrong	Exodus 21:21	Injury to slave
	Exodus 21:22	Pay for miscarriage
	Exodus 21:30	Pay for animals
	Exodus 21:32	Accidental death of slave
	Exodus 22:1	Pay for theft of an animal
	Exodus 22:3–4	Pay for burglary
	Exodus 22:5	Pay for loose animal
	Exodus 22:6	Pay for fire damages
	Exodus 22:7	Theft of entrusted property
	Exodus 22:8	Liability for fiduciary
	Exodus 22:9	Penalty for breach of trust
	Exodus 22:12–13	Liability for borrowed goods
	Exodus 22:17	Penalty for violating virgin
	Leviticus 5:15	Guilt offering
	Leviticus 6:1–5	Penalty for theft, deceit
	Numbers 5:7	Restitution to victim
	Deuteronomy 22:19	Restitution for violating a virgin
	Deuteronomy 22:29	Restitution for violating a virgin
	Joshua 7:24–25	Restitution for theft (Achan stoned)
	I Samuel 12:3	Samuel's defense of his actions

Subtopic:	Scripture:	Comments:
11. Restitution—*cont'd*	II Samuel 12:4–6	Nathan's accusation of David
	II Samuel 21:4	David's restitution to Gibeonites
	I Kings 20:39	Responsibility of agent
	Matthew 5:23–24	Be reconciled to your brother
	Matthew 5:25–26	Settle before going to court
	Luke 19:8–9	Zaccheus' restitution

Work & Wages

For even when we were with you, we used to give you this order: if anyone will not work, neither let him eat. —II Thessalonians 3:10

This topic references God's Word on our labor (work) and our compensation (wages). Clearly these Scriptures present God's perspective on being a good witness in the workplace through our **quality**. Additionally, this also requires being content with our wages and paying a fair wage to those who work for us.

Subtopic:	Scripture:	Comments:
12.A. Work	Genesis 2:15	Cultivating Garden of Eden
God's direction to labor	Exodus 16:27–28	Sabbath day
	Exodus 20:9	Six days of work
	Leviticus 22:11	Feed slaves well
	Leviticus 23:3	Sabbath day
	Leviticus 25:10	Jubilee year
	I Kings 5:13–15	Solomon's forced labor
	Nehemiah 5:14–16	Nehemiah took no wages
	Job 7:1	Man is forced to work
	Proverbs 16:26	Worker's appetite
	Ecclesiastes 3:13	Good of labor
	Ecclesiastes 5:18–19	Reward of labor
	Ecclesiastes 9:16	Wisdom is better than strength
	Matthew 5:16	Men see good works
	Matthew 12:11	Work on Sabbath
	John 21:3	Peter fishing
	Acts 16:14	Lydia—seller of purple fabric
	Acts 18:3	Paul's tent-making
	Ephesians 4:28	Work, don't steal
	Colossians 3:23	Whatever you do, do well
	I Thessalonians 4:12	Those who work are not in need
	II Thessalonians 3:8	Paul's work
	II Thessalonians 3:10	No work, no eat
	II Timothy 2:4	Don't get too entangled
	II Timothy 2:6	Hard workers deserve a share

Subtopic:	Scripture:	Comments:
12.B. Wages	Genesis 29:15	Jacob's wages
Remuneration for labor	Genesis 30:14–16	Wages
	Genesis 30:18	Leah's wages
	Genesis 30:26	Jacob's wages
	Genesis 30:28	Jacob's wages
	Genesis 30:32	Jacob's wages
	Genesis 31:7–8	Jacob's wages
	Genesis 31:11–12	Jacob's wages
	Genesis 31:41–42	Jacob's wages
	Exodus 2:9	Wages for Moses' nurse
	Leviticus 19:13	Pay a hired man daily
	Leviticus 25:6	Sabbath year wages
	Leviticus 25:39–40	Jew to be hired man, not slave
	Deuteronomy 24:14–15	Pay a hired servant fairly
	Judges 8:24–26	Gideon's wages
	Judges 17:10	Wages for Micah's priest
	Ruth 2:12	Wages full from God
	I Samuel 30:23–24	Wages for baggage tenders
	I Kings 5:6	Wages for temple workers
	II Kings 22:5–9	Wages for temple workers
	I Chronicles 19:6–7	Wages for Ammon's hired warriors
	II Chronicles 25:6–9	Wages for Israel's troops
	Ezra 3:7	Wages for temple workers
	Nehemiah 5:18	Nehemiah took no wages
	Nehemiah 12:47	Wages for temple staff
	Job 7:2	Hired man's wages
	Proverbs 10:16	Wages of righteous life
	Jeremiah 22:13	Woe to those who withhold pay
	Jeremiah 52:34	King Jehoiachin's wages
	Ezekiel 29:18–19	Plunder, wages for Nebuchadnezzar's army
	Zechariah 11:12–13	Prophesy of Judas' wages
	Malachi 3:5	Do not oppress wage earner
	Matthew 10:9–10	Worker is worthy of his hire
	Luke 3:14	Be content with your wages
	Luke 10:7	Worker is worthy of his hire
	Romans 6:23	Wages of sin is death
	I Corinthians 9:7	Who works at his own expense?
	I Corinthians 9:9–11	Sow spiritual, reap material
	I Corinthians 9:14	Those who teach should be paid
	II Corinthians 11:7	Paul preached at Corinth without charge
	II Corinthians 11:8–9	Took his wages from others
	I Timothy 5:18	Laborer is worthy of wages
	James 5:4	Wages withheld wrongly
	III John 6–7	Pay God's workers well

Subtopic:	Scripture:	Comments:
12.C. Employee/Employer *Worker and authority*	Genesis 13:8 Leviticus 25:53	Strife between workers Be fair to hired workers
12.D. Quality *God's principles of excellence*	Proverbs 22:29	Skilled will stand before kings
12.E. Slothful *Failure to perform* *adequately*	Proverbs 6:9–11 Proverbs 10:4 Proverbs 12:27 Proverbs 13:4 Proverbs 14:4 Proverbs 15:19 Proverbs 18:9 Proverbs 19:15 Proverbs 19:24 Proverbs 20:4 Proverbs 20:13 Proverbs 21:25–26 Proverbs 22:13 Proverbs 23:21 Proverbs 24:10 Proverbs 24:30–34 Proverbs 26:13–14 Proverbs 26:15 Proverbs 26:16 II Thessalonians 3:10	Sleep will bring poverty Negligent is poor Lazy man doesn't even cook his prey Lazy craves, but gets nothing No oxen The way of the lazy is thorny He who is slack, destroys Laziness casts sleep Laziness won't even feed himself Lazy doesn't plow Love sleep, become poor Lazy is hungry Lazy man's excuses Heavy drinker is impoverished Lazy are depressed Observation of a lazy man Lazy man's excuses Lazy man won't feed himself Lazy man acts wise No work, no eat
12.F. Diligent *Trustworthy at assigned tasks*	I Chronicles 22:16 Proverbs 10:5 Proverbs 12:11 Proverbs 12:24 Proverbs 22:3 Proverbs 27:18 Proverbs 28:19 Ecclesiastes 9:10 Ecclesiastes 11:6 Daniel 6:1–3 Luke 12:42 Luke 12:44 Acts 20:33–35 I Corinthians 10:31 Galatians 6:9 Colossians 3:17 Colossians 3:23 II Thessalonians 3:8–10	Work, and the Lord is with you He who gathers acts wisely He who tills will have plenty Diligent will rule Prudent sees evil He who tends will eat He who tills will have plenty Whatever you do, do well Start work early Daniel's diligence Faithful will be in charge Diligent will be in charge Paul's work ethic Whatever you do, do well Don't lose heart in doing good Do all in Jesus' name Whatever you do, do well Paul's work ethic

Subtopic:	Scripture:	Comments:
12.F. Diligent—*cont'd*	I Peter 4:11 Revelation 2:19	Work to glorify Jesus Service and perseverance
12.G. Yoke *Bound together*	II Corinthians 6:14–15	Don't be yoked to non- believers

Part II—Scriptural Index

Genesis

Scripture:	Subtopic:

Genesis 2:12
And **the gold of that land is good;** the bdellium and the onyx stone are there.

6.D. Provision

Genesis 2:15
Then the LORD God took the man and put him into **the garden of Eden to cultivate it** and keep it.

12.A. Work

Genesis 4:3–4
[3]So it came about in the course of time that **Cain brought an offering** to the LORD of the fruit of the ground.   [4]And Abel, on his part also brought of the firstlings of his flock and of their fat portions. And the LORD had regard for Abel and for his offering.

4.D. Offerings
4.E. First Fruits

Genesis 12:5
And **Abram took Sarai his wife and Lot his nephew, and all their possessions** which they had accumulated, and the persons which they had acquired in Haran, and they set out for the land of Canaan; thus they came to the land of Canaan.

6.D. Provision

Genesis 12:16
Therefore **he treated Abram well for her sake;** and gave him sheep and oxen and donkeys and male and female servants and female donkeys and camels.

1.I. Fairness

Genesis 13:2
Now **Abram was very rich** in livestock, in silver and in gold.

6.D. Provision

Genesis 13:6
And **the land could not sustain them while dwelling together;** for their possessions were so great that they were not able to remain together.

6.D. Provision

Genesis 13:8
Then Abram said to Lot, **"Please let there be no strife between you and me,** nor between my herdsmen and your herdsmen, for we are brothers."

12.C. Employee/ Employer

Genesis 14:11–12
[11]Then **they took all the goods of Sodom and Gomorrah and all their food supply, and departed.**   [12]And they also took Lot, Abram's nephew, and his possessions and departed, for he was living in Sodom.

6.D. Provision

Genesis 14:16
And **he brought back all the goods,** and also brought back his relative Lot with his possessions, and also the women, and the people.

6.D. Provision

Genesis 14:20
"And blessed be God Most High, Who has delivered your enemies into your hand." And **he gave him a tenth of all.**

4.C. Tithe*

Genesis 14:23
". . . I will not take a thread or a sandal thong or anything that is yours, **lest you should say, 'I have made Abram rich.' "**

6.D. Provision

Genesis 15:2–4
²And Abram said, "O LORD GOD, what wilt Thou give me, since I am childless, and the heir of my house is Eliezer of Damascus?" ³And Abram said, "Since Thou has given no offspring to me, one born in my house is my heir." ⁴Then behold, the word of the LORD came to him, saying, "This man will not be your heir; but **one who shall come forth from your own body, he shall be your heir."**

5.A. Inheritance

Genesis 15:14
"But I will also judge the nation whom they will serve; and afterward **they will come out with many possessions."**

6.C. Blessings

Genesis 17:12
"¹²And every male among you who is eight days old shall be circumcised throughout your generations, **a servant who is born in the house or who is bought with money** from any foreigner, who is not of your descendants." ¹³"A servant who is born in your house **or who is bought with your money** shall surely be circumcised; thus shall My covenant be in your flesh for an everlasting covenant."

9.E. Buying

Genesis 17:23
Then Abraham took Ishmael his son, and all the servants who were born in his house and **all who were bought with his money,** every male among the men of Abraham's household, and circumcised the flesh of their foreskin in the very same day, as God had said to him.

9.E. Buying

Genesis 17:27
And all the men of his household, **who were born in the house or bought with money from a foreigner,** were circumcised with him.

9.E. Buying

Genesis 20:16
And to Sarah he said, "Behold, **I have given your brother a thousand pieces of silver;** behold, it is your vindication before all who are with you, and before all men you are cleared."

9.E. Buying

Genesis 23:9
". . . that he may give me the cave of Machpelah which he owns, which is at the end of his field; for **the full price let him give it to me in your presence for a burial site."**

9.E. Buying

---

*Further explanation of this tithe is given in Hebrews 7:1–10.

Scripture:	Subtopic:

Genesis 23:15–18, 20
¹⁵"My lord, listen to me; a piece of land worth four hundred shekels of silver, what is that between me and you? So bury your dead." ¹⁶And Abraham listened to Ephron; and **Abraham weighed out for Ephron the silver** which he had named in the hearing of the sons of Heth, four hundred shekels of silver, commercial standard. ¹⁷So Ephron's field, which was in Machpelah, which faced Mamre, the field and cave which was in it, and all the trees which were in the field, that were within all the confines of its border, were deeded over ¹⁸to Abraham for a possession in the presence of the sons of Heth, before all who went in at the gate of his city. . . . ²⁰So the field, and the cave that is in it, were deeded over to Abraham for a burial site by the sons of Heth.

9.E. Buying

Genesis 24:22
Then it came about, when the camels had finished drinking, that **the man took a gold ring weighing a half-shekel and two bracelets for her wrists** weighing ten shekels in gold.

4.B. Giving to Men

Genesis 24:35–36
³⁵"And **the LORD has greatly blessed my master,** so that he has become rich; and He has given him flocks and herds, and silver and gold, and servants and maids, and camels and donkeys. ³⁶. . . and he has given him all that he has."

6.C. Blessings

Genesis 24:53
And the servant brought out articles of silver and articles of gold, and garments, and gave them to Rebekah; **he also gave precious things to her brother and to her mother.**

4.B. Giving to Men

Genesis 25:5–6
⁵Now **Abraham gave all that he had to Isaac;** ⁶but to the sons of his concubines, Abraham gave gifts while he was still living, and sent them away from his son Isaac eastward, to the land of the east.

5.A. Inheritance

Genesis 25:8
And Abraham breathed his last and died . . . satisfied with life.

5.A. Inheritance

Genesis 25:10
. . . **The field which Abraham purchased from the sons of Heth;** there Abraham was buried with Sarah his wife.

9.E. Buying

Genesis 25:31–34
³¹But Jacob said, **"First sell me your birthright."** ³²And Esau said, "Behold, I am about to die; so of what use then is the birthright to me?" ³³And Jacob said, "First swear to me"; so he swore to him, and sold his birthright to Jacob. ³⁴. . . Thus Esau despised his birthright.

5.A. Inheritance*

---

*A classic picture of how many people trade long-term rewards for short-term gratification.

Genesis 26:3
"Sojourn in this land and I will be with you and bless you, for **to you and to your descendants I will give all these lands,** and I will establish the oath which I swore to your father Abraham."

6.C. Blessings

Genesis 26:12–14
¹²Now Isaac sowed in that land, and reaped in the same year a hundredfold. And **the LORD blessed him,** ¹³**and the man became rich,** and continued to grow richer until he became very wealthy; ¹⁴for he had possessions of flocks and herds and a great household, so that the Philistines envied him.

6.C. Blessings

Genesis 26:28
And they said, "We see plainly that the LORD has been with you; so we said, 'Let there now be an oath between us, even between you and us, and **let us make a covenant with you.**'"

1.K. Paying Vows

Genesis 27:30
Now it came about, as soon as Isaac had finished blessing Jacob, and Jacob had hardly gone out from the presence of Isaac his father, that Esau his brother came in from his hunting.

5.A. Inheritance

Genesis 27:35–36
³⁵And he said, **"Your brother came deceitfully, and has taken away your blessing."** ³⁶Then he said, "Is he not rightly named Jacob, for he has supplanted me these two times? He took away my birthright, and behold, now he has taken away my blessing." And he said, "Have you not reserved a blessing for me?"

2.F. Dishonesty

Genesis 27:41
So **Esau bore a grudge against Jacob** because of the blessing with which his father had blessed him; and Esau said to himself, "The days of mourning for my father are near; then I will kill my brother Jacob."

2.G. Envy

Genesis 28:4
"May He also give you the blessing of Abraham, to you and to your descendants with you; that **you may possess the land of your sojournings,** which God gave to Abraham."

6.D. Provision

Genesis 28:22
"And this stone, which I have set up as a pillar, will be God's house; and of all that Thou dost give me **I will surely give a tenth to Thee.**"

4.C. Tithe

Genesis 29:15
Then Laban said to Jacob, "Because you are my relative, **should you therefore serve me for nothing? Tell me, what shall your wages be?**"

6.B. Counsel of God
12.B. Wages

Genesis 29:18
Now Jacob loved Rachel, so he said, **"I will serve you seven years for your younger daughter Rachel."**

9.E. Buying

Genesis 29:25
So it came about in the morning that, behold, it was Leah! And he
said to Laban, "What is this you have done to me? Was it not for
Rachel that I served with you? **Why then have you deceived me?**"

2.F. Dishonesty

Genesis 30:14–16
¹⁴Now in the days of wheat harvest Reuben went and found mandrakes in the field, and brought them to his mother Leah. Then
Rachel said to Leah, "Please give me some of your son's mandrakes." ¹⁵But she said to her, "Is it a small matter for you to take
my husband? And would you take my son's mandrakes also?" So
Rachel said, "Therefore he may lie with you tonight in return for
your son's mandrakes." ¹⁶When Jacob came in from the field in
the evening, then Leah went out to meet him and said, "You must
come in to me, for I have surely hired you with my son's mandrakes." So he lay with her that night.

12.B. Wages

Genesis 30:18
Then Leah said, **"God has given me my wages,** because I gave my
maid to my husband." So she named him Issachar.

12.B. Wages

Genesis 30:20
Then Leah said, **"God has endowed me with a good gift;** now my
husband will dwell with me, because I have borne him six sons." So
she named him Zebulun.

6.D. Provision

Genesis 30:26
"Give me my wives and my children for whom I have served you,
and let me depart; for you yourself know my service which I have
rendered you."

12.B. Wages

Genesis 30:28
And he continued, **"Name me your wages,** and I will give it."

12.B. Wages

Genesis 30:32–33
³²". . . and **such shall be my wages.** ³³So my honesty will answer
for me later, when you come concerning my wages. Every one that
is not speckled and spotted among the goats and black among the
lambs, if found with me, will be considered stolen."

12.B. Wages
1.B. Honesty

Genesis 30:43
So the man became exceedingly prosperous, and had large flocks
and female and male servants and camels and donkeys.

6.D. Provision

Genesis 31:1
Now Jacob heard the words of Laban's sons, saying, **"Jacob has
taken away all that was our father's,** and from what belonged to
our father he has made all this wealth."

2.G. Envy

Genesis 31:7
"Yet **your father has cheated me and changed** my wages ten times;
however, God did not allow him to hurt me."

2.F. Dishonesty
12.B. Wages

Genesis 31:8
"If he spoke thus, '**The speckled shall be your wages,**' then all the
flock brought forth speckled; and if he spoke thus, '**The striped
shall be your wages,**' then all the flock brought forth striped."

12.B. Wages

Genesis 31:9
"Thus **God has taken away your father's livestock** and given them
to me."

6.C. Blessings

Genesis 31:11–12
[11]"Then the angel of God said to me in the dream, 'Jacob,' and I
said, 'Here I am.' [12]And he said, 'Lift up, now, your eyes and see
that all the male goats which are mating are striped, speckled, and
mottled; for I have seen all that Laban has been doing to you.'"

2.F. Dishonesty
12.B. Wages

Genesis 31:14–16
[14]And Rachel and Leah answered and said to him, "**Do we still have
any portion or inheritance in our father's house?** [15]Are we not
reckoned by him as foreigners? For he has sold us, and has also
entirely consumed our purchase price. [16]Surely all the wealth
which God has taken away from our father belongs to us and our
children; now then, do whatever God has said to you."

5.A. Inheritance

Genesis 31:19–20
[19]When Laban had gone to shear his flock, then **Rachel stole the
household idols that were her father's.** [20]And Jacob deceived Laban the Aramean, by not telling him that he was fleeing.

2.F. Dishonesty

Genesis 31:30–32
". . . [30]but **why did you steal my gods?**" [31]Then Jacob answered
and said to Laban, "Because I was afraid, too I said, 'Lest you
would take your daughter from me by force.' [32]The one with
whom you find your gods shall not live. . . ." For Jacob did not
know that Rachel had stolen them.

2.E. Greed

Genesis 31:39
"That which was torn of beasts I did not bring to you; **I bore the
loss of it myself.** You required it of my hand whether stolen by day
or stolen by night."

1.I. Fairness

Genesis 31:41–42
[41]". . . and **you changed my wages ten times.** [42]. . . God has seen
my affliction and the toil of my hands, so He rendered judgment
last night."

12.B. Wages

Scripture:	Subtopic:

Genesis 32:17–18
[17]And he commanded the one in front, saying, "When my brother Esau meets you and asks you, saying, 'To whom do you belong, and where are you going, and to whom do these animals in front of you belong?' [18]then you shall say, 'These belong to your servant Jacob; **it is a present sent to my lord Esau.** And behold, he also is behind us.'" [19]Then he commanded also the second and the third, and all those who followed the droves, saying, "After this manner you shall speak to Esau when you find him; [20]and you shall say, 'Behold, your servant Jacob also is behind us.'" For he said, "**I will appease him with the present that goes before me.** Then afterward I will see his face; perhaps he will accept me."

4.B. Giving to Men

Genesis 33:10–11
[10]And Jacob said, "No, please, if now I have found favor in your sight, **then take my present from my hand,** for I see your face as one sees the face of God, and you have received me favorably. [11]Please take my gift which has been brought to you, because God has dealt graciously with me, and because I have plenty." Thus he urged him and he took it.

4.B. Giving to Men

Genesis 33:19
And **he bought the piece of land where he had pitched his tent** from the hand of the sons of Hamor, Shechem's father, for one hundred pieces of money.

9.E. Buying

Genesis 34:10
"Thus you shall live with us, and the land shall be open before you; **live and trade in it, and acquire property in it.**"

9.E. Buying

Genesis 34:12
"**Ask me ever so much bridal payment and gift,** and I will give according as you say to me; but give me the girl in marriage."

9.E. Buying

Genesis 34:29
. . . and **they captured and looted all their wealth** and all their little ones and their wives, even all that was in the houses.

6.E. Discipline

Genesis 36:6–7
[6]Then **Esau took his wives** and his sons and his daughters and all his household, and his livestock and all his cattle and all his goods which he had acquired in the land of Canaan, **and went to another land away from his brother Jacob.** [7]For their property had become too great for them to live together, and the land where they sojourned could not sustain them because of their livestock.

1.I. Fairness

Genesis 37:26–28
[26]And Judah said to his brothers, "What profit is it for us to kill our brother and cover up his blood? [27]**Come and let us sell him to the Ishmaelites and not lay our hands on him;** for he is our brother, our own flesh." And his brothers listened to him. [28]. . . sold him to the Ishmaelites for twenty shekels of silver. Thus they brought Joseph into Egypt.

2.J. Injustice

Genesis 37:36
Meanwhile, **the Midianites sold him in Egypt to Potiphar**, Pharaoh's officer, the captain of the bodyguard.

9.D. Selling

Genesis 38:20
When Judah sent the kid by his friend the Adullamite, **to receive the pledge from the woman's hand**, he did not find her.

3.F. Paying Debts

Genesis 39:2–3
²And **the LORD was with Joseph, so he became a successful man.** And he was in the house of his master, the Egyptian. ³Now his master saw that the LORD was with him and how the LORD caused all that he did to prosper in his hand.

6.C. Blessings

Genesis 39:4–6
⁴. . . all that he owned he put in his charge. ⁵. . . the LORD blessed the Egyptian's house on account of Joseph; thus **the LORD's blessing was upon all that he owned,** in the house and in the field. ⁶So he left everything he owned in Joseph's charge; . . . .

6.C. Blessings

Genesis 39:8
But he refused and said to his master's wife, "Behold, with me here, my master does not concern himself with anything in the house, and he has put all that he owns in my charge."

6.C. Blessings

Genesis 39:23
The chief jailer did not supervise anything under Joseph's charge because the LORD was with him; and **whatever he did, the LORD made to prosper.**

6.C. Blessings

Genesis 41:34–36
³⁴"Let Pharaoh take action to appoint overseers in charge of the land, and **let him exact a fifth of the produce of the land of Egypt** in the seven years of abundance. ³⁵Then let them gather all the food of these good years that are coming, and store up the grain for food in the cities under Pharaoh's authority, and let them guard it. ³⁶And let the food become as a reserve for the land for the seven years of famine which will occur in the land of Egypt, so that the land may not perish during the famine."

10. Planning

Genesis 41:52
And he named the second Ephraim, "For," he said, **"God has made me fruitful in the land of my affliction."**

6.D. Provision

Genesis 41:56–57
When the famine was spread over all the face of the earth, then **Joseph opened all the storehouses, and sold to the Egyptians;** and the famine was severe in the land of Egypt. And the people of all the earth came to Egypt to buy grain from Joseph, because the famine was severe in all the earth.

9.D. Selling
9.E. Buying

Scripture:	Subtopic:

Genesis 42:2–3
And he said, "Behold, I have heard that there is grain in Egypt; **go down there and buy some for us** from that place, so that we may live and not die." ³Then ten brothers of Joseph went down to buy grain from Egypt.

9.E. Buying

Genesis 42:5–7
⁵So the sons of Israel came to buy grain among those who were coming, for the famine was in the land of Canaan also. ⁶Now Joseph was the ruler over the land; he was the one who sold to all the people of the land. And Joseph's brothers came and bowed down to him with their faces to the ground. . . . ⁷Where have you come from?" And they said, **"From the land of Canaan, to buy food."**

9.E. Buying

Genesis 42:10
Then they said to him, "No, my lord, but your servants have come to buy food."

9.E. Buying

Genesis 42:25–28
Then **Joseph gave orders** to fill their bags with grain and **to restore every man's money** in his sack, and to give them provisions for the journey. . . . ²⁶So they loaded their donkeys with their grain, and departed from there. ²⁷And as one of them opened his sack to give his donkey fodder at the lodging place, he saw his money; and behold, it was in the mouth of his sack. ²⁸Then he said to his brothers, **"My money has been returned,** and behold, it is even in my sack." And their hearts sank, and they turned trembling to one another, saying, **"What is this that God has done to us?"**

4.B. Giving to Men

Genesis 42:35
Now it came about as they were emptying their sacks, that behold, **every man's bundle of money was in his sack;** and when they and their father saw their bundles of money, they were dismayed.

4.B. Giving to Men

Genesis 43:4
"If you send our brother with us, we will go down and buy you food."

9.E. Buying

Genesis 43:9
"**I myself will be surety for him;** you may hold me responsible for him. . . ."

3.E. Surety

Genesis 43:12
"And **take double the money** in your hand, and take back in your hand the money that was returned in the mouth of your sacks; perhaps it was a mistake."

9.E. Buying

Genesis 43:15
So the men took this present, and they took double the money in their hand, and Benjamin; then they arose and went down to Egypt and stood before Joseph.

9.E. Buying

Scripture:	Subtopic:

Genesis 43:18
Now the men were afraid, because they were brought to Joseph's house; and they said, "**It is because of the money that was returned in our sacks** the first time that we are being brought in, that he may seek occasion against us and fall upon us, and take us for slaves with our donkeys."

4.B. Giving to Men

Genesis 43:20
. . . and said, "Oh, my lord, we indeed came down the first time to buy food."

9.E. Buying

Genesis 43:21–23
²¹". . . and it came about when we came to the lodging place, that we opened our sacks, and behold, each man's money was in the mouth of his sack, our money in full. So we have brought it back in our hand. ²²We have also brought down other money in our hand to buy food; we do not know who put our money in our sacks." ²³And he said, "**Be at ease do not be afraid. Your God and the God of your father has given you treasure** in your sacks; I had your money." Then he brought Simeon out to them.

9.E. Buying

Genesis 43:26
When Joseph came home, they brought into the house to him the present which was in their hand and bowed to the ground before him.

4.B. Giving to Men

Genesis 44:1–2
¹Then he commanded his house steward, saying, "**Fill the men's sacks** with food, as much as they can carry, and **put each man's money in the mouth of his sack.** ²And put my cup, the silver cup, in the mouth of the sack of the youngest, and his money for the grain." And he did as Joseph had told him.

4.B. Giving to Men

Genesis 44:8
"Behold, the money which we found in the mouth of our sacks we have brought back to you from the land of Canaan. How then could we steal silver or gold from your lord's house?"

9.E. Buying

Genesis 44:32
"For your servant became surety for the lad to my father, saying, 'If I do not bring him back to you, then let me bear the blame before my father forever.'"

3.E. Surety

Genesis 45:4
Then Joseph said to his brothers, "Please come closer to me." And they came closer. And he said, "I am your brother Joseph, whom you sold into Egypt."

1.I. Fairness
6.D. Provision

Genesis 45:5
"And now do not be grieved or angry with yourselves, because you sold me here; **for God sent me before you to preserve life.**"

6.D. Provision

Scripture:	Subtopic:

Genesis 45:17
Then Pharaoh said to Joseph, "Say to your brothers, 'Do this: load your beasts and **go to the land of Canaan.**'"

4.B. Giving to Men

Genesis 45:20
"'And do not concern yourselves with your goods, for **the best of all the land of Egypt is yours.**'"

4.B. Giving to Men

Genesis 45:22
To each of them he gave changes of garments, but to Benjamin he gave three hundred pieces of silver and five changes of garments.

4.B. Giving to Men

Genesis 46:6
And they took their livestock and their property, which they had acquired in the land of Canaan, and came to Egypt, Jacob and all his descendants with him.

6.D. Provision

Genesis 47:11
So Joseph settled his father and his brothers, and gave them a possession in the land of Egypt, in the best of the land, in the land of Rameses, as Pharaoh had ordered.

4.B. Giving to Men

Genesis 47:14–17
[14]And **Joseph gathered all the money that was found in the land of Egypt and in the land of Canaan** for the grain which they bought, and Joseph brought the money into Pharaoh's house.   [15]And when the money was all spent in the land of Egypt and in the land of Canaan, all the Egyptians came to Joseph and said, "Give us food, for why should we die in your presence? For our money is gone." [16]Then Joseph said, "Give up your livestock, and I will give you food for you livestock, since your money is gone."   [17]**So they brought their livestock to Joseph,** and Joseph gave them food in exchange for the horses and the flocks and the herds and the donkeys; and he fed them with food in exchange for all their livestock that year.

9.F. Profit

Genesis 47:18–20
. . . "We will not hide from my lord that **our money is all spent,** and the cattle are my lord's. There is nothing left for my lord except our bodies and our lands. . . . Buy us and our land for food, and **we and our land will be slaves to Pharaoh. . . .**" So **Joseph bought all the land of Egypt for Pharaoh,** for every Egyptian sold his field, because the famine was severe upon them. Thus the land became Pharaoh's.

9.E. Buying

Genesis 47:22
Only the land of the priests he did not buy, for the priests had an allotment from Pharaoh, and they lived off the allotment which Pharaoh gave them. Therefore, they did not sell their land.

9.E. Buying

Scripture:	Subtopic:

Genesis 47:24
"And **at the harvest you shall give a fifth to Pharaoh,** and four-fifths shall be your own for seed of the field and for your food and for those of your households and as food for your little ones."

10. Planning

Genesis 47:26
And **Joseph made it a statute** concerning the land of Egypt valid to this day, that Pharaoh should have the fifth; only the land of the priests did not become Pharaoh's.

8.B. Administrative Tax

Genesis 49:20
"As for Asher, his food shall be rich, and he shall yield royal dainties."

6.A. God's Promises

Genesis 50:15
When Joseph's brothers saw that their father was dead, they said, "What if Joseph should bear a grudge against us and pay us back in full for all the wrong which we did to him!"

2.M. Fear

Exodus

Scripture:	Subtopic:

Exodus 2:9
Then Pharaoh's daughter said to her, "**Take this child** away and nurse him for me and **I shall give you your wages.**" So the woman took the child and nursed him.

12.B. Wages

Exodus 3:21–22
[21]"And I will grant this people favor in the sight of the Egyptians; and it shall be that when you go, you will not go empty-handed. [22]But every woman shall ask of her neighbor and the woman who lives in her house, articles of silver and articles of gold, and clothing; and you will put them on your sons and daughters. **Thus you will plunder the Egyptians.**"

6.D. Provision

Exodus 6:8
"'And **I will bring you to the land which I swore to give to Abra-ham,** Isaac, and Jacob, and I will give it to you for a possession; I am the LORD.'"

6.D. Provision

Exodus 9:4
"But the LORD will make a distinction between the livestock of Israel and the livestock of Egypt, so that **nothing will die of all that belongs to the sons of Israel.**"

6.D. Provision

Exodus 9:29
". . . the earth is the LORD's."

6.G. Wealth

Exodus 11:2–3
[2]"Speak now in the hearing of the people that **each man ask from his neighbor and each woman from her neighbor for articles of silver and articles of gold.**" [3]And the LORD gave the people favor in the sight of the Egyptians. Furthermore, the man Moses himself was greatly esteemed in the land of Egypt, both in the sight of Pharaoh's servants and in the sight of the people.

6.D. Provision

Exodus 12:35–36
[35]Now the sons of Israel had done according to the word of Moses, for they had requested from the Egyptians articles of silver and articles of gold, and clothing; [36]and the LORD had given the people favor in sight of the Egyptians, so that they let them have their request. **Thus they plundered the Egyptians.**

6.D. Provision

Exodus 12:44
". . . but **every man's slave purchased with money,** after you have circumcised him, then he may eat of it."

9.E. Buying

Scripture:	Subtopic:

Exodus 16:4
Then the LORD said to Moses, "Behold, **I will rain bread from heaven for you;** and the people shall go out and gather a day's portion every day, that I may test them, whether or not they will walk in My instruction."

6.D. Provision

Exodus 16:16
"This is what the LORD has commanded, '**Gather of it every man as much as he should eat;** you shall take an omer apiece according to the number of persons each of you has in his tent.'"

6.D. Provision

Exodus 16:18–21
When they measured it with an omer, he who had gathered much had no excess, and he who had gathered little had no lack; **every man gathered as much as he should eat.** [19]And Moses said to them, **"Let no man leave any of it until morning."** [20]But they did not listen to Moses, and some left part of it until morning, and it bred worms and became foul; and Moses was angry with them. [21]And they gathered it morning by morning, every man as much as he should eat; but when the sun grew hot, it would melt.

6.D. Provision*

Exodus 16:27–28
[27]And it came about **on the seventh day that some of the people went out to gather, but they found none.** [28]Then the LORD said to Moses, "How long do you refuse to keep My commandments and My instructions?"

12.A. Work[†]

Exodus 16:32
Then Moses said, "This is what the LORD has commanded, '**Let an omerful of it be kept throughout your generations,** that they may see the bread that I fed you in the wilderness, when I brought you out of the land of Egypt.'"

6.D. Provision

Exodus 17:2–3
[2]Therefore the people quarreled with Moses and said, "Give us water that we may drink." And Moses said to them, "Why do you quarrel with me? **Why do you test the LORD?"** [3]But the people thirsted there for water; and they grumbled against Moses and said, "Why, now, have you brought us up from Egypt, to kill us and our children and our livestock with thirst?"

2.I. Disobedient

Exodus 17:6
"Behold, I will stand before you there on the rock at Horeb; and you shall strike the rock, and **water will come out of it, that the people may drink.**" And Moses did so in the sight of the elders of Israel.

6.D. Provision

---

*Note that each gathered what he "should" eat, not what he "could" eat. Paul quotes this passage in II Corinthians 8:15 as a principle of sharing.

[†]Clearly God's plan for the Jew was to do no work on the sabbath day, not even gathering manna. See Colossians 2:16 for New Testament principle.

Scripture:	Subtopic:

Exodus 17:12
But Moses' hands were heavy. Then they took a stone and put it under him, and he sat on it; and Aaron and Hur supported his hands, one on one side and one on the other. Thus his hands were steady until the sun set.

6.A. God's Promises

Exodus 18:21
"Furthermore, you shall select out of all the people able men who fear God, men of truth, **those who hate dishonest gain;** and you shall place these over them, as leaders of thousands, of hundreds, of fifties and of tens."

1.B. Honesty*

Exodus 19:12
"And you shall set bounds for the people all around, saying, 'Beware that you do not go up on the mountain or touch the border of it; whoever touches the mountain shall surely be put to death.'"

1.B. Honesty

Exodus 20:5
"You shall not worship them or serve them; for I, the LORD your God, am a jealous God, visiting the iniquity of the fathers on the children, on the third and the fouth generations of those who hate Me."

7.B. False Gods

Exodus 20:9
"Six days you shall labor and do all your work."

12.A. Work

Exodus 20:15
"You shall not steal."

2.F. Dishonesty

Exodus 20:17
"You **shall not covet your neighbor's house;** you shall not covet your neighbor's wife or his male servant or his female servant or his ox or his donkey or anything that belongs to your neighbor."

2.D. Coveteousness

Exodus 20:23
"**You shall not make other gods besides Me;** gods of silver or gods of gold, you shall not make for yourselves."

7.B. False Gods

Exodus 21:2
"**If you buy a Hebrew slave, he shall serve for six years;** but on the seventh he shall go out as a free man without payment."

9.E. Buying†

Exodus 21:7–8
7"**And if a man sells his daughter** as a female slave, she is not to go free as the male slaves do. 8. . . He does not have authority to sell her to a foreign people because of his unfairness to her."

9.D. Selling

---

*See Nehemiah 5:14–17 for definition of a leader's role.
†Coincides with the year of remission. See Deuteronomy 15:1–11.

Scripture:	Subtopic:

Exodus 21:11
"And if he will not do these three things for her, then **she shall go out for nothing, without payment of money.**"

9.D. Selling

Exodus 21:16
"And he who kidnaps a man, whether he sells him or he is found in his possession, shall surely be put to death."

11. Restitution

Exodus 21:19
"If he gets up and walks around outside on his staff, then he who struck him shall go unpunished; **he shall only pay for his loss of time,** and shall take care of him until he is completely healed."

11. Restitution

Exodus 21:21
"If, however, **he survives a day or two, no vengeance shall be taken;** for he is his property."

11. Restitution

Exodus 21:22
"And if men struggle with each other and strike a woman with child so that **she has a miscarriage,** yet there is no further injury, **he shall surely be fined as the woman's husband may demand of him;** and he shall pay as the judges decide."

11. Restitution

Exodus 21:30
"If a ransom is demanded of him, then he shall give for the redemption of his life whatever is demanded of him."

11. Restitution

Exodus 21:32
"**If the ox gores a male or female slave,** the owner shall give his or her master thirty shekels of silver, and the ox shall be stoned."

11. Restitution

Exodus 22:1
"**If a man steals an ox or a sheep,** and slaughters it or sells it, he shall pay five oxen for the ox and four sheep for the sheep."

11. Restitution*

Exodus 22:3–4
³"**. . . He shall surely make restitution;** if he owns nothing, then he shall be sold for his theft. ⁴If what he stole is actually found alive in his possession, whether an ox or a donkey or a sheep, he shall pay double."

11. Restitution

Exodus 22:5
"**If a man lets a field or vineyard be grazed bare** and lets his animal loose so that it grazes in another man's field, he shall make restitution from the best of his own field and the best of his own vineyard."

11. Restitution

---

*Luke 19:8–9 for application of this principle.

Scripture:	Subtopic:

Exodus 22:6
"If a fire breaks out and spreads to thorn bushes, so that stacked grain or the standing grain or the field itself is consumed, he who started the fire shall surely make restitution."

11. Restitution

Exodus 22:7–8
[7]**"If a man gives his neighbor money or goods to keep for him,** and it is stolen from the man's house, if the thief is caught, he shall pay double.   [8]If the thief is not caught, then the owner of the house shall appear before the judges, to determine whether he laid his hands on his neighbor's property."

11. Restitution

Exodus 22:9
"For every breach of trust, whether it is for ox, for donkey, for sheep, for clothing, or for any lost thing about which one says, 'This is it,' the case of both parties shall come before the judges; he whom the judges condemn shall pay double to his neighbor."

11. Restitution

Exodus 22:12–13
[12]**"But if it is actually stolen from him,** he shall make restitution to its owner.   [13]If it is all torn to pieces, let him bring it as evidence; he shall not make restitution for what has been torn to pieces."

11. Restitution

Exodus 22:14–15
[14]**"And if a man borrows anything from his neighbor,** and it is injured or dies while its owner is not with it, he shall make full restitution.   [15]If its owner is with it, he shall not make restitution; if it is hired, it came for its hire."

3.A. Borrowing

Exodus 22:17
"If her father absolutely refuses to give her to him, **he shall pay money equal to the dowry for virgins."**

11. Restitution

Exodus 22:25
"If you lend money to My people, to the poor among you, you are not to act as a creditor to him; you shall not charge him interest."

3.B. Lending*

Exodus 22:26
"If you ever take your neighbor's cloak as a pledge, you are to return it to him before the sun sets."

3.E. Surety

Exodus 22:29–30
"You shall not delay the offering from your harvest and your vintage. The first-born of your sons you shall give to Me. You shall do the same with your oxen and with your sheep. It shall be with its mother seven days; on the eighth day you shall give it to Me."

4.D. Offerings
4.E. First Fruits

Exodus 23:3
". . . **nor shall you be partial to a poor man** in his dispute."

1.I. Fairness

---

*All loans to "God's people" should be interest free.

Scripture:	Subtopic:

Exodus 23:8
"**And you shall not take a bribe,** for a bribe blinds the clear-sighted and subverts the cause of the just."

2.B. Bribe

Exodus 23:11
". . . but **on the seventh year you shall let it rest** and lie fallow, so that the needy of your people may eat; and whatever they leave the beast of the field may eat. You are to do the same with your vineyard and your olive grove."

4.H. Helping Needy

Exodus 25:2–3
²"**Tell the sons of Israel to raise a contribution for Me;** from every man whose heart moves him you shall raise My contribution. ³And this is the contribution which you are to raise from them: gold, silver and bronze."

4.D. Offerings*

Exodus 25:11
"And **you shall overlay it with pure gold,** inside and out you shall overlay it, and you shall make a gold molding around it."

6.G. Wealth

Exodus 25:17–18
¹⁷"And **you shall make a mercy seat of pure gold,** two and a half cubits long and one and a half cubits wide. ¹⁸And you shall make two cherubim of gold, make them of hammered work at the two ends of the mercy seat."

6.G. Wealth

Exodus 25:24–26
²⁴"And **you shall overlay it with pure gold** and make a gold border around it. ²⁵And you shall make for it a rim of a handbreadth around it; and you shall make a gold border for the rim around it. ²⁶And you shall make four gold rings for it. . . ."

6.G. Wealth

Exodus 25:28–29
²⁸"And **you shall make the poles of acacia wood and overlay them with gold,** so that with them the table may be carried. ²⁹And you shall make its dishes and its pans and its jars and its bowls, with which to pour libations; you shall make them of pure gold."

6.G. Wealth

Exodus 25:31
"Then you shall make a lampstand of pure gold. . . ."

6.G. Wealth

Exodus 25:36
"Their bulbs and their branches shall be of one piece with it; all of it shall be one piece of hammered work of pure gold."

6.G. Wealth

Exodus 25:38–39
³⁸"And its snuffers and their trays shall be of pure gold. ³⁹It shall be made from a talent of pure gold, with all these utensils."

6.G. Wealth

---

*God's plan for "church" financing.

Scripture:	Subtopic:

Exodus 26:6
"And you shall make fifty clasps of gold. . . ."

6.G. Wealth

Exodus 26:11
"And you shall make fifty clasps of bronze. . . ."

6.G. Wealth

Exodus 26:21
". . . and their forty sockets of silver; . . ."

6.G. Wealth

Exodus 26:25
"And there shall be eight boards with their sockets of silver, sixteen sockets; two sockets under one board and two sockets under another board."

6.G. Wealth

Exodus 26:29
"And you shall overlay the boards with gold and make their rings of gold as holders for the bars; and you shall overlay the bars with gold."

6.G. Wealth

Exodus 26:32
"And you shall hang it on four pillars of acacia overlaid with gold, their hooks also being of gold, on four sockets of silver."

6.G. Wealth

Exodus 26:37
"And you shall make five pillars of acacia for the screen, and overlay them with gold, their hooks also being of gold; and you shall cast five sockets of bronze for them."

6.G. Wealth

Exodus 27:10–11
". . . and its pillars shall be twenty, with their twenty sockets of bronze; the hooks of the pillars and their bands shall be of silver. And likewise for the north side . . . the hooks of the pillars and their bands shall be of silver."

6.G. Wealth

Exodus 27:17
"All the pillars around the court shall be furnished with silver bands with their hooks of silver and their sockets of bronze."

6.G. Wealth

Exodus 28:5–6
[5]"And they shall take the gold and the blue and the purple and the scarlet material and the fine linen. [6]They shall also make the ephod of gold, of blue and purple and scarlet material and fine twisted linen, the work of the skillful workman."

6.G. Wealth

Exodus 28:8
". . . of the same material: of gold, . . ."

6.G. Wealth

Exodus 28:11
". . . you shall set them in filigree settings of gold."

6.G. Wealth

Exodus 28:13–14
[13]"And you shall make filigree settings of gold, [14]and two chains of pure gold; . . ."

6.G. Wealth

Exodus 28:15
"And you shall make a breastpiece of judgment, the work of a skillful workman; like the work of the ephod you shall make it; of gold, of blue and purple and scarlet material and fine twisted linen you shall make it."

6.G. Wealth

Exodus 28:22
"And you shall make on the breastpiece chains of twisted cordage work in pure gold."

6.G. Wealth

Exodus 28:23
". . . two rings of gold, . . ."

6.G. Wealth

Exodus 28:24
"And you shall put the two cords of gold on the two rings at the ends of the breastpiece."

6.G. Wealth

Exodus 28:26
"And you shall make two rings of gold. . . ."

6.G. Wealth

Exodus 28:27
"And you shall make two rings of gold. . . ."

6.G. Wealth

Exodus 28:33–34
[33]". . . and bells of gold between them all around: [34]a golden bell and a pomegranate, a golden bell and a pomegranate, all around on the hem of the robe."

6.G. Wealth

Exodus 28:36
"You shall also make a plate of pure gold and shall engrave on it, like the engravings of a seal, 'Holy to the LORD.'"

6.G. Wealth

Exodus 30:3–4
[3]"And you shall overlay it with pure gold, its top and its sides all around, and its horns; and you shall make a gold molding all around for it. [4]. . . make two gold rings. . . ."

6.G. Wealth

Exodus 30:5
". . . overlay them with gold."

6.G. Wealth

Scripture:	Subtopic:

Exodus 30:12–16

[12]"When you take a census of the sons of Israel to number them, then **each one of them shall give a ransom for himself to the LORD,** when you number them, that there may be no plague among them when you number them.   [13]This is what everyone who is numbered shall give: half a shekel according to the shekel of the sanctuary (the shekel is twenty gerahs), half a shekel as a contribution to the LORD.   [14]Everyone who is numbered, from twenty years old and over, shall give the contribution to the LORD.   [15]**The rich shall not pay more, and the poor shall not pay less** than the half shekel, when you give the contribution to the LORD make atonement for yourselves.   [16]And you shall take the atonement money from the sons of Israel, and shall give it for the service of the tent of meeting, that it may be a memorial for the sons of Israel before the LORD, to make atonement for yourselves."

4.D. Offerings

Exodus 31:4

". . . to make artistic designs for work in gold, in silver, and in bronze."

6.G. Wealth

Exodus 31:8

". . . the table also and its utensils, and the pure gold lampstand with all its utensils, and the altar of incense. . ."

6.G. Wealth

Exodus 32:2–3

[2]And Aaron said to them, "Tear off the gold rings which are in the ears of your wives, your sons, and your daughters, and bring them to me."   [3]Then **all the people tore off the gold rings which were in their ears, and brought them to Aaron.**

7.B. False Gods

Exodus 32:24

"And I said to them, '**Whoever has any gold, let them tear it off.**' So they gave it to me, and I threw it into the fire, and out came this calf."

7.B. False Gods

Exodus 32:31

". . . and **they have made a god of gold** for themselves."

7.B. False Gods

Exodus 34:19

"The first offspring from every womb belongs to Me, and all your male livestock, the first offspring from cattle and sheep."

4.E. First Fruits

Exodus 34:26

"You shall bring the very first of the first fruits of your soil into the house of the LORD your God. You shall not boil a kid in its mother's milk."

4.E. First Fruits

Scripture:	Subtopic:

Exodus 35:5
"Take from among you a contribution to the LORD; whoever is of a willing heart, let him bring it as the LORD's contribution: gold, silver, and bronze."

4.D. Offerings*

Exodus 35:21–22
²¹And everyone whose heart stirred him and everyone whose spirit moved him came and **brought the LORD's contribution for the work of the tent of meeting** and for all its service and for the holy garments. ²²Then all whose hearts moved them, both men and women, came and brought brooches and earrings and signet rings and bracelets, all articles of gold; so did every man who presented an offering of gold to the LORD.

4.D. Offerings

Exodus 35:24
Everyone who could make a contribution of silver and bronze brought the LORD's contribution; and every man, who had in his possession acacia wood for any work of the service, brought it.

4.D. Offerings

Exodus 35:31–32
³¹"And He has filled him with the Spirit of God, in wisdom, in understanding and in knowledge and in all craftsmanship; ³²to make designs for working in gold and in silver and in bronze."

6.C. Blessings

Exodus 36:3
And they received from Moses all the contributions which the sons of Israel had brought to perform the work in the construction of the sanctuary. And **they still continued bringing to him freewill offerings every morning.**

4.D. Offerings

Exodus 36:5–6
⁵And they said to Moses, **"The people are bringing much more than enough for the construction work** which the LORD commanded us to perform." ⁶So Moses issued a command, and a proclamation was circulated throughout the camp, saying, "Let neither man nor woman any longer perform work for the contributions of the sanctuary." Thus the people were restrained from bringing any more.

4.D. Offerings†

Exodus 36:13
And he made fifty clasps of gold, and joined the curtains to one another with the clasps, so the tabernacle was a unit.

6.G. Wealth

Exodus 36:24
And he made forty sockets of silver under the twenty boards; . . .

6.G. Wealth

Exodus 36:26
. . . and their forty sockets of silver; . . .

6.G. Wealth

---

*God's plan for building His house.
†God's people gave **more** than enough to build the Tabernacle.

Scripture:	Subtopic:

Exodus 37:6
". . . mercy seat of pure gold, . . ." 6.G. Wealth

Exodus 37:7
". . . two cherubim of gold; . . ." 6.G. Wealth

Exodus 37:16–17
[16]And he made the utensils which were on the table, its dishes and 6.G. Wealth
its pans and its bowls and its jars, with which to pour out libations,
of pure gold. [17]Then he made the lampstand of pure gold. . . .

Exodus 37:22–24
[22]Their bulbs and their branches were of one piece with it; the 6.G. Wealth
whole of it was a single hammered work of pure gold. [23]And he
made its seven lamps with its snuffers and its trays of pure
gold. [24]He made it and all its utensils from a talent of pure gold.

Exodus 38:10
. . . bands were of silver. 6.G. Wealth

Exodus 38:11
. . . bands were of silver. 6.G. Wealth

Exodus 38:12
. . . bands were of silver. 6.G. Wealth

Exodus 38:17
. . . bands, of silver; and the overlaying of their tops, of silver, . . . 6.G. Wealth

Exodus 38:19
. . . hooks were of silver, . . . bands were of silver. 6.G. Wealth

Exodus 38:24–25
[24]All the gold that was used for the work, in all the work of the 6.G. Wealth*
sanctuary, even the gold of the wave offering, was 29 talents and
730 shekels, according to the shekel of the sanctuary. [25]And the
silver of those of the congregation who were numbered was 100
talents and 1,775 shekels, according to the shekel of the sanctuary; . . .

Exodus 39:2
And he made the ephod of gold. . . . 6.G. Wealth

Exodus 39:3
Then they hammered out gold sheets. . . . 6.G. Wealth

Exodus 40:26
Then he placed the gold altar in the tent of meeting in front of the 6.G. Wealth
veil.

---

*The gold was calculated to be twenty-eight thousand pounds and the silver, ninety-six thousand
pounds.

Leviticus

Scripture:	Subtopic:

Leviticus 5:15
". . . according to your valuation in silver by shekels, in terms of the shekel of the sanctuary, **for a guilt offering.**"

11. Restitution

Leviticus 6:1–5
¹THEN the LORD spoke to Moses, saying, ²"When a person sins and acts unfaithfully against the LORD, and deceives his companion in **regard to a deposit or a security entrusted to him, or through robbery,** or if he has extorted from his companion, ³or has found what was lost and lied about it and sworn falsely, so that he sins in regard to any one of the things a man may do; ⁴then it shall be, when he sins and becomes guilty, that he shall restore what he took by robbery, or what he got by extortion, or the deposit which was entrusted to him, or the lost thing which he found, ⁵or anything about which he swore falsely; **he shall make restitution for it in full, and add to it one-fifth more.** He shall give it to the one to whom it belongs on the day he presents his guilt offering."

11. Restitution*

Leviticus 14:21–22
²¹"**But if he is poor,** and his means are insufficient, **then he is to take one male lamb for a guilt offering** as a wave offering to make atonement for him, and one-tenth of an ephah of fine flour mixed with oil for a grain offering, and a log of oil, ²²and two turtledoves or two young pigeons which are within his means, the one shall be a sin offering and the other a burnt offering."

4.D. Offerings†

Leviticus 14:30–31
³⁰"He shall then offer one of the turtledoves or young pigeons, which are within his means. ³¹**He shall offer what he can afford,** the one for a sin offering, and the other for a burnt offering, together with the grain offering. So the priest shall make atonement before the LORD on behalf of the one to be cleansed."

4.D. Offerings

Leviticus 19:10
"**Nor shall you glean your vineyard,** nor shall you gather the fallen fruit of your vineyard; you shall leave them for the needy and for the stranger. I am the LORD your God."

1.I. Fairness
4.H. Helping Needy

Leviticus 19:11
"**You shall not steal,** nor deal falsely, nor lie to one another."

2.F. Dishonesty

Leviticus 19:12
"And **you shall not swear falsely** by My name, so as to profane the name of your God; I am the LORD."

1.B. Honesty

---

*God's plan requires repayment with interest for any theft.
†One ephah equaled about ⅔ bushel.

Scripture:	Subtopic:

Leviticus 19:13
"You shall not oppress your neighbor, nor rob him. The wages of a hired man are not to remain with you all night until morning."

12.B. Wages

Leviticus 19:15
"You shall do no injustice in judgment; you shall not be partial to the poor nor defer to the great, but you are to judge your neighbor fairly."

2.J. Injustice

Leviticus 19:35–36
[35]"You shall do no wrong in judgment, in measurement of weight, or capacity. [36]**You shall have just balances, just weights,** a just ephah, and a just hin: I am the LORD your God, who brought you out from the land of Egypt."

1.B. Honesty

Leviticus 22:11
"But **if a priest buys a slave** as his property with his money, that one may eat of it, and those who are born in his house may eat of his food."

9.E. Buying
12.A. Work

Leviticus 22:21
"And **when a man offers a sacrifice of peace offerings** to the LORD to fulfill a special vow, or for a freewill offering, of the herd or of the flock, **it must be perfect** to be accepted; there shall be no defect in it."

4.D. Offerings

Leviticus 23:3
"For six days work may be done; but on the seventh day there is a sabbath of complete rest, a holy convocation. You shall not do any work; it is a sabbath to the LORD in all your dwellings."

12.A. Work

Leviticus 23:10–11
[10]"Speak to the sons of Israel, and say to them, 'When you enter the land which I am going to give to you and reap its harvest, then **you shall bring in the sheaf of the first fruits of your harvest** to the priest. [11]And he shall wave the sheaf before the LORD for you to be accepted; on the day after the sabbath the priest shall wave it.'"

4.D. Offerings
4.E. First Fruits

Leviticus 23:22
"When you reap the harvest of your land, moreover, **you shall not reap to the very corners of your field,** nor gather the gleaning of your harvest; you are to leave them for the needy and the alien. I am the LORD your God."

4.H. Helping
Needy

Leviticus 25:6
"And all of you shall have the sabbath products of the land for food; yourself, and your male and female slaves, and your hired man and your foreign resident, those who live as aliens with you."

12.B. Wages

Leviticus 25:10
"You shall thus consecrate the fiftieth year and proclaim a release through the land to all its inhabitants. **It shall be a jubilee for you, and each of you shall return to his own property, and each of you shall return to his family.**"

12.A. Work*

Leviticus 25:13–17
¹³"**On this year of jubilee** each of you shall return to his own property. ¹⁴If you make a sale, moreover, to your friend, or buy from your friend's hand, you shall not wrong one another. ¹⁵Corresponding to the number of years after the jubilee, you shall buy from your friend; he is to sell to you according to the number of years of crops. ¹⁶In proportion to the extent of the years you shall increase its price, and in proportion to the fewness of the years, you shall diminish its price; for it is a number of crops he is selling to you. ¹⁷So you shall not wrong one another, but you shall fear your God; for I am the LORD your God."

9.E. Buying

Leviticus 25:19
"Then the land will yield its produce, so that you can eat your fill and live securely on it."

6.D. Provision

Leviticus 25:23
"**The land,** moreover, **shall not be sold permanently,** for the land is Mine; for you are but aliens and sojourners with Me."

9.D. Selling

Leviticus 25:24
"Thus for every piece of your property, you are to provide for the redemption of the land."

9.D. Selling

Leviticus 25:25–28
²⁵"**If a fellow countryman of yours becomes so poor he has to sell part of his property, then his nearest kinsman is to come and buy back what his relative has sold.** ²⁶Or in case a man has no kinsman, but so recovers his means as to find sufficient for its redemption, ²⁷then he shall calculate the years since its sale and refund the balance to the man to whom he sold it, and so return to his property. ²⁸But if he has not found sufficient means to get it back for himself, then what he has sold shall remain in the hands of its purchaser until the year of jubilee; but at the jubilee it shall revert, that he may return to his property."

9.D. Selling†
9.E. Buying

Leviticus 25:35–37
³⁵"Now in case a countryman of yours becomes poor and his means with regard to you falter, then you are to sustain him, like a stranger or a sojourner, that he may live with you. ³⁶Do not take usurious interest from him, but revere your God, that your countryman may live with you. ³⁷**You shall not give him your silver at interest,** nor your food for gain."

3.D. Usury†
4.H. Helping Needy

---

*God's plan was that all land in Canaan would revert to the original family every fiftieth year. This was every seventh year of remission or 7x7.
　†See note on Leviticus 25:10.
　†See note on Exodus 22:25.

Leviticus 25:39–40

[39]"And **if a countryman** of yours becomes so poor with regard to you that he **sells himself to you, you shall not subject him to a slave's service.** [40]He shall be with you as a hired man, as if he were a sojourner; he shall serve with you until the year of jubilee."

12.B. Wages

Leviticus 25:42

"For they are My servants whom I brought out from the land of Egypt; they are not to be sold in a slave sale."

9.D. Selling

Leviticus 25:47–50

[47]"Now if the means of a stranger or of a sojourner with you becomes sufficient, and a countryman of yours becomes so poor with regard to him as to sell himself to a stranger who is sojourning with you, or to the descendants of a stranger's family, [48]then he shall have redemption right after he has been sold. One of his brothers may redeem him, [49]or his uncle, or his uncle's son, may redeem him, or one of his blood relatives from his family may redeem him; or if he prospers, he may redeem himself. [50]He then with his purchaser shall calculate from the year when he sold himself to him up to the year of jubilee; and the price of his sale shall correspond to the number of years. It is like the days of a hired man that he shall be with him."

9.D. Selling

Leviticus 25:53

"**Like a man hired year by year he shall be with him;** he shall not rule over him with severity in your sight."

12.C. Employee/ Employer

Leviticus 27:1–9

[1]Again, the LORD spoke to Moses, saying, [2]"Speak to the sons of Israel, and say to them, '**When a man makes a difficult vow,** he shall be valued according to your valuation of persons belonging to the LORD. [3]If your valuation is of the male from twenty years even to sixty years old, then your valuation shall be fifty shekels of silver, after the shekel of the sanctuary. [4]Or if it is a female, then your valuation shall be thirty shekels. [5]And if it be from five years even to twenty years old then your valuation for the male shall be twenty shekels, and for the female ten shekels. [6]But if they are from a month even up to five years old, then your valuation shall be five shekels of silver for the male, and for the female your valuation shall be three shekels of silver. [7]And if they are from sixty years old and upward, if it is a male, then your valuation shall be fifteen shekels, and for the female ten shekels. [8]But if he is poorer than your valuation, then he shall be placed before the priest, and the priest shall value him; according to the means of the one who vowed, the priest shall value him. [9]Now if it is an animal of the kind which men can present as an offering to the LORD, any such that one gives to the LORD shall be holy.'"

1.K. Paying Vows*

---

*Also on vows see Ecclesiastes 5:4–5.

Scripture:	Subtopic:

Leviticus 27:13
"But **if he should ever wish to redeem it,** then he shall add one-fifth of it to your valuation."

4.D. Offerings

Leviticus 27:15–28
[15]"Yet **if the one who consecrates it should wish to redeem his house, then he shall add one-fifth of your valuation price to it,** so that it may be his.   [16]Again, if a man consecrates to the LORD part of the fields of his own property, then your valuation shall be proportionate to the seed needed for it: a homer of barley seed at fifty shekels of silver.   [17]If he consecrates his field as of the year of jubilee, according to your valuation it shall stand.   [18]If he consecrates his field after the jubilee, however, then the priest shall calculate the price for him proportionate to the years that are left until the year of jubilee; and it shall be deducted from your valuation.   [19]And if the one who consecrates it should ever wish to redeem the field, then he shall add one-fifth of your valuation price to it, so that it may pass to him.   [20]Yet if he will not redeem the field, but has sold the field to another man, it may no longer be redeemed;   [21]and when it reverts in the jubilee, the field shall be holy to the LORD, like a field set apart; it shall be for the priest as his property.   [22]Or if he consecrates to the LORD a field which he has bought, which is not a part of the field of his own property,   [23]then the priest shall calculate for him the amount of your valuation up to the year of jubilee; and he shall on that day give your valuation as holy to the LORD.   [24]In the year of jubilee the field shall return to the one from whom he bought it, to whom the possession of the land belongs.   [25]Every valuation of yours, moreover, shall be after the shekel of the sanctuary. The shekel shall be twenty gerahs.   [26]However, a first-born among animals, which as a first-born belongs to the LORD, no man may consecrate it; whether ox or sheep, it is the LORD's.   [27]But if it is among the unclean animals, then he shall redeem it according to your valuation, and add to it one-fifth of it; and if it is not redeemed, then it shall be sold according to your valuation.   [28]Nevertheless, anything which a man sets apart to the LORD out of all that he has, of man or animal or of the fields of his own property, shall not be sold or redeemed. Anything devoted to destruction is most holy to the LORD."

4.D. Offerings*

Leviticus 27:30–33
[30]"Thus **all the tithe of the land,** of the seed of the land or of the fruit of the tree, is the LORD's; it is holy to the LORD.   [31]**If, therefore, a man wishes to redeem part of his tithe, he shall add to it one-fifth of it.**   [32]And for every tenth part of herd or flock, whatever passes under the rod, the tenth one shall be holy to the LORD.   [33]He is not to be concerned whether it is good or bad, nor shall he exchange it; or if he does exchange it, then both it and its substitute shall become holy. It shall not be redeemed."

4.C. Tithe

---

*Note that all property is valued in relation to the year of jubilee when it had to be returned to the original owner.

Numbers

Scripture:	Subtopic:

Numbers 3:13
"For **all the first-born are Mine;** on the day that I struck down all
the first-born in the land of Egypt, I sanctified to Myself all the
first-born in Israel, from man to beast. They shall be Mine; I am
the LORD."

4.E. First Fruits

Numbers 3:45–49
⁴⁵"Take the Levites instead of all the first-born among the sons of
Israel and the cattle of the Levites. And the Levites shall be Mine; I
am the LORD.   ⁴⁶And for the ransom of the 273 of the first-born of
the sons of Israel who are in excess beyond the Levites,   ⁴⁷you shall
take five shekels apiece, per head; you shall take them in terms of
the shekel of the sanctuary (the shekel is twenty gerahs),   ⁴⁸and
give the money, the ransom of those who are in excess among them,
to Aaron and to his sons."   ⁴⁹**So Moses took the ransom money from
those who were in excess,** beyond those ransomed by the Levites.

4.B. Giving to
Men

Numbers 3:51
Then **Moses gave the ransom money to Aaron** and to his sons, at the
command of the LORD, just as the LORD had commanded Moses.

1.F. Obedience

Numbers 5:7
"Then he shall confess his sins which he has committed, and he
shall make restitution in full for his wrong, and add to it one-fifth
of it, and give it to him whom he has wronged."

11. Restitution

Numbers 5:9–10
⁹"Also every contribution pertaining to all the holy gifts of the sons
of Israel, which they offer to the priest, shall be his.   ¹⁰**So every
man's holy gifts shall be his;** whatever any man gives to the priest,
it becomes his."

4.F. Gifts

Numbers 7:13–14
¹³And his offering was one silver dish whose weight was one hundred and thirty shekels, one silver bowl of seventy shekels, according to the shekel of the sanctuary, both of them full of fine flour
mixed with oil for a grain offering;   ¹⁴one gold pan of ten shekels,
full of incense.

4.D. Offerings

Numbers 11:4
And **the rabble who were among them had greedy desires;** and also
the sons of Israel wept again and said, "Who will give us meat to
eat?"

2.E. Greed

Numbers 11:20
"But a whole month, until it comes out of your nostrils and becomes loathsome to you; because **you have rejected the LORD** who is among you and have wept before Him, saying, 'Why did we ever leave Egypt?'"

2.I. Disobedient

Numbers 11:34
So the name of that place was called Kibroth-hattaavah, because there **they buried the people who had been greedy.**

2.E. Greed

Numbers 15:6–7
⁶"Or for a ram you shall prepare **as a grain offering** two-tenths of an ephah of fine flour mixed with one-third of a hin of oil; ⁷and for the libation you shall offer one-third of a hin of wine as a soothing aroma to the LORD."

4.D. Offerings
4.E. First Fruits

Numbers 15:18–21
¹⁸"Speak to the sons of Israel, and say to them, 'When you enter the land where I bring you, ¹⁹then it shall be, that when you eat of the food of the land, **you shall lift up an offering to the LORD.** ²⁰Of the first of your dough you shall lift up a cake as an offering; as the offering of the threshing floor, so you shall lift it up. ²¹From the first of your dough you shall give to the LORD an offering throughout your generations.'"

4.D. Offerings
4.E. First Fruits

Numbers 16:32
And **the earth opened its mouth and swallowed them** up, and their households, and all the men who belonged to Korah, with their possessions.

7.B. False Gods

Numbers 18:8–9
⁸Then the LORD spoke to Aaron, "Now behold, I **Myself have given you charge of My offerings**, even all the holy gifts of the sons of Israel, I have given them to you as a portion, and to your sons as a perpetual allotment. ⁹This shall be yours from the most holy gifts, reserved from the fire; every offering of theirs, even every grain offering and every sin offering and every guilt offering, which they shall render to Me, shall be most holy for you and for your sons."

4.D. Offerings

Numbers 18:12–13
¹²"All the best of the fresh oil and all the best of the fresh wine and of the grain, **the first fruits of those which they give to the LORD, I** give them to you. ¹³The first ripe fruits of all that is in their land, which they bring to the LORD, shall be yours; everyone of your household who is clean may eat it."

4.E. First Fruits

Numbers 18:20–21
²⁰Then the LORD said to Aaron, "**You shall have no inheritance in their land**, nor own any portion among them; I am your portion and your inheritance among the sons of Israel. ²¹And to the sons of Levi, behold, I have given all the tithe in Israel for an inheritance, in return for their service which they perform, the service of the tent of meeting."

5.A. Inheritance

Numbers 18:24
"**For the tithe of the sons of Israel,** which they offer as an offering to the LORD, I have given to the Levites for an inheritance; therefore I have said concerning them, 'They shall have no inheritance among the sons of Israel.'"

5.A. Inheritance

Numbers 18:26
"Moreover, you shall speak to the Levites and say to them, 'When you take from the sons of Israel the tithe which I have given you from them for your inheritance; then you shall present an offering from it to the LORD, **a tithe of the tithe.**'"

4.C. Tithe*

Numbers 18:28–29
²⁸"So you shall also present an offering to the LORD from your tithes, which you receive from the sons of Israel; and from it **you shall give the LORD's offering to Aaron the priest.** ²⁹Out of all your gifts you shall present every offering due to the LORD, from all the best of them, the sacred part from them."

4.C. Tithe

Numbers 20:19
Again, the sons of Israel said to him, "We shall go up by the highway, and **if I and my livestock do drink any of your water, then I will pay its price.** Let me only pass through on my feet, nothing else."

9.E. Buying

Numbers 22:7
So the elders of Moab and the elders of Midian departed with the **fees for divination** in their hand; and they came to Balaam and repeated Balak's words to him.

2.B. Bribe

Numbers 22:17–18
¹⁷"For **I will indeed honor you richly,** and I will do whatever you say to me. Please come then, curse this people for me." ¹⁸And Balaam answered and said to the servants of Balak, "Though Balak were to give me his house full of silver and gold, I could not do anything, either small or great, contrary to the command of the LORD my God."

1.F. Obedience

Numbers 24:13
"**Though Balak were to give me his house full of silver and gold, I** could not do anything contrary to the command of the LORD, either good or bad, of my own accord. What the LORD speaks, that I will speak."

1.F. Obedience

---

*Even the Levites that were paid by tithes were expected to tithe.

Numbers 26:54–56

[54]"**To the larger group you shall increase their inheritance,** and to the smaller group you shall diminish their inheritance; each shall be given their inheritance according to those who were numbered of them.   [55]But the land shall be divided by lot. **They shall receive their inheritance according to the names of the tribes** of their fathers.   [56]According to the selection by lot, their inheritance shall be divided between the larger and the smaller groups."

5.A. Inheritance

Numbers 27:7

"**The daughters of Zelophehad** are right in their statements. You shall surely give them a hereditary possession among their father's brothers, and **you shall transfer the inheritance of their father to them.**"

5.A. Inheritance

Numbers 27:8–11

[8]". . . **If a man dies and has no son, then you shall transfer his inheritance to his daughter.**   [9]And if he has no daughter, then you shall give his inheritance to his brothers.   [10]And if he has no brothers, then you shall give his inheritance to his father's brothers. [11]And if his father has no brothers, then you shall give his inheritance to his nearest relative in his own family, and he shall possess it; and it shall be a statutory ordinance to the sons of Israel, just as the LORD commanded Moses."

5.A. Inheritance

Numbers 30:2

"**If a man makes a vow to the LORD,** or takes an oath to bind himself with a binding obligation, **he shall not violate his word;** he shall do according to all that proceeds out of his mouth."

1.K. Paying Vows*

Numbers 31:21–22

[21]. . . "This is the statute of the law which the LORD has commanded Moses: [22]only the gold and the silver, the bronze, the iron, the tin and the lead."

6.G. Wealth

Numbers 31:26–29

[26]"You and Eleazar the priest and the heads of the fathers' households of the congregation, take a count of the booty that was captured, both of man and of animal;   [27]and divide the booty between the warriors who went out to battle and all the congregation.   [28]And **levy a tax for the LORD from the men of war who went out to battle,** one in five hundred of the persons and of the cattle and of the donkeys and of the sheep;   [29]take it from their half and give it to Eleazar the priest, as an offering to the LORD."

8.A. Church Tax

---

*See Ecclesiastes 5:4–5 also.

Scripture:	Subtopic:

Numbers 31:50–54

[50]"So **we have brought as an offering to the LORD** what each man found, articles of gold, armlets and bracelets, signet rings, earrings and necklaces, to make atonement for ourselves before the LORD." [51]And Moses and Eleazar the priest took the gold from them, all kinds of wrought articles. [52]And all the gold of the offering which they offered up to the LORD, from the captains of thousands and the captains of hundreds, was 16,750 shekels. [53]The men of war had taken booty, every man for himself. [54]So Moses and Eleazar the priest took the gold from the captains of thousands and of hundreds, and brought it to the tent of meeting as a memorial for the sons of Israel before the LORD.

4.D. Offerings

Numbers 33:54

"And **you shall inherit the land by lot** according to your families; to the larger you shall give more inheritance, and to the smaller you shall give less inheritance. Wherever the lot falls to anyone, that shall be his. You shall inherit according to the tribes of your fathers."

5.A. Inheritance

Numbers 35:2

"Command the sons of Israel that they **give to the Levites from the inheritance of their possession,** cities to live in; and you shall give to the Levites pasture lands around the cities."

5.A. Inheritance

Numbers 35:8

"As for the cities which you shall give from the possession of the sons of Israel, you shall take more from the larger and you shall take less from the smaller; each shall give some of his cities to the Levites in proportion to his possession which he inherits."

5.A. Inheritance

Numbers 35:31–32

[31]"Moreover, **you shall not take ransom for the life of a murderer** who is guilty of death, but he shall surely be put to death. [32]And you shall not take ransom for him who has fled to his city of refuge, that he may return to live in the land before the death of the priest."

2.B. Bribe

Numbers 36:3–4

[3]"But **if they marry one of the sons of the other tribes** of the sons of Israel, **their inheritance will be withdrawn** from the inheritance of our fathers and will be added to the inheritance of the tribe to which they belong; thus it will be withdrawn from our allotted inheritance. [4]And when the jubilee of the sons of Israel comes, then their inheritance will be added to the inheritance of the tribe to which they belong; so their inheritance will be withdrawn from the inheritance of the tribe of our fathers."

5.A. Inheritance

Numbers 36:6–7

[6]". . . 'Let them marry whom they wish; only they must marry within the family of the tribe of their father.' [7]Thus **no inheritance of the sons of Israel shall be transferred from tribe to tribe,** for the sons of Israel shall each hold to the inheritance of the tribe of his fathers."

5.A. Inheritance

Numbers 36:9

"Thus **no inheritance shall be transferred from one tribe to another tribe,** for the tribes of the sons of Israel shall each hold to his own inheritance."

5.A. Inheritance

Deuteronomy

Scripture:	Subtopic:

Deuteronomy 1:17
"**You shall not show partiality in judgment;** you shall hear the small and the great alike. You shall not fear man, for the judgment is God's. And the case that is too hard for you, you shall bring to me, and I will hear it."

1.I. Fairness

Deuteronomy 2:6
"**You shall buy food from them** with money so that you may eat, and you shall also purchase water from them with money so that you may drink."

9.E. Buying

Deuteronomy 2:7
"**For the LORD your God has blessed you** in all that you have done; He has known your wanderings through this great wilderness. These forty years the LORD your God has been with you; you have not lacked a thing."

6.D. Provision

Deuteronomy 2:28
"**You will sell me food for money so that I may eat,** and give me water for money so that I may drink, only let me pass through on foot."

9.D. Selling

Deuteronomy 5:32
"So you shall observe to do just as the LORD your God has commanded you; **you shall not turn aside to the right or to the left.**"

1.F. Obedience

Deuteronomy 7:10
"But repays those who hate Him to their faces, to destroy them; **He will not delay with him who hates Him,** He will repay him to his face."

7.A. To Wicked

Deuteronomy 7:25
"**The graven images of their gods you are to burn with fire;** you shall not covet the silver or the gold that is on them, nor take it for yourselves, lest you be snared by it, for it is an abomination to the LORD your God."

2.E. Greed

Deuteronomy 8:13–14
[13]". . . and when your herds and your flocks multiply, and your silver and gold multiply, and all that you have multiplies, [14]**then your heart becomes proud,** and you forget the LORD your God who brought you out from the land of Egypt, out of the house of slavery."

2.C. Pride

Deuteronomy 8:17
"Otherwise, you may say in your heart, '**My power and the strength of my hand made me this wealth.**'"

2.C. Pride

Deuteronomy 8:18
"But **you shall remember the LORD your God,** for it is He who is giving you power to make wealth, that He may confirm His covenant which He swore to your fathers, as it is this day."

6.D. Provision

Deuteronomy 8:20
"Like the nations that the LORD makes to perish before you, so **you shall perish; because you would not listen to the voice of the LORD your God.**"

2.I. Disobedient

Deuteronomy 10:17
"For the LORD your God is the God of gods and the Lord of lords, the great, the mighty, and the awesome **God who does not show partiality,** nor take a bribe."

2.B. Bribe
6.A. God's Promises

Deuteronomy 10:18–19
[18]"**He executes justice for the orphan and the widow,** and shows His love for the alien by giving him food and clothing. [19]So show your love for the alien, for you were aliens in the land of Egypt."

4.H. Helping Needy
6.D. Provision

Deuteronomy 11:17
"Or the anger of the LORD will be kindled against you, and **He will shut up the heavens** so that there will be no rain and the ground will not yield its fruit; and you will perish quickly from the good land which the LORD is giving you."

7.A. To Wicked

Deuteronomy 12:6–7
[6]"And **there you shall bring your burnt offerings,** your sacrifices, your tithes, the contribution of your hand, your votive offerings, your freewill offerings, and the first-born of your herd and of your flock. [7]There also you and your households shall eat before the LORD your God, and rejoice in all your undertakings in which the LORD your God has blessed you."

4.C. Tithe
4.D. Offerings

Deuteronomy 12:11
". . . Then it shall come about that the place in which the LORD your God shall choose for His name to dwell, **there you shall bring all that I command you:** your burnt offerings and your sacrifices, your tithes and the contribution of your hand, and all your choice votive offerings which you will vow to the LORD."

4.C. Tithe
4.D. Offerings

Deuteronomy 12:17
"**You are not allowed to eat within your gates the tithe of your grain,** or new wine, or oil, or the first-born of your herd or flock, or any of your votive offerings which you vow, or your freewill offerings, or the contribution of your hand."

4.C. Tithe
4.E. First Fruits

Deuteronomy 12:19
"**Be careful that you do not forsake the Levite** as long as you live in your land."

4.B. Giving To Men

Deuteronomy 14:21

"You shall not eat anything which dies of itself. You may give it to the alien who is in your town, so that he may eat it, or you may sell it to a foreigner, for you are a holy people to the LORD your God. You shall not boil a kid in its mother's milk."

9.D. Selling

Deuteronomy 14:22–29

[22]**"You shall surely tithe all the produce from what you sow,** which comes out of the field every year. [23]And you shall eat in the presence of the LORD your God, at the place where He chooses to establish His name, the tithe of your grain, your new wine, your oil, and the first-born of your herd and your flock, in order that you may learn to fear the LORD your God always. [24]And if the distance is so great for you that you are not able to bring the tithe, since the place where the LORD your God chooses to set His name is too far away from you when the LORD your God blesses you, [25]then you shall exchange it for money, and bind the money in your hand and go to the place which the LORD your God chooses. [26]And you may spend the money for whatever your heart desires, for oxen, or sheep, or wine, or strong drink, or whatever your heart desires; and there you shall eat in the presence of the LORD your God and rejoice, you and your household. [27]Also you shall not neglect the Levite who is in your town, for he has no portion or inheritance among you. [28]At the end of every third year you shall bring out all the tithe of your produce in that year, and shall deposit it in your town. [29]And the Levite, because he has no portion or inheritance among you, and the alien, the orphan and the widow who are in your town, shall come and eat and be satisfied, in order that the LORD your God may bless you in all the work of your hand which you do."

4.C. Tithe*

---

*Tithe (dekatos) literally means one-tenth.

Deuteronomy 15:1–11

¹"**At the end of every seven years you shall grant a remission of debts.** ²And this is the manner of remission: every creditor shall release what he has loaned to his neighbor; he shall not exact it of his neighbor and his brother, because the LORD's remission has been proclaimed. ³From a foreigner you may exact it, but your hand shall release whatever of yours is with your brother. ⁴However, there shall be no poor among you, since the LORD will surely bless you in the land which the LORD your God is giving you as an inheritance to possess, ⁵if only you listen obediently to the voice of the LORD your God, to observe carefully all this commandment which I am commanding you today. ⁶For the LORD your God shall bless you as He has promised you, and you will lend to many nations, but you will not borrow; and you will rule over many nations, but they will not rule over you. ⁷If there is a poor man with you, one of your brothers, in any of your towns in your land which the LORD your God is giving you, you shall not harden your heart, nor close your hand from your poor brother; ⁸but you shall freely open your hand to him, and shall generously lend him sufficient for his need in whatever he lacks. ⁹Beware, lest there is a base thought in your heart, saying, 'The seventh year, the year of remission, is near,' and your eye is hostile toward your poor brother, and you give him nothing; then he may cry to the LORD against you, and it will be a sin in you. ¹⁰You shall generously give to him, and your heart shall not be grieved when you give to him, because for this thing the LORD your God will bless you in all your work and in all your undertakings. ¹¹For the poor will never cease to be in the land; therefore I command you, saying, 'You shall freely open your hand to your brother, to your needy and poor in your land.'"

3.B. Lending
3.F. Paying Debts*
4.H. Helping Needy

Deuteronomy 16:17

"**Every man shall give as he is able,** according to the blessing of the LORD your God which He has given you."

4.D. Offerings

Deuteronomy 16:19–20

¹⁹"**You shall not distort justice;** you shall not be partial, and you shall not take a bribe, for a bribe blinds the eyes of the wise and perverts the words of the righteous. ²⁰Justice, and only justice, you shall pursue, that you may live and possess the land which the LORD your God is giving you."

1.I. Fairness
2.B. Bribe

Deuteronomy 17:1

"**You shall not sacrifice to the LORD your God an ox or a sheep which has a blemish** or any defect, for that is a detestable thing to the LORD your God."

4.D. Offerings

---

*No debt to a brother extended beyond the seventh year.

Deuteronomy 17:15–17

¹⁵**"You shall surely set a king** over you whom the LORD your God chooses, one from among your countrymen you shall set as king over yourselves; you may not put a foreigner over yourselves who is not your countryman. ¹⁶Moreover, **he shall not multiply horses for himself,** nor shall he cause the people to return to Egypt to multiply horses, since the LORD has said to you, 'You shall never again return that way.' ¹⁷Neither shall he multiply wives for himself, lest his heart turn away; nor shall he greatly increase silver and gold for himself."

1.B. Honesty

Deuteronomy 18:1–2

¹**"The Levitical priests,** the whole tribe of Levi, **shall have no portion or inheritance with Israel;** they shall eat the LORD's offerings by fire and His portion. ²And they shall have no inheritance among their countrymen; the LORD is their inheritance, as He promised them."

5.A. Inheritance

Deuteronomy 18:4

"You shall give him the first fruits of your grain, your new wine, and your oil, and the first shearing of your sheep."

4.E. First Fruits

Deuteronomy 18:8

"They shall eat equal portions, except what they receive from the sale of their fathers' estates."

5.A. Inheritance

Deuteronomy 20:5

"The officers also shall speak to the people, saying, '**Who is the man that has built a new house** and has not dedicated it? Let him depart and return to his house, lest he die in the battle and another man dedicate it.'"

5.C. Provision

Deuteronomy 21:14

"And it shall be, if you are not pleased with her, then you shall let her go wherever she wishes; but **you shall certainly not sell her for money,** you shall not mistreat her, because you have humbled her."

9.D. Selling

Deuteronomy 21:17

"But he shall acknowledge the first-born, the son of the unloved, by giving him a double portion of all that he has, for he is the beginning of his strength; to him belongs the right of the first-born."

5.A. Inheritance

Deuteronomy 22:1–2

¹**"You shall not see your countryman's ox or his sheep straying away, and pay no attention to them;** you shall certainly bring them back to your countryman. ²And if your countryman is not near you, or if you do not know him, then you shall bring it home to your house, and it shall remain with you until your countryman looks for it; then you shall restore it to him."

1.I. Fairness

Scripture:	Subtopic:

Deuteronomy 22:4
"**You shall not see your countryman's donkey or his ox fallen down on the way, and pay no attention** to them; you shall certainly help him to raise them up."

1.I. Fairness

Deuteronomy 22:19
"And **they shall fine him a hundred shekels of silver** and give it to the girl's father, because he publicly defamed a virgin of Israel. And she shall remain his wife; he cannot divorce her all his days."

11. Restitution

Deuteronomy 22:29
"Then **the man who lay with her shall give to the girl's father fifty shekels of silver,** and she shall become his wife because he has violated her; he cannot divorce her all his days."

11. Restitution

Deuteronomy 23:6
"You shall never seek their peace or their prosperity all your days."

4.G. Worthless Gifts

Deuteronomy 23:18
"**You shall not bring the hire of a harlot** or the wages of a dog into the house of the LORD your God for any votive offering, for both of these are an abomination to the LORD your God."

4.G. Worthless Gifts

Deuteronomy 23:19–20
[19]"**You shall not charge interest to your countrymen:** interest on money, food, or anything that may be loaned at interest.   [20]You may charge interest to a foreigner, but to your countryman you shall not charge interest, so that the LORD your God may bless you in all that you undertake in the land which you are about to enter to possess."

3.C. Interest*

Deuteronomy 23:21
"**When you make a vow to the LORD your God,** you shall not delay to pay it, for it would be sin in you, and the LORD your God will surely require it of you."

1.K. Paying Vows

Deuteronomy 23:23
"**You shall be careful to perform what goes out from your lips,** just as you have voluntarily vowed to the LORD your God, what you have promised."

1.K. Paying Vows

Deuteronomy 24:7
"If a man is caught **kidnapping** any of his countrymen of the sons of Israel, and he deals with him violently, or sells him, then that thief shall die; so you shall purge the evil from among you."

9.D. Selling

---

*Note that countrymen (brothers) are never charged interest.

Scripture:	Subtopic:

Deuteronomy 24:10–13
[10]"**When you make your neighbor a loan of any sort, you shall not enter his house to take his pledge.** [11]You shall remain outside, and the man to whom you make the loan shall bring the pledge out to you. [12]And if he is a poor man, you shall not sleep with his pledge. [13]When the sun goes down you shall surely return the pledge to him, that he may sleep in his cloak and bless you; and it will be righteousness for you before the LORD your God."

3.E. Surety*

Deuteronomy 24:14–15
[14]"**You shall not oppress a hired servant who is poor and needy,** whether he is one of your countrymen or one of your aliens who is in your land in your towns. [15]**You shall give him his wages** on his day before the sun sets, for he is poor and sets his heart on it; so that he may not cry against you to the LORD and it become sin in you."

4.H. Helping Needy
12.B. Wages

Deuteronomy 24:17
"**You shall not pervert the justice due an alien** or an orphan, nor take a widow's garment in pledge."

1.I. Fairness
2.J. Injustice

Deuteronomy 24:19–21
[19]"**When you reap your harvest** in your field and have forgotten a sheaf in the field, **you shall not go back to get it;** it shall be for the alien, for the orphan, and for the widow, in order that the LORD your God may bless you in all the work of your hands. [20]When you beat your olive tree, you shall not go over the boughs again; it shall be for the alien, for the orphan, and for the widow. [21]When you gather the grapes of your vineyard, you shall not go over it again; it shall be for the alien, for the orphan, and for the widow."

4.H. Helping Needy

Deuteronomy 25:13–15
[13]"**You shall not have in your bag differing weights,** a large and a small. [14]You shall not have in your house differing measures, a large and a small. You shall have a full and just weight; [15]you shall have a full and just measure, that your days may be prolonged in the land which the LORD your God gives you."

2.F. Dishonesty†

Deuteronomy 26:2
". . . That you shall take some of **the first of all the produce of the ground** which you shall bring in from your land that the LORD your God gives you, and you shall put it in a basket and go to the place where the LORD your God chooses to establish His name."

4.E. First Fruits

---

*Limits were placed on recovering pledges. God always expects mercy from His people.
†Charging varying amounts, having false weights, any form of deceit in business transactions are wrong.

Deuteronomy 26:10–13

[10]"'And now behold, I have brought the first of the produce of the ground which Thou, O LORD hast given me.' And you shall set it down before the LORD your God, and worship before the LORD your God; [11]and you and the Levite and the alien who is among you shall rejoice in all the good which the LORD your God has given you and your household. [12]When you have finished paying all **the tithe of your increase in the third year, the year of tithing, then you shall give it to the Levite,** to the stranger, to the orphan and to the widow, that they may eat in your towns, and be satisfied. [13]And you shall say before the LORD your God, 'I have removed the sacred portion from my house, and also have given it to the Levite and the alien, the orphan and the widow, according to all Thy commandments which Thou has commanded me; I have not transgressed or forgotten any of Thy commandments.'"

4.C. Tithe
4.E. First Fruits

Deuteronomy 27:17

"'**Cursed is he who moves his neighbor's boundary mark.**' And all the people shall say, 'Amen.'"

2.F. Dishonesty

Deuteronomy 27:18

"'**Cursed is he who misleads a blind person** on the road.' And all the people shall say, 'Amen.'"

2.F. Dishonesty

Deuteronomy 27:19

"'**Cursed is he who distorts the justice due an alien,** orphan, and widow.' And all the people shall say, 'Amen.'"

2.F. Dishonesty

Deuteronomy 27:25

"'**Cursed is he who accepts a bribe** to strike down an innocent person.' And all the people shall say, 'Amen.'"

2.B. Bribe

Deuteronomy 28:8

"**The LORD will command the blessing upon you** in your barns and in all that you put your hand to, and He will bless you in the land which the LORD your God gives you."

6.C. Blessings

Deuteronomy 28:11

"And **the LORD will make you abound in prosperity,** in the offspring of your body and in the offspring of your beast and in the produce of your ground, in the land which the LORD swore to your fathers to give you."

6.C. Blessings

Deuteronomy 28:12

"**The LORD will open for you His good storehouse,** the heavens, to give rain to your land in its season and to bless all the work of your hand; and you shall lend to many nations, but you shall not borrow."

3.B. Lending

Scripture:	Subtopic:

Deuteronomy 28:13
"And **the LORD shall make you the head and not the tail,** and you only shall be above, and you shall not be underneath, if you will listen to the commandments of the LORD your God, which I charge you today, to observe them carefully."

1.F. Obedience

Deuteronomy 28:15–20
¹⁵"But it shall come about, if you will not obey the LORD your God, to observe to do all His commandments and His statutes with which I charge you today, that all these curses shall come upon you and overtake you. ¹⁶Cursed shall you be in the city, and cursed shall you be in the country. ¹⁷Cursed shall be your basket and your kneading bowl. ¹⁸Cursed shall be the offspring of your body and the produce of your ground, the increase of your herd and the young of your flock. ¹⁹Cursed shall you be when you come in, and cursed shall you be when you go out. ²⁰The LORD will send upon you curses, confusion, and rebuke, in all you undertake to do, until you are destroyed and until you perish quickly, on account of the evil of your deeds, because you have forsaken Me."

7.A. To Wicked

Deuteronomy 28:43–45
⁴³"The alien who is among you shall rise above you higher and higher, but you shall go down lower and lower. ⁴⁴**He shall lend to you, but you shall not lend to him;** he shall be the head, and you shall be the tail. ⁴⁵So all these curses shall come on you and pursue you and overtake you until you are destroyed, because you would not obey the LORD your God by keeping His commandments and His statutes which He commanded you."

3.A. Borrowing

Deuteronomy 28:68
"And the LORD will bring you back to Egypt in ships, by the way about which I spoke to you, 'You will never see it again!' And there **you shall offer yourselves for sale to your enemies** as male and female slaves, but there will be no buyer."

7.A. To Wicked
9.D. Selling

Deuteronomy 29:9
"So keep the words of this covenant to do them, **that you may prosper** in all that you do."

6.C. Blessings

Deuteronomy 30:8–11
⁸"And you shall again obey the LORD, and observe all His commandments which I command you today. ⁹Then **the LORD your God will prosper you abundantly in all the work of your hand,** in the offspring of your body and in the offspring of your cattle and in the produce of your ground, for the LORD will again rejoice over you for good, just as He rejoiced over your fathers; ¹⁰if you obey the LORD your God to keep His commandments and His statutes which are written in this book of the law, if you turn to the LORD your God with all your heart and soul. ¹¹For this commandment which I command you today is not too difficult for you, nor is it out of reach."

6.C. Blessings

Scripture:	Subtopic:

Deuteronomy 30:14–15

[14]"But the word is very near you, in your mouth and in your heart, that you may observe it. [15]See, I have set before you today **life and prosperity, and death and adversity.**"

1.F. Obedience

Deuteronomy 31:10

Then Moses commanded them, saying, "At the end of every seven years, at the time of the year of remission of debts, at the Feast of Booths."

3.F. Paying Debts

Joshua

Scripture:	Subtopic:

Joshua 1:8
"**This book of the law shall not depart from your mouth,** but you shall meditate on it day and night, so that you may be careful to do according to all that is written in it; for then you will make your way prosperous, and then you will have success."

6.C. Blessings

Joshua 6:18–19
[18]"But as for you, only **keep yourselves from the things under the ban, lest you covet them** and take some of the things under the ban, so you would make the camp of Israel accursed and bring trouble on it.   [19]But all the silver and gold and articles of bronze and iron are holy to the LORD; they shall go into the treasury of the LORD."

2.E. Greed

Joshua 6:24
And they burned the city with fire, and all that was in it. Only the silver and gold and articles of bronze and iron, they put into the treasury of the house of the LORD.

4.F. Gifts

Joshua 7:1
But **the sons of Israel acted unfaithfully in regard to the things under the ban,** for Achan, the son of Carmi, the son of Zabdi, the son of Zerah, from the tribe of Judah, took some of the things under the ban, therefore the anger of the LORD burned against the sons of Israel.

2.E. Greed

Joshua 7:11
"Israel has sinned, and they have also transgressed My covenant which I commanded them. And they have even taken some of the things under the ban and have both stolen and deceived. Moreover, they have also put them among their own things."

2.F. Dishonesty

Joshua 7:21–22
[21]"When I saw among the spoil a beautiful mantle from Shinar and two hundred shekels of silver and a bar of gold fifty shekels in weight, then **I coveted them and took them;** and behold, they are concealed in the earth inside my tent with the silver underneath it."   [22]So Joshua sent messengers, and they ran to the tent; and behold, it was concealed in his tent with the silver underneath it.

2.E. Greed

Joshua 7:24–25
[24]Then Joshua and all Israel with him, took Achan the son of Zerah, the silver, the mantle, the bar of gold, his sons, his daughters, his oxen, his donkeys, his sheep, his tent and all that belonged to him; and they brought them up to the valley of Achor.   [25]And Joshua said, "Why have you troubled us? The LORD will trouble you this day." And all Israel stoned them with stones; and they burned them with fire after they had stoned them with stones.

11. Restitution

Scripture:	Subtopic:

Joshua 9:14–15
[14]So the men of Israel took some of their provisions, and did not ask for the counsel of the LORD.   [15]And **Joshua made peace with them and made a covenant with them,** to let them live; and the leaders of the congregation swore an oath to them.

6.B. Counsel of God

Joshua 9:20
"This we will do to them, even let them live, lest wrath be upon us for the oath which we swore to them."

6.F. Justice

Joshua 9:22–23
[22]Then Joshua called for them and spoke to them, saying, "Why have you deceived us, saying, 'We are very far from you,' when you are living within our land?   [23]Now therefore, you are cursed, and you shall never cease being slaves, both hewers of wood and drawers of water for the house of my God."

7.A. To Wicked

Joshua 11:23
So Joshua took the whole land, according to all that the LORD had spoken to Moses, and **Joshua gave it for an inheritance to Israel** according to their divisions by their tribes. Thus the land had rest from war.

5.A. Inheritance

Joshua 13:14
Only to the tribe of Levi he did not give an inheritance; the offerings by fire to the LORD, the God of Israel, are their inheritance, as He spoke to them.

5.A. Inheritance

Joshua 13:33
But to the tribe of Levi, Moses did not give an inheritance; the LORD, the God of Israel, is their inheritance, as He had promised to them.

5.A. Inheritance

Joshua 14:1
Now these are the territories which the sons of Israel inherited in the land of Canaan, which Eleazar the priest, and Joshua the son of Nun, and the heads of the households of the tribes of the sons of Israel apportioned to them for an inheritance.

5.A. Inheritance

Joshua 14:4
For the sons of Joseph were two tribes, Manasseh and Ephraim, and they did not give a portion to the Levites in the land, except cities to live in, with their pasture lands for their livestock and for their property.

5.A. Inheritance

Joshua 14:14
Therefore, Hebron became the inheritance of Caleb the son of Jephunneh the Kenizzite until this day, because he followed the LORD God of Israel fully.

5.A. Inheritance

Joshua 17:6
. . . because the **daughters of Manasseh received an inheritance** among his sons. And the land of Gilead belonged to the rest of the sons of Manasseh.

5.A. Inheritance

Joshua 18:3
So Joshua said to the sons of Israel, "How long will you put off entering to take possession of the land which the LORD, the God of your fathers, has given to you?"

2.I. Disobedient

Joshua 22:8
. . . and said to them, "**Return to your tents with great riches** and with very much livestock, with silver, gold, bronze, iron, and with very many clothes; divide the spoil of your enemies with your brothers."

6.D. Provision

Joshua 24:13
"And **I gave you a land on which you had not labored,** and cities which you had not built, and you have lived in them; you are eating of vineyards and olive groves, which you did not plant."

6.D. Provision

Joshua 24:15
"And if it is disagreeable in your sight to serve the LORD, **choose for yourselves today whom you will serve:** whether the gods which your fathers served which were beyond the River, or the gods of the Amorites in whose land you are living; but as for me and my house, we will serve the LORD."

1.F. Obedience

Joshua 24:32
Now **they buried the bones of Joseph,** which the sons of Israel brought up from Egypt, at Shechem, in the piece of ground which Jacob had bought from the sons of Hamor the father of Shechem for one hundred pieces of money; and they became the inheritance of Joseph's sons.

5.A. Inheritance

Judges

Scripture:	Subtopic:

Judges 3:8–9
8Then the anger of the LORD was kindled against Israel, so that **He sold them into the hands of Cushan-rishathaim** king of Mesopotamia; and the sons of Israel served Cushan-rishathaim eight years. 9And when the sons of Israel cried to the LORD, the LORD raised up a deliverer for the sons of Israel to deliver them, Othniel the son of Kenaz, Caleb's younger brother.

7.A. To Wicked

Judges 4:1–2
1Then the sons of Israel again did evil in the sight of the LORD, after Ehud died. 2And **the LORD sold them into the hand of Jabin** king of Canaan, who reigned in Hazor; and the commander of his army was Sisera, who lived in Harosheth-hagoyim.

7.A. To Wicked

Judges 4:9
And she said, "I will surely go with you; nevertheless, the honor shall not be yours on the journey that you are about to take, for **the LORD will sell Sisera into the hands of a woman.**" Then Deborah arose and went with Barak to Kedesh.

2.I. Disobedient

Judges 8:24–26
24Yet Gideon said to them, "**I would request of you, that each of you give me an earring from his spoil.**" (For they had gold earrings, because they were Ishmaelites.) 25And they said, "We will surely give them." So they spread out a garment, and every one of them threw an earring there from his spoil. 26And the weight of the gold earrings that he requested was 1,700 shekels of gold, besides the crescent ornaments and the pendants and the purple robes which were on the kings of Midian, and besides the neck bands that were on their camels' necks.

12.B. Wages

Judges 8:27
And Gideon made it into an ephod, and placed it in his city, Ophrah, and all Israel played the harlot with it there, so that it became a snare to Gideon and his household.

2.I. Disobedient

Judges 9:4
And they gave him seventy pieces of silver from the house of Baal-berith with which **Abimelech hired worthless and reckless fellows,** and they followed him.

2.B. Bribe

Judges 10:7
And the anger of the LORD burned against Israel, and **He sold them into the hands of the Philistines,** and into the hands of the sons of Ammon.

7.A. To Wicked

Judges 11:2
And Gilead's wife bore him sons; and when his wife's sons grew up,   **5.A. Inheritance**
they drove **Jephthah** out and said to him, "You shall not have an
inheritance in our father's house, for you are the son of another
woman."

Judges 16:5
And the lords of the Philistines came up to her, and said to her,   **2.B. Bribe**
"**Entice him, and see where his great strength lies** and how we may
overpower him that we may bind him to afflict him. Then **we will
each give you eleven hundred pieces of silver.**"

Judges 16:18
When Delilah saw that he had told her all that was in his heart, she   **2.B. Bribe**
sent and called the lords of the Philistines, saying, "Come up once
more, for he has told me all that is in his heart." Then the lords of
the Philistines came up to her, and brought the money in their
hands.

Judges 17:2–4
²And he said to his mother, "The eleven hundred pieces of silver   **2.I. Disobedient**
which were taken from you, about which you uttered a curse in my
hearing, behold, the silver is with me; I took it." And his mother
said, "Blessed be my son by the LORD." ³He then returned the
eleven hundred pieces of silver to his mother, and his mother said,
"**I wholly dedicate the silver from my hand to the LORD for my son
to make a graven image and a molten image;** now therefore, I will
return them to you." ⁴So when he returned the silver to his
mother, his mother took two hundred pieces of silver and gave them
to the silversmith who made them into a graven image and a molten image, and they were in the house of Micah.

Judges 17:10
Micah then said to him, "**Dwell with me** and be a father and a   **12.B. Wages**
priest to me, **and I will give you ten pieces of silver a year,** a suit of
clothes, and your maintenance." So the Levite went in.

Judges 18:1
In those days there was no king of Israel; and in those days the tribe   **5.A. Inheritance**
of the Danites was seeking an inheritance for themselves to live in,
for until that day an inheritance had not been allotted to them as a
possession among the tribes of Israel.

Ruth

Scripture:	Subtopic:

Ruth 2:12
"May the LORD reward your work, and **your wages be full from the LORD,** the God of Israel, under whose wings you have come to seek refuge."

12.B. Wages

Ruth 3:10
Then he said, "May you be blessed of the LORD, my daughter. You have shown your last kindness to be better than the first by not going after young men, whether poor or rich."

6.C. Blessings

Ruth 4:3–7
³Then he said to the closest relative, "**Naomi,** who has come back from the land of Moab, has to sell the piece of land which belonged to our brother Elimelech. ⁴So I thought to inform you, saying, '**Buy it before those who are sitting here,** and before the elders of my people. If you will redeem it, redeem it; but if not, tell me that I may know; for there is no one but you to redeem it, and I am after you.'" And he said, "I will redeem it." ⁵Then Boaz said, "On the day you buy the field from the hand of Naomi, you must also acquire Ruth the Moabitess, the widow of the deceased, in order to raise up the name of the deceased on his inheritance." ⁶And the closest relative said, "**I cannot redeem it for myself, lest I jeopardize my own inheritance.** Redeem it for yourself; you may have my right of redemption, for I cannot redeem it." ⁷Now **this was the custom in former times in Israel concerning the redemption and the exchange of land to confirm any matter:** a man removed his sandal and gave it to another; and this was the manner of attestation in Israel.

5.A. Inheritance
9.E. Buying

Ruth 4:11
And all the people who were in the court, and the elders, said, "We are witnesses. May the LORD make the woman who is coming into your home like Rachel and Leah, both of whom built the house of Israel; and may you achieve wealth in Ephrathah and become famous in Bethlehem."

6.C. Blessings

I Samuel

Scripture:	Subtopic:

I Samuel 2:3
"Boast no more so very proudly, do not let arrogance come out of your mouth; for the LORD is a God of knowledge, and with Him actions are weighed."

6.A. God's Promises

I Samuel 2:7
"**The LORD makes poor and rich;** He brings low, He also exalts."

6.A. God's Promises

I Samuel 2:29
"**Why do you kick at My sacrifice and at My offering** which I have commanded in My dwelling, and honor your sons above Me, by making yourselves fat with the choicest of every offering of My people Israel?"

4.G. Worthless Gifts

I Samuel 2:30
". . . for **those who honor Me I will honor,** and those who despise Me will be lightly esteemed."

6.C. Blessings

I Samuel 2:35–36
[35]"But **I will raise up for Myself a faithful priest** who will do according to what is in My heart and in My soul; and I will build him an enduring house, and he will walk before My anointed always. [36]And it shall come about that everyone who is left in your house shall come and bow down to him for a piece of silver or a loaf of bread, and say, 'Please assign me to one of the Priest's offices so that I may eat a piece of bread.'"

1.F. Obedience

I Samuel 3:13
"For I have told him that **I am about to judge his house forever** for the iniquity which he knew, because his sons brought a curse on themselves and **he did not rebuke them.**"

7.A. To Wicked

I Samuel 8:3
His sons, however, did not walk in his ways, but turned aside after dishonest gain and took bribes and perverted justice.

2.B. Bribe

I Samuel 8:14–19
[14]"And **he will take the best of your fields** and your vineyards and your olive groves, **and give them to his servants.** [15]And he will take a tenth of your seed and of your vineyards, and give to his officers and to his servants. [16]He will also take your male servants and your female servants and your best young men and your donkeys, and use them for his work. [17]**He will take a tenth of your flocks,** and you yourselves will become his servants. [18]Then you will cry out in that day because of your king whom you have chosen for yourselves, but the LORD will not answer you in that day." [19]Nevertheless, the people refused to listen to the voice of Samuel, and they said, "No, but there shall be a king over us."

8.B. Administrative Tax

I Samuel 9:8
And the servant answered Saul again and said, "Behold, I have in my hand a fourth of a shekel of silver; I will give it to the man of God and he will tell us our way."

4.B. Giving to Men

I Samuel 12:3
"Here I am; bear witness against me before the LORD and His anointed. Whose ox have I taken, or whose donkey have I taken, or **whom have I defrauded? Whom have I oppressed,** or from whose hand have I taken a bribe to blind my eyes with it? I will restore it to you."

1.B. Honesty
11. Restitution

I Samuel 12:9
"But they forgot the LORD their God, so **He sold them into the hand of Sisera,** captain of the army of Hazor, and into the hand of the Philistines and into the hand of the king of Moab, and they fought against them."

7.A. To Wicked

I Samuel 15:21
"But **the people took some of the spoil,** sheep and oxen, the choicest of the things devoted to destruction, to sacrifice to the LORD your God at Gilgal."

2.I. Disobedient

I Samuel 17:25
And the men of Israel said, "Have you seen this man who is coming up? Surely he is coming up to defy Israel. And it will be that **the king will enrich the man who kills him** with great riches and will give him his daughter and make his father's house free in Israel."

2.B. Bribe

I Samuel 18:23
So Saul's servants spoke these words to David. But David said, "Is it trivial in your sight to become the king's son-in-law, since **I am a poor man and lightly esteemed?**"

4.H. Helping Needy

I Samuel 22:2
And everyone who was in distress, and **everyone who was in debt,** and everyone who was discontented, **gathered to him;** and he became captain over them. Now there were about four hundred men with him.

4.H. Helping Needy

I Samuel 25:2–3
²Now there was a man in Maon whose business was in Carmel; and **the man was very rich,** and he had three thousand sheep and a thousand goats. And it came about while he was shearing his sheep in Carmel ³(**now the man's name was Nabal,** and his wife's name was Abigail. And the woman was intelligent and beautiful in appearance, but the man was harsh and evil in his dealings, and he was a Calebite).

2.E. Greed

I Samuel 25:27
"And now **let this gift which your maidservant has brought** to my lord be given to the young men who accompany my lord."

4.B. Giving to Men

Scripture: Subtopic:

I Samuel 30:23–24

²³Then David said, "You must not do so, my brothers, with what   12.B. Wages
the LORD has given us, who has kept us and delivered into our
hand the band that came against us.   ²⁴And who will listen to you
in this matter? For as his share is who goes down to the battle, **so
shall his share be who stays by the baggage;** they shall share alike."

II Samuel

Scripture:	Subtopic:

II Samuel 8:6–7
⁶Then David put garrisons among the Arameans of Damascus, and **the Arameans became servants to David, bringing tribute.** And the LORD helped David wherever he went. ⁷And David took the shields of gold which were carried by the servants of Hadadezer, and brought them to Jerusalem.

8.B. Administrative Tax

II Samuel 8:10–11
¹⁰Toi sent Joram his son to King David to greet him and bless him, because he had fought against Hadadezer and defeated him; for Hadadezer had been at war with Toi. And **Joram brought with him articles of silver, of gold and of bronze.** ¹¹King David also dedicated these to the LORD, with the silver and gold that he had dedicated from all the nations which he had subdued.

4.B. Giving to Men

II Samuel 12:1–3
¹**Then the LORD sent Nathan to David.** And he came to him, and said, "There were two men in one city, the one rich and the other poor. ²The rich man had a great many flocks and herds. ³But the poor man had nothing except one little ewe lamb which he bought and nourished; And it grew up together with him and his children. It would eat of his bread and drink of his cup and lie in his bosom, and was like a daughter to him."

2.E. Greed

II Samuel 12:4–6
⁴"Now a traveler came to the rich man, and he was unwilling to take from his own flock or his own herd, to prepare for the wayfarer who had come to him; **rather he took the poor man's ewe lamb and prepared it for the man who had come to him.**" ⁵Then David's anger burned greatly against the man, and he said to Nathan, "As the LORD lives, surely the man who has done this deserves to die. ⁶And he must make restitution for the lamb fourfold, because he did this thing and had no compassion."

2.J. Injustice
11. Restitution

II Samuel 18:11–12
¹¹Then Joab said to the man who had told him, "Now behold, you saw him! Why then did you not strike him there to the ground? And I would have given you ten pieces of silver and a belt." ¹²And the man said to Joab, "**Even if I should receive a thousand pieces of silver in my hand, I would not put out my hand against the king's son;** for in our hearing the king charged you and Abishai and Ittai, saying, 'Protect for me the young man Absalom!'"

2.B. Bribe

II Samuel 21:4
Then the Gibeonites said to him, "We have no concern of silver or gold with Saul or his house, nor is it for us to put any man to death in Israel." And he said, "I will do for you whatever you say."

11. Restitution

Scripture:

II Samuel 24:24

However, the king said to Araunah, "No, but I will surely buy it from you for a price, for I will not offer burnt offerings to the LORD my God which cost me nothing." So David bought the threshing floor and the oxen for fifty shekels of silver.

Subtopic:

4.D. Offerings
9.E. Buying

I Kings

Scripture:	Subtopic:

I Kings 3:11–13

[11]And God said to him, "Because you have asked this thing and have not asked for yourself long life, nor have asked riches for yourself, nor have you asked for the life of your enemies, but have asked for yourself discernment to understand justice, [12]behold, I have done according to your words. Behold, I have given you a wise and discerning heart, so that there has been no one like you before you, nor shall one like you arise after you. [13]And **I have also given you what you have not asked, both riches and honor, so that there will not be any among the kings like you all your days.**"

6.A. God's Promises

I Kings 5:6

"Now therefore, command that they cut for me cedars from Lebanon, and my servants will be with your servants; and **I will give you wages for your servants according to all that you say,** for you know that there is no one among us who knows how to cut timber like the Sidonians."

12.B. Wages

I Kings 5:10–11

[10]So Hiram gave Solomon as much as he desired of the cedar and cypress timber. [11]Solomon then gave Hiram 20,000 kors of wheat as food for his household, and twenty kors of beaten oil; thus **Solomon would give Hiram year by year.**

4.B. Giving to Men

I Kings 5:13–15

[13]Now King Solomon levied forced laborers from all Israel; and the forced laborers numbered 30,000 men. [14]And he sent them to Lebanon, 10,000 a month in relays; they were in Lebanon a month and two months at home. And Adoniram was over the forced laborers. [15]Now Solomon had 70,000 transporters, and 80,000 hewers of stone in the mountains.

12.A. Work

I Kings 5:17

Then the king commanded, and they quarried great stones, costly stones, to lay the foundation of the house with cut stones.

4.D. Offerings

I Kings 6:20–22

And the inner sanctuary was twenty cubits in length, twenty cubits in width, and twenty cubits in height, and he overlaid it with pure gold. He also overlaid the altar with cedar. So Solomon overlaid the inside of the house with pure gold. And he drew chains of gold across the front of the inner sanctuary; and he overlaid it with gold. And he overlaid the whole house with gold, until all the house was finished. Also the whole altar which was by the inner sanctuary he overlaid with gold.

4.D. Offerings

I Kings 6:28
He also overlaid the cherubim with gold.

4.D. Offerings

I Kings 7:51
Thus all the work that King Solomon performed in the house of the LORD was finished. And Solomon brought in the things dedicated by his father David, the silver and the gold and the utensils, and he put them in the treasuries of the house of the LORD.

4.D. Offerings

I Kings 9:14
And Hiram sent to the king 120 talents of gold.

4.B. Giving to Men

I Kings 9:28
And they went to Ophir, and took four hundred and twenty talents of gold from there, and brought it to King Solomon.

4.B. Giving to Men

I Kings 10:2
So she came to Jerusalem with a very large retinue, with camels carrying spices and very much gold and precious stones. When she came to Solomon, she spoke with him about all that was in her heart.

4.B. Giving to Men

I Kings 10:7
"Nevertheless I did not believe the reports, until I came and my eyes had seen it. And behold, the half was not told me. **You exceed in wisdom and prosperity the report which I heard.**"

1.L. Wisdom

I Kings 10:10
And **she gave the king a hundred and twenty talents of gold,** and a very great amount of spices and precious stones. Never again did such abundance of spices come in as that which the queen of Sheba gave King Solomon.

4.B. Giving to Men

I Kings 10:14
Now the weight of gold which came in to Solomon in one year was 666 talents of gold.

4.B. Giving to Men

I Kings 10:16–18
[16]And King Solomon made 200 large shields of beaten gold, using 600 shekels of gold on each large shield. [17]And he made 300 shields of beaten gold, using three minas of gold on each shield, and the king put them in the house of the forest of Lebanon. [18]Moreover, the king made a great throne of ivory and overlaid it with refined gold.

4.D. Offerings

I Kings 10:21
And **all King Solomon's drinking vessels were of gold,** and all the vessels of the house of the forest of Lebanon were of pure gold. None was of silver; it was not considered valuable in the days of Solomon.

6.G. Wealth

Scripture:	Subtopic:

I Kings 10:23
So King **Solomon became greater than all the kings of the earth in riches and in wisdom.**

6.A. God's Promises
6.G. Wealth

I Kings 10:27
And **the king made silver as common as stones** in Jerusalem, and he made cedars as plentiful as sycamore trees that are in the lowland.

6.G. Wealth

I Kings 10:29
And a chariot was imported from Egypt for 600 shekels of silver, and a horse for 150; and by the same means they exported them to all the kings of the Hittites and to the kings of the Arameans.

9.E. Buying

I Kings 12:28
So **the king consulted, and made two golden calves,** and he said to them, "It is too much for you to go up to Jerusalem; behold your gods, O Israel, that brought you up from the land of Egypt."

2.I. Disobedient

I Kings 13:7–8
[7]Then the king said to the man of God, "Come home with me and refresh yourself, and I will give you a reward." [8]But the man of God said to the king, **"If you were to give me half your house I would not go with you,** nor would I eat bread or drink water in this place."

2.B. Bribe

I Kings 14:25–26
[25]Now it came about in the fifth year of King Rehoboam, that Shishak the king of Egypt came up against Jerusalem. [26]And he **took away the treasures of the house of the** LORD and the treasures of the king's house, and he took everything, even taking all the shields of gold which Solomon had made.

7.A. To Wicked

I Kings 15:15
And he brought into the house of the LORD the dedicated things of his father and his own dedicated things: silver and gold and utensils.

4.D. Offerings

I Kings 15:18
Then **Asa took all the silver** and the gold which were left in the treasuries of the house of the LORD and the treasuries of the king's house, and **delivered them into the hand of his servants.** And King Asa sent them to Ben-hadad the son of Tabrimmon, the son of Hezion, king of Aram, who lived in Damascus. . . .

6.E. Discipline

I Kings 17:13–14
[13]Then Elijah said to her, "Do not fear; go, do as you have said, but make me a little bread cake from it first, and bring it out to me, and afterward you may make one for yourself and for your son. [14]For thus says the LORD God of Israel, '**The bowl of flour shall not be exhausted, nor shall the jar of oil be empty, until the day that the LORD sends rain on the face of the earth.**'"

6.D. Provision

Scripture:		Subtopic:
I Kings 17:16 The bowl of flour was not exhausted nor did the jar of oil become empty, according to the word of the LORD which He spoke through Elijah.		6.D. Provision
I Kings 20:3 **"Your silver and your gold are mine;** your most beautiful wives and children are also mine."		2.E. Greed
I Kings 20:7 Then the king of Israel called all the elders of the land and said, "Please observe and see how this man is looking for trouble; for he sent to me for my wives and my children and my silver and my gold, and I did not refuse him."		2.E. Greed
I Kings 20:39 And as the king passed by, he cried to the king and said, "Your servant went out into the midst of the battle; and behold, a man turned aside and brought a man to me and said, 'Guard this man; if for any reason he is missing, then your life shall be for his life, or else you shall pay a talent of silver.'"		11. Restitution
I Kings 21:2 ". . . it is close beside my house, and **I will give you a better vineyard than it in its place;** if you like, I will give you the price of it in money."		2.E. Greed
I Kings 21:20 And **Ahab** said to Elijah, "Have you found me, O my enemy?" And he answered, "I have found you, because **you have sold yourself to do evil** in the sight of the LORD."		7.A. To Wicked
I Kings 21:25 Surely **there was no one like Ahab who sold himself to do evil** in the sight of the LORD, because Jezebel his wife incited him.		7.A. To Wicked

II Kings

Scripture:	Subtopic:
II Kings 3:4 Now **Mesha** king of Moab was a sheep breeder, and **used to pay the king of Israel** 100,000 lambs and the wool of 100,000 rams.	8.B. Administrative Tax
II Kings 4:1 Now a certain woman of the wives of the sons of the prophets cried out to Elisha, "Your servant my husband is dead, and you know that your servant feared the LORD; and **the creditor has come to take my two children** to be his slaves."	3.F. Paying Debts
II Kings 4:7 Then she came and told the man of God. And he said, "**Go, sell the oil and pay your debt,** and you and your sons can live on the rest."	3.F. Paying Debts
II Kings 5:5 Then the king of Aram said, "Go now, and I will send a letter to the king of Israel." And he departed and took with him ten talents of silver and six thousand shekels of gold and ten changes of clothes.	4.B. Giving to Men

Scripture:	Subtopic:

II Kings 5:15–27

[15]When he returned to the man of God with all his company, and came and stood before him, he said, "Behold now, **I know that there is no God in all the earth, but in Israel;** so please take a present from your servant now." [16]But he said, "As the LORD lives, before whom I stand, I will take nothing." And he urged him to take it, but he refused. [17]And Naaman said, "If not, please let your servant at least be given two mules' load of earth; for your servant will no more offer burnt offering nor will he sacrifice to other gods, but to the LORD. [18]In this matter may the LORD pardon your servant; when my master goes into the house of Rimmon to worship there, and he leans on my hand and I bow myself in the house of Rimmon, when I bow myself in the house of Rimmon, the LORD pardon your servant in this matter." [19]And he said to him, "Go in peace." So he departed from him some distance. [20]But Gehazi, the servant of Elisha the man of God, thought, "Behold, my master has spared this Naaman the Aramean, by not receiving from his hands what he brought. As the LORD lives, I will run after him and take something from him." [21]So Gehazi pursued Naaman. When Naaman saw one running after him, he came down from the chariot to meet him and said, "Is all well?" [22]And he said, "All is well. My master has sent me, saying, 'Behold, just now two young men of the sons of the prophets have come to me from the hill country of Ephraim. **Please give them a talent of silver and two changes of clothes.**'" [23]And Naaman said, "Be pleased to take two talents." And he urged him, and bound two talents of silver in two bags with two changes of clothes, and gave them to two of his servants; and they carried them before him. [24]When he came to the hill, he took them from their hand and deposited them in the house, and he sent the men away, and they departed. [25]But he went in and stood before his master. And Elisha said to him, "Where have you been, Gehazi?" And he said, "Your servant went nowhere." [26]Then he said to him, "Did not my heart go with you, when the man turned from his chariot to meet you? Is it a time to receive money and to receive clothes and olive groves and vineyards and sheep and oxen and male and female servants? [27]Therefore, the leprosy of Naaman shall cleave to you and to your descendants forever." So he went out from his presence a leper as white as snow.

2.E. Greed
2.F. Dishonesty
4.B. Giving to Men

II Kings 6:25

And there was a great famine in Samaria; and behold, they besieged it, until **a donkey's head was sold for eighty shekels of silver,** and a fourth of a kab of dove's dung for five shekels of silver.

9.D. Selling

II Kings 7:8–9
[8]When these lepers came to the outskirts of the camp, they entered one tent and ate and drank, and carried from there silver and gold and clothes, and went and hid them; and they returned and entered another tent and carried from there also, and went and hid them. [9]Then they said to one another, "We are not doing right. This day is a day of good news, but we are keeping silent; if we wait until morning light, punishment will overtake us. Now therefore come, let us go and tell the king's household."

6.F. Justice

II Kings 7:16
So the people went out and plundered the camp of the Arameans. Then a measure of fine flour was sold for a shekel and two measures of barley for a shekel, according to the word of the LORD.

6.D. Provision

II Kings 7:19–20
[19]Then the royal officer answered the man of God and said, "Now behold, if the LORD should make windows in heaven, could such a thing be?" And he said, "Behold, you shall see it with your own eyes, but you shall not eat of it." [20]And so it happened to him, for the people trampled on him at the gate, and he died.

7.A. To Wicked

II Kings 12:4–7
[4]Then Jehoash said to the priests, "All the money of the sacred things which is brought into the house of the LORD, in current money, both the money of each man's assessment and all the money which any man's heart prompts him to bring into the house of the LORD, [5]let the priests take it for themselves, each from his acquaintance; and they shall repair the damages of the house wherever any damage may be found." [6]But it came about that in the twenty-third year of King Jehoash the priests had not repaired the damages of the house. [7]Then King Jehoash called for Jehoiada the priest, and for the other priests and said to them, "Why do you not repair the damages of the house? Now therefore take no more money from your acquaintances, but pay it for the damages of the house."

4.D. Offerings

II Kings 12:9–16

⁹But Jehoiada the priest took a chest and bored a hole in its lid, and put it beside the altar, on the right side as one comes into the house of the LORD; and the priests who guarded the threshold put in it all the money which was brought into the house of the LORD.   ¹⁰And when they saw that there was much money in the chest, the king's scribe and the high priest came up and tied it in bags and counted the money which was found in the house of the LORD.   ¹¹And they gave the money which was weighed out into the hands of those who did the work, who had the oversight of the house of the LORD; and they paid it out to the carpenters and the builders, who worked on the house of the Lord;   ¹²and to the masons and the stonecutters, and for buying timber and hewn stone to repair the damages to the house of the LORD, and for all that was laid out for the house to repair it.   ¹³But there were not made for the house of the LORD silver cups, snuffers, bowls, trumpets, any vessels of gold, or vessels of silver from the money which was brought into the house of the LORD;   ¹⁴for **they gave that to those who did the work, and with it they repaired the house of the Lord.**   ¹⁵Moreover, they did not require an accounting from the men into whose hand they gave the money to pay to those who did the work, for they dealt faithfully.   ¹⁶The money from the guilt offerings and the money from the sin offerings, was not brought in to the house of the LORD; it was for the priests.

4.D. Offerings

II Kings 14:14

And he took all the gold and silver and all the utensils which were found in the house of the LORD, and in the treasuries of the king's house, the hostages also, and returned to Samaria.

6.E. Discipline

II Kings 15:19–20

¹⁹Pul, king of Assyria, came against the land, and Menahem gave Pul a thousand talents of silver so that his hand might be with him to strengthen the kingdom under his rule.   ²⁰**Then Menahem exacted the money from Israel,** even from all the mighty men of wealth, from each man fifty shekels of silver to pay the king of Assyria. So the king of Assyria returned and did not remain there in the land.

8.B. Administrative Tax

II Kings 16:8

And **Ahaz** took the silver and gold that was found in the house of the LORD and in the treasuries of the king's house, and **sent a present to the king of Assyria.**

2.B. Bribe
4.B. Giving to Men

II Kings 17:3–4

³Shalmaneser king of Assyria came up against him, and **Hoshea became his servant and paid him tribute.**   ⁴But the king of Assyria found conspiracy in Hoshea, who had sent messengers to So king of Egypt and had offered no tribute to the king of Assyria, as he had done year by year; so the king of Assyria shut him up and bound him in prison.

8.B. Administrative Tax

II Kings 17:7–9
⁷Now this came about, because the sons of Israel had sinned against the LORD their God, who had brought them up from the land of Egypt from under the hand of Pharaoh, king of Egypt, and they had feared other gods ⁸and walked in the customs of the nations whom the LORD had driven out before the sons of Israel, and in the customs of the kings of Israel which they had introduced. ⁹And the sons of Israel did things secretly which were not right, against the LORD their God. Moreover, they built for themselves high places in all their towns, from watchtower to fortified city.

2.I. Disobedient

II Kings 17:17
Then they made their sons and their daughters pass through the fire, and practiced divination and enchantments, and **sold themselves to do evil in the sight of the LORD**, provoking Him.

2.I. Disobedient

II Kings 18:14–16
¹⁴Then **Hezekiah** king of Judah sent to the king of Assyria at Lachish, saying, "I have done wrong. **Withdraw from me; whatever you impose on me I will bear.**" So the king of Assyria required of Hezekiah king of Judah three hundred talents of silver and thirty talents of gold. ¹⁵And Hezekiah gave him all the silver which was found in the house of the LORD, and in the treasuries of the king's house. ¹⁶At that time Hezekiah cut off the gold from the doors of the temple of the LORD, and from the doorposts which Hezekiah king of Judah had overlaid, and gave it to the king of Assyria.

8.B. Administrative Tax

II Kings 20:13
And **Hezekiah listened to them, and showed them all his treasure house,** the silver and the gold and the spices and the precious oil and the house of his armor and all that was found in his treasuries. There was nothing in his house, nor in all his dominion, that Hezekiah did not show them.

2.C. Pride

II Kings 22:4–9
⁴"Go up to Hilkiah the high priest that he may count the money brought in to the house of the LORD which the door keepers have gathered from the people. ⁵And let them deliver it into the hand of the workmen who have the oversight of the house of the LORD, and **let them give it to the workmen who are in the house of the LORD to repair the damages of the house,** ⁶to the carpenters and the builders and the masons and for buying timber and hewn stone to repair the house. ⁷Only no accounting shall be made with them for the money delivered into their hands, for they deal faithfully." ⁸Then Hilkiah the high priest said to Shaphan the scribe, "I have found the book of the law in the house of the LORD." And Hilkiah gave the book to Shaphan who read it. ⁹And Shaphan the scribe came to the king and brought back word to the king and said, "Your servants have emptied out the money that was found in the house, and have delivered it into the hand of the workmen who have the oversight of the house of the LORD."

1.H. Trust
4.D. Offerings
12.B. Wages

Scripture:	Subtopic:

II Kings 23:33
And **Pharaoh Neco** imprisoned him at Riblah in the land of Hamath, that he might not reign in Jerusalem; and he **imposed on the
land a fine of one hundred talents of silver** and a talent of gold.

8.B. Administrative
Tax

II Kings 23:35
So **Jehoiakim gave the silver and gold to Pharaoh,** but he taxed the
land in order to give the money at the command of Pharaoh. He
exacted the silver and gold from the people of the land, each according to his valuation, to give it to Pharaoh Neco.

8.B. Administrative
Tax

II Kings 24:13
And **he carried out from there all the treasures of the house of the
LORD,** and the treasures of the king's house, and cut in pieces all
the vessels of gold which Solomon king of Israel had made in the
temple of the LORD, just as the LORD had said.

6.E. Discipline

II Kings 24:14
Then he led away into exile all Jerusalem and all the captains and
all the mighty men of valor, ten thousand captives, and all the
craftsmen and the smiths. **None remained except the poorest people of the land.**

6.E. Discipline

II Kings 25:15
The captain of the guard also took away the firepans and the basins, what was fine gold and what was fine silver.

6.E. Discipline

II Kings 25:30
And **for his allowance, a regular allowance was given him by the
king,** a portion for each day, all the days of his life.

4.B. Giving to
Men

I Chronicles

Scripture:	Subtopic:

I Chronicles 18:7
And **David took the shields of gold** which were carried by the servants of Hadadezer, and brought them to Jerusalem.

6.G. Wealth

I Chronicles 18:10–11
¹⁰. . . And Hadoram brought all kinds of articles of gold and silver and bronze. ¹¹**King David also dedicated these to the LORD** with the silver and the gold which he had carried away from all the nations: from Edom, Moab, the sons of Ammon, the Philistines, and from Amalek.

6.G. Wealth

I Chronicles 19:6–7
⁶When the sons of Ammon saw that they had made themselves odious to David, Hanun and the **sons of Ammon sent 1,000 talents of silver to hire for themselves chariots and horsemen from Mesopotamia,** from Aram-maacah, and from Zobah. ⁷So they hired for themselves 32,000 chariots, and the king of Maacah and his people, who came and camped before Medeba. And the sons of Ammon gathered together from their cities and came to battle.

9.E. Buying
12.B. Wages

I Chronicles 20:2
And **David took the crown of their king** from his head, and he found it to weigh a talent of gold, and there was a precious stone in it; and it was placed on David's head. And he brought out the spoil of the city, a very great amount.

6.G. Wealth

I Chronicles 21:22
Then David said to Ornan, "**Give me the site of this threshing floor,** that I may build on it an altar to the LORD; for the full price you shall give it to me, that the plague may be restrained from the people."

9.D. Selling

I Chronicles 21:23
And **Ornan said to David, "Take it for yourself;** and let my lord the king do what is good in his sight. See, I will give the oxen for burnt offerings and the threshing sledges for wood and the wheat for the grain offering; I will give it all."

4.D. Offerings

I Chronicles 21:24
But King David said to Ornan, "No, **but I will surely buy it for the full price; for I will not take what is yours for the LORD,** or offer a burnt offering which costs me nothing."

9.E. Buying

Scripture:	Subtopic:

I Chronicles 22:5
And David said, "My son Solomon is young and inexperienced, and the house that is to be built for the LORD shall be exceedingly magnificent, famous and glorious throughout all lands. Therefore now I will make preparation for it." So **David made ample preparations before his death.**

10. Planning

I Chronicles 22:14
"Now behold, with great pains **I have prepared for the house of the LORD 100,000 talents of gold and 1,000,000 talents of silver,** and bronze and iron beyond weight, for they are in great quantity; also timber and stone I have prepared, and you may add to them."

10. Planning*

I Chronicles 22:16
"Of the gold, the silver and the bronze and the iron, there is no limit. **Arise and work, and may the LORD be with you.**"

12.F. Diligent

I Chronicles 23:27–28
²⁷For by the last words of David the sons of Levi were numbered, from twenty years old and upward. ²⁸For their office is to assist the sons of Aaron with the service of the house of the LORD, in the courts and in the chambers and in the purifying of all holy things, even the work of the service of the house of God.

5.A. Inheritance

I Chronicles 26:20
And **the Levites, their relatives, had charge of the treasures** of the house of God, and of the treasures of the dedicated gifts.

4.A. Storehouse

I Chronicles 26:22
The sons of Jehieli, Zetham and Joel his brother, **had charge of the treasures** of the house of the LORD.

4.A. Storehouse

I Chronicles 26:24
Shebuel the son of Gershom, the son of Moses, was officer over the treasures.

4.A. Storehouse

I Chronicles 26:26–27
²⁶This Shelomoth and his relatives had charge of all the treasures of the dedicated gifts, which King David and the heads of the fathers' households, the commanders of thousands and hundreds, and commanders of the army, had dedicated. ²⁷**They dedicated part of the spoil won in battles to repair the house of the LORD.**

4.D. Offerings

---

*About one billion ounces of gold and 1.2 billion ounces of silver.

I Chronicles 28:14–18

[14] **. . . for the golden utensils,** the weight of gold for all utensils for every kind of service; for the silver utensils, the weight of silver for all utensils for every kind of service; [15]and the weight of gold for the golden lampstands and their golden lamps, with the weight of each lampstand and its lamps; and the weight of silver for the silver lampstands, with the weight of each lampstand and its lamps according to the use of each lampstand; [16]and the gold by weight for the tables of showbread, for each table; and silver for the silver tables; [17]and the forks, the basins, and the pitchers of pure gold; and for the golden bowls with the weight for each bowl; and for the silver bowls with the weight for each bowl; [18]and for the altar of incense refined gold by weight; and gold for the model of the chariot, even the cherubim, that spread out their wings, and covered the ark of the covenant of the LORD.

6.G. Wealth

I Chronicles 29:2–5

[2]**"Now with all my ability I have provided for the house of my God the gold for the things of gold,** and the silver for the things of silver, and the bronze for the things of bronze, the iron for the things of iron, and wood for the things of wood, onyx stones and inlaid stones, stones of antimony, and stones of various colors, and all kinds of precious stones, and alabaster in abundance. [3]And moreover, in my delight in the house of my God, the treasure I have of gold and silver, I give to the house of my God, over and above all that I have already provided for the holy temple, [4]namely, 3,000 talents of gold, of the gold of Ophir, and 7,000 talents of refined silver, to overlay the walls of the buildings; [5]of gold for the things of gold, and of silver for the things of silver, that is, for all the work done by the craftsmen. Who then is willing to consecrate himself this day to the LORD?"

4.F. Gifts

I Chronicles 29:7

. . . and **for the service for the house of God they gave 5,000 talents** and 10,000 darics of gold, and 10,000 talents of silver, and 18,000 talents of brass, and 100,000 talents of iron.

4.D. Offerings*

I Chronicles 29:12–14

[12]**"Both riches and honor come from Thee, and Thou dost rule over all,** and in Thy hand is power and might; and it lies in Thy hand to make great, and to strengthen everyone. [13]Now therefore, our God, we thank Thee, and praise Thy glorious name. [14]But who am I and who are my people that we should be able to offer as generously as this? For all things come from Thee, and from Thy hand we have given Thee."

6.D. Provision

I Chronicles 29:28

Then **he died** in a ripe old age, **full of days, riches and honor;** and his son Solomon reigned in his place.

6.C. Blessings

---

*About 6.5 million ounces of gold and 12 million ounces in silver.

II Chronicles

Scripture:	Subtopic:

II Chronicles 1:11–12

[11]And God said to Solomon, "Because you had this in mind, and did not ask for riches, wealth, or honor, or the life of those who hate you, nor have you even asked for long life, but you have asked for yourself [12]wisdom and knowledge, that you may rule My people, over whom I have made you king, wisdom and knowledge have been granted to you. And **I will give you riches and wealth and honor,** such as none of the kings who were before you has possessed, nor those who will come after you."

6.A. God's Promises

II Chronicles 1:15

And **the king made silver and gold as plentiful** in Jerusalem as stones, and he made cedars as plentiful as sycamores in the lowland.

6.A. God's Promises

II Chronicles 1:17

And **they imported chariots from Egypt** for 600 shekels of silver apiece, and horses for 150 apiece, and by the same means they exported them to all the kings of the Hittites and the kings of Aram.

9.E. Buying

II Chronicles 3:4–17

⁴And **the porch which was in front** of the house was as long as the width of the house, twenty cubits, and the height 120; and inside he overlaid it with pure gold.   ⁵And he overlaid the main room with cypress wood and overlaid it with fine gold, and ornamented it with palm trees and chains.   ⁶Further, he adorned the house with precious stones; and the gold was gold from Parvaim.   ⁷He also overlaid the house with gold—the beams, the thresholds, and its walls, and its doors; and he carved cherubim on the walls.   ⁸Now he made the room of the holy of holies: its length, across the width of the house, was twenty cubits, and its width was twenty cubits; and he overlaid it with fine gold, amounting to 600 talents.   ⁹And the weight of the nails was fifty shekels of gold. He also overlaid the upper rooms with gold.   ¹⁰Then he made two sculptured cherubim in the room of the holy of holies and overlaid them with gold.   ¹¹And the wingspan of the cherubim was twenty cubits; the wing of one, of five cubits, touched the wall of the house, and its other wing, of five cubits, touched the wing of the other cherub.   ¹²And the wing of the other cherub, of five cubits, touched the wall of the house; and its other wing of five cubits, was attached to the wing of the first cherub.   ¹³The wings of these cherubim extended twenty cubits, and they stood on their feet facing the main room.   ¹⁴And he made the veil of violet, purple, crimson and fine linen, and he worked cherubim on it.   ¹⁵He also made two pillars for the front of the house, thirty-five cubits high, and the capital on the top of each was five cubits.   ¹⁶And he made chains in the inner sanctuary, and placed them on the tops of the pillars; and he made one hundred pomegranates and placed them on the chains.   ¹⁷And he erected the pillars in front of the temple, one on the right and the other on the left, and named the one on the right Jachin and the one on the left Boaz.

6.D. Provision

II Chronicles 4:7–8

⁷Then he made **the ten golden lampstands** in the way prescribed for them, and he set them in the temple, five on the right side and five on the left.   ⁸He also made ten tables and placed them in the temple, five on the right side and five on the left. And he made one hundred golden bowls.

6.G. Wealth

II Chronicles 4:19–22

¹⁹**Solomon also made all the things that were in the house of God:** even the golden altar, the tables with the bread of the Presence on them,   ²⁰the lampstands with their lamps of pure gold, to burn in front of the inner sanctuary in the way prescribed;   ²¹the flowers, the lamps, and the tongs of gold, of purest gold;   ²²and the snuffers, the bowls, the spoons, and the firepans of pure gold; and the entrance of the house, its inner doors for the holy of holies, and the doors of the house, that is, of the nave, of gold.

6.D. Provision

II Chronicles 5:1

. . . even the silver and the gold and all the utensils, and put them in the treasuries of the house of God.

6.D. Provision

Scripture:	Subtopic:

II Chronicles 7:14
". . . and My people who **are called by my name humble themselves and pray,** and seek My face and turn from their wicked ways, then I will hear from heaven, will forgive their sin, and will heal their land."

1.C. Humility

II Chronicles 8:18
. . . and took from there four hundred and fifty talents of gold, and brought them to King Solomon.

4.B. Giving to Men

II Chronicles 9:1
. . . **She had a very large retinue,** with camels carrying spices, and a large amount of gold and precious stones; and when she came to Solomon, she spoke with him about all that was on her heart.

4.B. Giving to Men

II Chronicles 9:9–10
9Then **she gave the king one hundred and twenty talents of gold,** and a very great amount of spices and precious stones; there had never been spice like that which **the queen of Sheba** gave to King Solomon. 10And the servants of Huram and the servants of Solomon who brought gold from Ophir, also brought algum trees and precious stones.

4.B. Giving to Men

II Chronicles 9:13
Now **the weight of gold** which came to Solomon in one year was 666 talents of gold.

4.B. Giving to Men*

II Chronicles 9:15–18
15And King Solomon made 200 large shields of beaten gold, using 600 shekels of beaten gold on each large shield. 16And he made 300 shields of beaten gold, using three hundred shekels of gold on each shield, and the king put them in the house of the forest of Lebanon. 17Moreover, **the king made a great throne of ivory and overlaid it with pure gold.** 18And there were six steps to the throne and a footstool in gold attached to the throne, and arms on each side of the seat, and two lions standing beside the arms.

6.G. Wealth

II Chronicles 9:20–22
20And **all King Solomon's drinking vessels were of gold,** and all the vessels of the house of the forest of Lebanon were of pure gold; silver was not considered valuable in the days of Solomon . . . 21the ships of Tarshish came bringing gold and silver, ivory and apes and peacocks. 22So King Solomon became greater than all the kings of the earth in riches and wisdom.

6.A. God's Promises

II Chronicles 9:24
And **they brought every man his gift,** articles of silver and gold, garments, weapons, spices, horses, and mules, so much year by year.

4.B. Giving to Men

_____
*About 800,000 ounces in gold.

Scripture:	Subtopic:

II Chronicles 9:27
And **the king made silver as common as stones** in Jerusalem, and he
made cedars as plentiful as sycamore trees that are in the lowland.

6.G. Wealth

II Chronicles 12:9
So **Shishak** king of Egypt came up against Jerusalem, and **took the
treasures of the house of the LORD** and the treasures of the king's
palace. He took everything; he even took the golden shields which
Solomon had made.

6.E. Discipline

II Chronicles 13:8
"So now you intend to resist the kingdom of the LORD through the
sons of David, being a great multitude and having with you the
golden calves which Jeroboam made for gods for you."

2.I. Disobedient

II Chronicles 15:1–2
¹Now the Spirit of God came on Azariah the son of Oded, ²and he
went out to meet Asa and said to him, "Listen to me, Asa, and all
Judah and Benjamin: the LORD is with you when you are with
Him. And if you seek Him, He will let you find Him; but if you
forsake Him, He will forsake you."

6.A. God's Promises

II Chronicles 15:18
And he brought into the house of God the dedicated things of his
father and his own dedicated things: silver and gold and utensils.

4.F. Gifts

II Chronicles 16:2–3
²Then **Asa brought out silver and gold from the treasuries of the
house of the LORD** and the king's house, and **sent them to Ben-
hadad king of Aram**, who lived in Damascus, saying, ³"Let there
be a treaty between you and me, as between my father and your
father. Behold, I have sent you silver and gold; go, break your
treaty with Baasha king of Israel so that he will withdraw from
me."

2.B. Bribe
4.B. Giving to
Men

II Chronicles 16:9
"For **the eyes of the LORD** move to and fro throughout the earth
that He may strongly support those whose heart is completely His.
You have acted foolishly in this. Indeed, from now on you will
surely have wars."

2.I. Disobedient

II Chronicles 17:5
So the LORD established the kingdom in his control, and all
Judah brought tribute to Jehoshaphat, and he had great riches and
honor.

6.A. God's Promises
8.B. Administrative
Tax

II Chronicles 17:11
And some of the Philistines brought gifts and silver as tribute to
Jehoshaphat; the Arabians also brought him flocks, 7,700 rams and
7,700 male goats.

4.B. Giving to
Men

Scripture:	Subtopic:

II Chronicles 18:1
Now **Jehoshaphat had great riches and honor;** and he allied himself
by marriage with Ahab. .... 6.C. Blessings

II Chronicles 19:7
"Now then let the fear of the LORD be upon you; be very careful
what you do, for **the LORD our God will have no part in unright-**
eousness, or partiality, or the taking of a bribe." .... 2.B. Bribe

II Chronicles 20:25
And when **Jehoshaphat and his people came to take their spoil,**
they found much among them, including goods, garments, and
valuable things which they took for themselves, more than they
could carry. And they were three days taking the spoil because
there was so much. .... 7.A. To Wicked

II Chronicles 21:3
And their father gave them many gifts of silver, gold and precious
things, with fortified cities in Judah, **but he gave the kingdom to**
Jehoram because he was the first-born. .... 5.A. Inheritance

II Chronicles 24:5
And he gathered the priests and Levites, and said to them, "Go out
to the cities of Judah, and **collect money from all Israel to repair the**
house of your God annually, and you shall do the matter quickly."
But the Levites did not act quickly. .... 8.A. Church Tax

II Chronicles 24:9
And they made a proclamation in Judah and Jerusalem to **bring to**
the LORD the levy fixed by Moses the servant of God on Israel in
the wilderness. .... 8.A. Church Tax

II Chronicles 24:11–12
[11]And it came about whenever the chest was brought in to the king's
officer by the Levites, and when they saw that there was much
money, then the king's scribe and the chief priest's officer would
come, empty the chest, take it, and return it to its place. Thus they
did daily and collected much money. [12]And the king and Jehoiada
gave it to those who did the work of the service of the house of the
LORD; and they hired masons and carpenters to restore the house of
the LORD, and also workers in iron and bronze to repair the house
of the LORD. .... 4.D. Offerings / 8.A. Church Tax

II Chronicles 24:14
And when they had finished, they brought the rest of the money
before the king and Jehoiada; and it was made into utensils for the
house of the LORD, utensils for the service and the burnt offering,
and pans and utensils of gold and silver. And they offered burnt
offerings in the house of the LORD continually all the days of Jehoiada. .... 4.D. Offerings

Scripture:	Subtopic:

II Chronicles 25:6–9
⁶He hired also 100,000 valiant warriors out of Israel for one hundred talents of silver.   ⁷But a man of God came to him saying, "O king, do not let the army of Israel go with you, for the LORD is not with Israel nor with any of the sons of Ephraim.   ⁸But if you do go, do it, be strong for the battle; yet God will bring you down before the enemy, for God has power to help and to bring down."   ⁹And Amaziah said to the man of God, "But **what shall we do for the hundred talents which I have given to the troops of Israel?**" And the man of God answered, "The LORD has much more to give you than this."

1.H. Trust
12.B. Wages

II Chronicles 25:24
And he took all the gold and silver, and all the utensils which were found in the house of God with Obed-edom, and the treasures of the king's house, the hostages also, and returned to Samaria.

7.A. To Wicked

II Chronicles 26:5
And he continued to seek God in the days of Zechariah, who had understanding through the vision of God; and as long as he sought the LORD, **God prospered him.**

6.A. God's Promises

II Chronicles 26:8
The Ammonites also gave tribute to Uzziah, and his fame extended to the border of Egypt, for he became very strong.

8.B. Administrative Tax

II Chronicles 27:5
He fought also with the king of the Ammonites and prevailed over them so that the **Ammonites gave him during that year one hundred talents of silver,** ten thousand kors of wheat and ten thousand of barley. The Ammonites also paid him this amount in the second and in the third year.

8.B. Administrative Tax

II Chronicles 28:21
And **Ahaz** took a portion out of the house of the LORD and out of the palace of the king and of the princes, and **gave it to the king of Assyria; but it did not help him.**

2.B. Bribe
6.E. Discipline

II Chronicles 31:14–15
¹⁴And Kore the son of Imnah the Levite, the keeper of the eastern gate, was over the freewill offerings of God, to apportion the contributions for the LORD and the most holy things.   ¹⁵And under his authority were Eden, Miniamin, Jeshua, Shemaiah, Amariah, and Shecaniah in the the cities of the priests, to distribute faithfully their portions to their brothers by divisions, whether great or small,

4.D. Offerings

II Chronicles 32:25
But Hezekiah gave no return for the benefit he received because his heart was proud; therefore wrath came on him and on Judah and Jerusalem.

2.C. Pride

II Chronicles 32:27–29

[27]Now **Hezekiah had immense riches and honor;** and he made for himself treasuries for silver, gold, precious stones, spices, shields and all kinds of valuable articles,   [28]storehouses also for the produce of grain, wine and oil, pens for all kinds of cattle and sheepfolds for the flocks.   [29]And he made cities for himself, and acquired flocks and herds in abundance; for God had given him very great wealth.

6.A. God's Promises

II Chronicles 34:9

And they came to Hilkiah the high priest and delivered the money that was brought into the house of God, which the Levites, the doorkeepers, had collected from Manasseh and Ephraim, and from all the remnant of Israel, and from all Judah and Benjamin and the inhabitants of Jerusalem.

4.F. Gifts

II Chronicles 34:11

They in turn gave it to the carpenters and to the builders to buy quarried stone and timber for couplings and to make beams for the houses which the kings of Judah had let go to ruin.

9.E. Buying

II Chronicles 34:14

When they were bringing out the money which had been brought into the house of the LORD, **Hilkiah the priest found the book of the law of the LORD given by Moses.**

4.F. Gifts

II Chronicles 34:17

"They have also emptied out the money which was found in the house of the LORD, and have delivered it into the hands of the supervisors and the workmen."

8.B. Administrative Tax

II Chronicles 36:3

Then the king of Egypt deposed him at Jerusalem, and **imposed on the land a fine of one hundred talents of silver** and one talent of gold.

8.B. Administrative Tax

II Chronicles 36:18

And **all the articles of the house of God,** great and small, and the treasures of the house of the LORD, and the treasures of the king and of his officers, **he brought them all to Babylon.**

7.A. To Wicked

Ezra

Scripture:	Subtopic:

Ezra 1:4
"**And** every survivor, at whatever place he may live, **let the men of that place support him with silver and gold,** with goods and cattle, together with a freewill offering for the house of God which is in Jerusalem."

4.D. Offerings

Ezra 1:6
And **all those about them encouraged them with articles of silver,** with gold, with goods, with cattle, and with valuables, aside from all that was given as a freewill offering.

4.F. Gifts

Ezra 1:9–11
⁹Now this was their number: 30 gold dishes, 1,000 silver dishes, 29 duplicates; ¹⁰30 gold bowls, 410 silver bowls of a second kind, and 1,000 other articles. ¹¹**All the articles of gold and silver numbered 5,400.** Sheshbazzar brought them all up with the exiles who went up from Babylon to Jerusalem.

6.D. Provision

Ezra 2:69
According to their ability they gave to the treasury for the work 61,000 gold drachmas, and 5,000 silver minas, and 100 priestly garments.

4.F. Gifts*

Ezra 3:7
Then they gave money to the masons and carpenters, and food, drink, and oil to the Sidonians and to the Tyrians, to bring cedar wood from Lebanon to the sea at Joppa, according to the permission they had from Cyrus king of Persia.

12.B. Wages

Ezra 4:13
"Now let it be known to the king, that if that city is rebuilt and the walls are finished, **they will not pay tribute,** custom, or toll, and it will damage the revenue of the kings."

8.B. Administrative Tax

Ezra 4:20–21
²⁰". . . that mighty kings have ruled over Jerusalem, governing all the provinces beyond the River, and that **tribute, custom, and toll were paid to them.** ²¹So, now issue a decree to make these men stop work, that the city may not be rebuilt until a decree is issued by me."

8.B. Administrative Tax

---

*About 277,000 ounces of gold and 6,250 pounds of silver.

Ezra 5:14
"And also the gold and silver utensils of the house of God which Nebuchadnezzar had taken from the temple in Jerusalem, and brought them to the temple of Babylon, these King Cyrus took from the temple of Babylon, and they were given to one whose name was Sheshbazzar, whom he had appointed governor."

6.D. Provision

Ezra 5:17
"And now, if it pleases the king let a search be conducted in the king's treasure house, which is there in Babylon, if it be that **a decree was issued by king Cyrus to rebuild this house** of God at Jerusalem; and let the king send to us his decision concerning this matter."

6.D. Provision

Ezra 6:1
Then **King Darius issued a decree**, and search was made in the archives, where the treasures were stored in Babylon.

6.D. Provision

Ezra 6:4–5
⁴". . . with three layers of huge stones, and one layer of timbers. And let the cost be paid from the royal treasury.   ⁵And also let the gold and silver utensils of the temple of God, which Nebuchadnezzar took from the temple in Jerusalem and brought to Babylon, be returned and brought to their places in the temple in Jerusalem; and you shall put them in the house of God."

6.D. Provision

Ezra 6:8
"Moreover, I issue a decree concerning what you are to do for these elders of Judah in the rebuilding of this house of God: **the full cost is to be paid to these people from the royal treasury out of the taxes** of the provinces beyond the River, and that without delay."

8.B. Administrative Tax

Ezra 7:15–18
¹⁵". . . and **to bring the silver and gold, which the king and his counselors have freely offered to the God of Israel,** whose dwelling is in Jerusalem,   ¹⁶with all the silver and gold which you shall find in the whole province of Babylon, along with the freewill offering of the people and of the priests, who offered willingly for the house of their God which is in Jerusalem;   ¹⁷with this money, therefore, you shall diligently buy bulls, rams, and lambs, with their grain offerings and their libations and offer them on the altar of the house of your God which is in Jerusalem.   ¹⁸And whatever seems good to you and to your brothers to do with **the rest of the silver and gold, you may do according to the will of your God."**

4.F. Gifts

Ezra 7:21–22
²¹"And I, even **I King Artaxerxes, issue a decree** to all the treasurers who are in the provinces beyond the River, that whatever Ezra the priest, the scribe of the law of the God of heaven, may require of you, it shall be done diligently,   ²²even up to 100 talents of silver, 100 kors of wheat, 100 baths of wine, 100 baths of oil, and salt as needed."

8.B. Administrative Tax

Ezra 7:24
"We also inform you that **it is not allowed to impose tax, tribute or toll on any of the priests,** Levites, singers, doorkeepers, Nethinim, or servants of this house of God."

8.B. Administrative Tax

Ezra 7:26
"And **whoever will not observe the law of your God** and the law of the king, **let judgement be executed upon him strictly,** whether for death or for banishment or for confiscation of goods or for imprisonment."

6.E. Discipline

Ezra 8:25–27
. . . and **I weighed out to them the silver, the gold,** and the utensils, the offering for the house of our God which the king and his counselors and his princes, and all Israel present there, had offered. [26]Thus I weighed into their hands **650 talents of silver,** and silver utensils worth 100 talents, and 100 gold talents, [27]and 20 gold bowls, worth 1,000 darics; and two utensils of fine shiny bronze, precious as gold.

4.D. Offerings*

Ezra 8:30
So the priests and the Levites accepted the weighed out silver and gold and the utensils, to bring them to Jerusalem to the house of our God.

4.D. Offerings

Ezra 9:12
". . . **never seek their peace or their prosperity, that you may be strong** and eat the good things of the land and leave it as an inheritance to your sons forever."

5.A. Inheritance

Ezra 10:8
. . . and that **whoever would not come within three days,** according to the counsel of the leaders and the elders, **all his possessions should be forfeited** and he himself excluded from the assembly of the exiles.

2.I. Disobedient

---

*Approximately 900,000 ounces of silver and 4,550 ounces of gold.

Nehemiah

Scripture:	Subtopic:

Nehemiah 2:8
". . . and a letter to Asaph the keeper of the king's forest, that he may give me timber to make beams for the gates of the fortress which is by the temple, for the wall of the city, and for the house to which I will go." And the king granted them to me because the good hand of my God was on me.

6.A. God's Promises
6.D. Provision

Nehemiah 2:20
So I answered them and said to them, **"The God of Heaven will give us success;** therefore we His servants will arise and build, but you have no portion, right, or memorial in Jerusalem."

6.A. God's Promises

Nehemiah 5:2–5
²For there were those who said, "We, our sons and our daughters, are many; therefore let us get grain that we may eat and live." ³And there were others who said, **"We are mortgaging our fields, our vineyards, and our houses** that we might get grain because of the famine." ⁴Also there were those who said, "We have borrowed money for the king's tax on our fields and our vineyards. ⁵And now our flesh is like the flesh of our brothers, our children like their children. Yet behold, we are forcing our sons and our daughters to be slaves, and some of our daughters are forced into bondage already, and we are helpless because our fields and vineyards belong to others."

3.A. Borrowing
8.B. Administrative Tax

Nehemiah 5:7–10
⁷And I consulted with myself, and contended with the nobles and the rulers and said to them, **"You are exacting usury, each from his brother!"** Therefore, I held a great assembly against them. ⁸And I said to them, "We according to our ability have redeemed our Jewish brothers who were sold to the nations; now would you even sell your brothers that they may be sold to us?" Then they were silent and could not find a word to say. ⁹Again I said, "The thing which you are doing is not good; should you not walk in the fear of our God because of the reproach of the nations, our enemies? ¹⁰And likewise I, **my brothers and my servants, are lending them money and grain. Please, let us leave off this usury."**

3.D. Usury

Nehemiah 5:11–13

[11]"**Please, give back to them this very day their fields,** their vineyards, their olive groves, and their houses, also the hundredth part of the money and of the grain, the new wine, and the oil that you are exacting from them." [12]Then they said, "We will give it back and will require nothing from them; we will do exactly as you say." So I called the priests and took an oath from them that they would do according to this promise. [13]I also shook out the front of my garment and said, "Thus may God shake out every man from his house and from his possessions who does not fulfill this promise; even thus may he be shaken out and emptied." And all the assembly said, "Amen!" And they praised the LORD. Then the people did according to this promise.

1.F. Obedience

Nehemiah 5:14–16

[14]Moreover, from the day that I was appointed to be their governor in the land of Judah, from the twentieth year to the thirty-second year of King Artaxerxes, for twelve years, **neither I nor my kinsmen have eaten the governor's food allowance.** [15]But the former governors who were before me laid burdens on the people and took from them bread and wine besides forty shekels of silver; even their servants domineered the people. But I did not do so because of the fear of God. [16]And I also applied myself to the work on this wall; we did not buy any land, and all my servants were gathered there for the work.

12.A. Work

Nehemiah 5:18

. . . for all this **I did not demand the governor's food allowance,** because the servitude was heavy on this people.

12.B. Wages

Nehemiah 7:70–72

[70]And some from among the heads of fathers' households gave to the work. The governor gave to the treasury 1,000 gold drachmas, 50 basins, 530 priests' garments. [71]And some of the heads of fathers' households gave into the treasury of the work 20,000 gold drachmas, and 2,200 silver minas. [72]And that which the rest of the people gave was 20,000 gold drachmas and 2,000 silver minas, and 67 priests' garments.

4.F. Gifts*

Nehemiah 9:21

"Indeed, forty years **Thou didst provide for them in the wilderness** and they were not in want; Their clothes did not wear out, nor did their feet swell."

6.D. Provision

Nehemiah 10:31–32

[31]As for the peoples of the land who bring wares or any grain on the sabbath day to sell, **we will not buy from them on the sabbath or a holy day;** and we will forego the crops the seventh year and the exaction of every debt. [32]We also placed ourselves under obligation to contribute yearly one third of a shekel for the service of the house of our God.

9.E. Buying

---

*Nehemiah never used his position to benefit himself.

Nehemiah 10:34–35

³⁴Likewise **we cast lots for the supply of wood among the priests,** the Levites, and the people in order that they might bring it to the house of our God, according to our fathers' households, at fixed times annually, to burn on the altar of the LORD our God as it is written in the law; ³⁵and in order that they might bring the first fruits of our ground and the first fruits of all the fruit of every tree to the house of the LORD annually.

4.D. Offerings
4.E. First Fruits

Nehemiah 10:37–39

³⁷**We will also bring the first of our dough, our contributions, the fruit of every tree,** the new wine and the oil to the priests at the chambers of the house of our God, and the tithe of our ground to the Levites, for the Levites are they who receive the tithes in all the rural towns. ³⁸And the priest, the son of Aaron, shall be with the Levites when the Levites receive tithes, and the Levites shall bring up the tenth of the tithes to the house of our God, to the chambers of the storehouse. ³⁹For the sons of Israel and **the sons of Levi shall bring the contribution of the grain,** the new wine and the oil, to the chambers; there are the utensils of the sanctuary, the priests who are ministering, the gatekeepers, and the singers. Thus we will not neglect the house of our God.

4.C. Tithe
4.E. First Fruits

Nehemiah 12:44

On that day men were also appointed over the chambers for the stores, **the contributions, the first fruits, and the tithes,** to gather into them from the fields of the cities the portions required by the law for the priests and Levites; for Judah rejoiced over the priests and Levites who served.

4.A. Storehouse
4.C. Tithe
4.E. First Fruits

Nehemiah 12:47

And so all Israel in the days of Zerubbabel and Nehemiah gave the portions due the singers and the gatekeepers as each day required, and **set apart the consecrated portion for the Levites,** and the Levites set apart the consecrated portion for the sons of Aaron.

12.B. Wages

Nehemiah 13:5

. . . had prepared a large room for him, where formerly they put the grain offerings, the frankincense, the utensils, and the tithes of grain, wine and oil prescribed for the Levites, the singers and the gatekeepers, and **the contributions for the priests.**

4.A. Storehouse
4.C. Tithe

Nehemiah 13:12

All Judah then brought **the tithe of the grain,** wine, and oil into the storehouses.

4.C. Tithe

Nehemiah 13:13

And **in charge of the storehouses I appointed Shelemiah** the priest, Zadok the scribe, and Pedaiah of the Levites, and in addition to them was Hanan the son of Zaccur, the son of Mattaniah; for they were considered reliable, and it was their task to distribute to their kinsmen.

4.A. Storehouse
4.C. Tithe

Esther

Scripture:	Subtopic:

Esther 1:4
And **he displayed the riches of his royal glory** and the splendor of his
great majesty for many days, 180 days.

2.K. Ego

Esther 1:6–7
⁶There were hangings of fine white and violet linen held by cords of
fine purple linen on silver rings and marble columns, and couches
of gold and silver on a mosaic pavement of porphyry, marble,
mother-of-pearl, and precious stones. ⁷**Drinks were served in
golden vessels** of various kinds, and the royal wine was plentiful
according to the king's bounty.

6.G. Wealth

Esther 3:9
"If it is pleasing to the king, let it be decreed that they be destroyed,
and **I will pay ten thousand talents of silver** into the hands of those
who carry on the king's business, to put into the king's treasuries."

2.B. Bribe

Esther 3:11
And the king said to Haman, "The silver is yours, and the people
also, to do with them as you please."

2.J. Injustice

Esther 3:13
. . . and **to seize their possessions as plunder.**

2.J. Injustice

Esther 4:7
And Mordecai told him all that had happened to him, and **the exact
amount of money that Haman had promised to pay** to the king's
treasuries for the destruction of the Jews.

2.J. Injustice

Esther 5:11
Then Haman recounted to them the glory of his riches, and the
number of his sons, and every instance where the king had magni-
fied him, and how he had promoted him above the princes and
servants of the king.

2.B. Bribe

Esther 5:13
"Yet all of this does not satisfy me every time I see Mordecai the Jew
sitting at the king's gate."

2.C. Pride

Esther 8:15
**Then Mordecai went out from the presence of the king in royal
robes** of blue and white, with a large crown of gold and a garment
of fine linen and purple; and the city of Susa shouted and rejoiced.

6.F. Justice

Esther 9:16
. . . and rid themselves of their enemies, and kill 75,000 of those
who hated them; but they did not lay their hands on the plunder.

6.F. Justice

Esther 9:22
. . . they should make them days of feasting and rejoicing and sending portions of food to one another and gifts to the poor.

4.H. Helping Needy

Esther 10:1
Now **King Ahasuerus laid a tribute on the land** and on the coast-lands of the sea.

8.B. Administrative Tax

Job

Scripture:	Subtopic:

Job 1:3
His possessions also were 7,000 sheep, 3,000 camels, 500 yoke of oxen, 500 female donkeys, and very many servants; and that man was the greatest of all the men of the east.

6.G. Wealth

Job 1:21
And he said, "**Naked I came from my mother's womb, and naked I shall return there.** The LORD gave and the LORD has taken away. Blessed be the name of the LORD."

1.G. Contentment
6.D. Provision

Job 2:3
And the LORD said to Satan, "**Have you considered My servant Job?** For there is no one like him on the earth, a blameless and upright man fearing God and turning away from evil. And he still holds fast his integrity, although you incited Me against him, to ruin him without cause."

1.B. Honesty

Job 2:10
But he said to her, "You speak as one of the foolish women speaks. **Shall we indeed accept good from God and not accept adversity?**" In all this Job did not sin with his lips.

1.G. Contentment
6.D. Provision

Job 3:15
"Or with princes who had gold, who were filling their houses with silver."

2.C. Pride

Job 5:5
". . . and **the schemer is eager for their wealth.**"

2.E. Greed
2.F. Dishonesty

Job 5:12–13
[12]"He frustrates the plotting of the shrewd, so that their hands cannot attain success. [13]**He captures the wise by their own shrewdness** And the advice of the cunning is quickly thwarted."

7.A. To Wicked

Job 5:15
"But He saves from the sword of their mouth, and the poor from the hand of the mighty."

6.F. Justice

Job 5:17–20
[17]"Behold, how happy is the man whom God reproves, so do not despise the discipline of the Almighty. [18]For He inflicts pain, and gives relief; he wounds, and His hands also heal. [19]From six troubles He will deliver you, even in seven evil will not touch you. [20]**In famine He will redeem you from death,** and in war from the power of the sword."

6.A. God's Promises

Scripture:	Subtopic:

Job 5:24
"And you will know that your tent is secure, for **you will visit your abode and fear no loss.**"

1.H. Trust

Job 6:4
"For the arrows of the Almighty are within me; their poison my spirit drinks; The terrors of God are arrayed against me."

7.A. To Wicked

Job 6:22
"Have I said, 'Give me something,' or, '**Offer a bribe for me from your wealth.**'"

2.B. Bribe

Job 6:27
"**You would even cast lots for the orphans, and barter over your friend.**"

2.J. Injustice

Job 7:1
"**Is not man forced to labor on earth,** and are not his days like the days of a hired man?"

12.A. Work

Job 7:2
"As a slave who pants for the shade, and **as a hired man who eagerly waits for his wages, . . .**"

12.B. Wages

Job 12:6
"**The tents of the destroyers prosper,** and those who provoke God are secure, whom God brings into their power."

2.J. Injustice

Job 15:29
"**He will not become rich, nor will his wealth endure;** and his grain will not bend down to the ground."

6.F. Justice

Job 15:31
"**Let him not trust in emptiness,** deceiving himself; for emptiness will be his reward."

2.L. Futility of Riches

Job 20:10
"**His sons favor the poor,** and his hands give back his wealth."

4.H. Helping Needy

Job 20:15
"**He swallows riches, but will vomit them up;** God will expel them from his belly."

6.F. Justice

Job 20:18–22
[18]"He returns what he has attained and cannot swallow it; **as to the riches of his trading, he cannot even enjoy them.** [19]For he has oppressed and forsaken the poor; he has seized a house which he has not built. [20]Because he knew no quiet within him he does not retain anything he desires. [21]Nothing remains for him to devour, therefore his prosperity does not endure. [22]In the fulness of his plenty he will be cramped; the hand of everyone who suffers will come against him."

2.F. Dishonesty
2.J. Injustice

Job 20:26
"Complete darkness is held in reserve for his treasures, and unfanned fire will devour him; it will consume the survivor in his tent."

6.F. Justice

Job 20:28–29
²⁸**"The increase of his house will depart;** his possessions will flow away in the day of His anger. ²⁹This is the wicked man's portion from God, even the heritage decreed to him by God."

6.F. Justice

Job 21:13
"They spend their days in prosperity, and suddenly they go down to Sheol."

6.F. Justice

Job 21:15–16
¹⁵**"'Who is the Almighty, that we should serve Him, and what would we gain if we entreat Him?'** ¹⁶Behold, **their prosperity is not in their hand;** the counsel of the wicked is far from me."

2.I. Disobedient

Job 22:6
⁶**"For you have taken pledges of your brothers without cause, and stripped men naked."**

3.E. Surety

Job 22:24–25
²⁴**"And place your gold in the dust, and the gold of Ophir among the stones of the brooks, ²⁵Then the Almighty will be your gold and choice silver to you."**

6.A. God's Promises

Job 23:10
". . . When He has tried me, **I shall come forth as gold."**

6.A. God's Promises

Job 23:12
". . . **I have treasured the words of His mouth more than my necessary food."**

1.H. Trust

Job 24:3–4
"They drive away the donkeys of the orphans; they take the widow's ox for a pledge. ⁴**They push the needy aside** from the road; the poor of the land are made to hide themselves altogether."

2.J. Injustice

Job 24:9–10
⁹**"Others snatch the orphan from the breast,** and against the poor they take a pledge. ¹⁰They cause the poor to go about naked without clothing, and they take away the sheaves from the hungry."

2.J. Injustice

Job 24:14
"The murderer arises at dawn; **he kills the poor and the needy,** and at night he is as a thief."

2.J. Injustice

Job 27:13–17

¹³"**This is the portion of a wicked man** from God, and the inheritance which tyrants receive from the Almighty.   ¹⁴Though his sons are many, they are destined for the sword; and his descendants will not be satisfied with bread.   ¹⁵His survivors will be buried because of the plague, and their widows will not be able to weep.   ¹⁶**Though he piles up silver like dust, and prepares garments as plentiful as the clay;   ¹⁷he may prepare it, but the just will wear it, and the innocent will divide the silver.**"

7.A. To Wicked

Job 27:19–20

¹⁹"**He lies down rich, but never again;** he opens his eyes, and it is no more.   ²⁰Terrors overtake him like a flood; a tempest steals him away in the night."

7.A. To Wicked

Job 28:1

"**Surely there is a mine for silver,** and a place where they refine gold."

6.G. Wealth

Job 28:6

"**Its rocks are the source of sapphires,** and its dust contains gold."

6.G. Wealth

Job 28:15–19

¹⁵"**Pure gold cannot be given in exchange for it,** nor can silver be weighed as its price.   ¹⁶It cannot be valued in the gold of Ophir, in precious onyx, or sapphire.   ¹⁷Gold or glass cannot equal it, nor can it be exchanged for articles of fine gold.   ¹⁸Coral and crystal are not to be mentioned; and the acquisition of wisdom is above that of pearls.   ¹⁹The topaz of Ethiopia cannot equal it, nor can it be valued in pure gold."

2.L. Futility of Riches

Job 29:12

"Because **I delivered the poor who cried for help, and the orphan who had no helper.**"

4.H. Helping Needy

Job 29:16

"**I was a father to the needy,** and I investigated the case which I did not know."

4.H. Helping Needy

Job 30:15

"Terrors are turned against me, they pursue my honor as the wind, and **my prosperity has passed away like a cloud.**"

2.L. Futility of Riches

Job 30:25

"Have I not wept for the one whose life is hard? **Was not my soul grieved for the needy?**"

4.H. Helping Needy

Job 31:12

"For it would be fire that consumes to Abaddon, and would uproot all my increase."

6.F. Justice

Scripture:	Subtopic:

Job 31:16–19
[16]"**If I have kept the poor from their desire,** or have caused the eyes of the widow to fail, [17]Or have eaten my morsel alone, and the orphan has not shared it [18](but from my youth he grew up with me as with a father, and from infancy I guided her), [19]if I have seen anyone perish for lack of clothing, or that the needy had no covering."

4.H. Helping Needy

Job 31:24–25
[24]"**If I have put my confidence in gold,** and called fine gold my trust, [25]if I have gloated because my wealth was great, and because my hand had secured so much."

2.C. Pride

Job 31:28
". . . For I would have denied God above."

2.C. Pride

Job 34:19
"**Who shows no partiality to princes,** nor regards the rich above the poor, for they all are the work of His hands?"

6.A. God's Promises

Job 36:11
"If they hear and serve Him, **they shall end their days in prosperity,** and their years in pleasures."

6.C. Blessings

Job 36:19
"**Will your riches keep you from distress,** or all the forces of your strength?"

2.C. Pride

Job 41:11
"**Who has given to Me that I should repay him?** Whatever is under the whole heaven is Mine."

4.I. Giving to Get*

Job 42:10
And the LORD restored the fortunes of Job when he prayed for his friends, and the LORD increased all that Job had twofold.

6.A. God's Promises

Job 42:11
. . . **And each one gave him one piece of money,** and each a ring of gold.

6.D. Provision
6.F. Justice

---

*Paul quotes this verse in Romans 11:35 in regard to those disobedient to God. This message is contrary to the "prosperity" message.

Psalms

Scripture:	Subtopic:

Psalms 1:1–2
[1]How blessed is the man who does not walk in the counsel of the wicked, nor stand in the path of sinners, nor sit in the seat of the scoffers! [2]But his delight is in the law of the LORD, and in His law he meditates day and night.

1.J. Counsel of Men*

Psalms 8:6
Thou dost make him to rule over the works of Thy hands; thou hast put all things under his feet.

6.D. Provision

Psalms 9:18
For the needy will not always be forgotten, nor the hope of the afflicted perish forever.

4.H. Helping Needy

Psalms 10:2
In pride the wicked hotly pursue the afflicted; let them be caught in the plots which they have devised.

2.J. Injustice

Psalms 10:3
For the wicked boasts of his heart's desire, and the greedy man curses and spurns the LORD.

2.E. Greed

Psalms 10:5
His ways prosper at all times; thy judgments are on high, out of his sight; as for all his adversaries, he snorts at them.

2.C. Pride

Psalms 12:5
"Because of the devastation of the afflicted, because of the groaning of the needy, now I will arise," says the LORD; "I will set him in the safety for which he longs."

4.H. Helping Needy

Psalms 14:1
The fool has said in his heart, "There is no God." They are corrupt, they have committed abominable deeds; there is no one who does good.

2.J. Injustice

Psalms 15:1–2
[1]O LORD, who may abide in Thy tent? Who may dwell on Thy holy hill? [2]He who walks with integrity, and works righteousness, and speaks truth in his heart.

6.A. God's Promises

---

*A counselor is one who "urges you to adopt his standards"; a non-Christian can only give intellectual advice, not godly wisdom.

Scripture:	Subtopic:

Psalms 15:5
He does not put out his money at interest, nor does he take a bribe against the innocent. He who does these things will never be shaken.

2.B. Bribe
3.C. Interest

Psalms 17:13–15
¹³Arise, O LORD, confront him, bring him low; deliver my soul from the wicked with Thy sword, ¹⁴**From men with Thy hand, O LORD, from men of the world, whose portion is in this life;** and whose belly Thou dost fill with Thy treasure; they are satisfied with children, and leave their abundance to their babes. ¹⁵As for me, I shall behold Thy face in righteousness; I will be satisfied with Thy likeness when I awake.

2.L. Futility of Riches
5.A. Inheritance

Psalms 19:9–10
⁹The fear of the LORD is clean, enduring forever; the judgments of the LORD are true; they are righteous altogether. ¹⁰They are more desirable than gold, yes, than much fine gold.

1.I. Fairness

Psalms 22:25
From Thee comes my praise in the great assembly; **I shall pay my vows before those who fear Him.**

1.K. Paying Vows*

Psalms 22:29
All the prosperous of the earth will eat and worship, all those who go down to the dust will bow before Him, even he who cannot keep his soul alive.

2.L. Futility of Riches

Psalms 24:1
The earth is the LORD's, and all it contains, the world, and those who dwell in it.

6.D. Provision†

Psalms 25:12–13
¹²Who is the man who fears the LORD? He will instruct him in the way he should choose. ¹³**His soul will abide in prosperity,** and his descendants will inherit the land.

6.D. Provision

Psalms 26:10
In whose hands is a wicked scheme, and whose right hand is full of bribes.

2.B. Bribe

Psalms 30:6
Now as for me, **I said in my prosperity, "I will never be moved."**

2.C. Pride

Psalms 32:8–9
⁸I will instruct you and teach you in the way which you should go; **I will counsel you with My eye upon you.** ⁹Do not be as the horse or as the mule which have no understanding, . . .

6.B. Counsel of God

---

*Also see Ecclesiastes 5:4–5. A vow is a "promise to perform."
†If God owns everything then we are stewards (managers).

Scripture:	Subtopic:

Psalms 32:10
Many are the sorrows of the wicked; but he who trusts in the LORD, lovingkindness shall surround him.

1.H. Trust
2.E. Greed

Psalms 33:6
By the word of the LORD the heavens were made, and by the breath of His mouth all their host.

6.G. Wealth

Psalms 33:18–19
[18]Behold, **the eye of the LORD is on those who fear Him,** on those who hope for His lovingkindness, [19]To deliver their soul from death, and **to keep them alive in famine.**

6.D. Provision

Psalms 34:6
This poor man cried and the LORD heard him, and saved him out of all his troubles.

4.H. Helping Needy

Psalms 34:9
O fear the LORD, you His saints; **for to those who fear Him, there is no want.**

6.D. Provision

Psalms 34:19
Many are the afflictions of the righteous; but the LORD delivers him out of them all.

6.A. God's Promises*

Psalmss 35:1
Contend, O LORD, with those who contend with me; fight against those who fight against me.

6.D. Provision

Psalms 37:1
Do not fret because of evildoers, **be not envious toward wrong-doers.**

2.G. Envy

Psalms 37:4
Delight yourself in the LORD; and He will give you the desires of your heart.

6.D. Provision

Psalms 37:7–9
[7]**Rest in the LORD** and wait patiently for Him; **do not fret because of him who prospers in his way,** because of the man who carries out wicked schemes. [8]Cease from anger, and forsake wrath; do not fret, it leads only to evildoing. [9]For evildoers will be cut off, but those who wait for the LORD, they will inherit the land.

1.H. Trust
6.D. Provision

Psalms 37:11
But **the humble will inherit the land,** and will delight themselves in abundant prosperity.

1.C. Humility

---

*God doesn't promise that we will avoid all problems (see James 1:1–3). He promises to see us through them if we trust Him (see Psalms 50:14–15). .

Scripture:	Subtopic:

Psalms 37:16
Better is the little of the righteous than the abundance of many wicked.

1.G. Contentment

Psalms 37:18–19
[18]**The LORD knows the days of the blameless; and their inheritance will be forever.** [19]They will not be ashamed in the time of evil; and in the days of famine they will have abundance.

6.D. Provision*

Psalms 37:21
The wicked borrows and does not pay back, but the righteous is gracious and gives.

3.A. Borrowing

Psalms 37:25
I have been young, and now I am old; yet **I have not seen the righteous forsaken,** or his descendants begging bread.

6.D. Provision†

Psalms 37:26
All day long he is gracious and lends; and his descendants are a blessing.

3.B. Lending

Psalms 37:28–29
[28]For the LORD loves justice, and does not forsake His godly ones; They are preserved forever; but the descendants of the wicked will be cut off. [29]**The righteous will inherit the land, and dwell in it forever.**

6.A. God's Promises

Psalms 37:34
Wait for the LORD, and keep His way, and He will exalt you to inherit the land; when the wicked are cut off, you will see it.

6.D. Provision

Psalms 37:37–38
[37]Mark the blameless man, and behold the upright; for the man of peace will have a posterity. [38]But transgressors will be altogether destroyed; **the posterity of the wicked will be cut off.**

7.A. To Wicked

Psalms 39:6
"Surely every man walks about as a phantom; surely they make an uproar for nothing; **he amasses riches, and does not know who will gather them.**"

2.L. Futility of Riches†

Psalms 40:17
Since I am afflicted and needy, let the LORD be mindful of me; Thou art my help and my deliverer; do not delay, O my God.

4.H. Helping Needy

---

*The inheritance addressed here is spiritual, not material.
†The "righteous" referenced here refers to a group, not an individual. Obviously many individuals have suffered for their faith. But, as a group, God's people prosper.
†See Solomon's commentary in Ecclesiastes 2:21–22 on legacy.

Scripture:	Subtopic:

Psalms 41:1
How blessed is he who considers the helpless; the LORD will deliver him in a day of trouble.

4.H. Helping Needy

Psalms 44:12
Thou dost sell Thy people cheaply, and hast not profited by their sale.

9.D. Selling

Psalms 49:6–7
⁶Even those who trust in their wealth, and boast in the abundance of their riches? ⁷No man can by any means redeem his brother, or give to God a ransom for him.

2.L. Futility of Riches

Psalms 49:10–12
¹⁰For he sees that **even wise men die;** the stupid and the senseless alike perish, **and leave their wealth to others.** ¹¹Their inner thought is, that their houses are forever, and their dwelling places to all generations; they have called their lands after their own names. ¹²**But man in his pomp will not endure;** he is like the beasts that perish.

2.L. Futility of Riches

Psalms 49:16–17
¹⁶**Do not be afraid when a man becomes rich,** when the glory of his house is increased; ¹⁷For when he dies he will carry nothing away; his glory will not descend after him.

2.L. Futility of Riches*

Psalms 50:12
"If I were hungry, I would not tell you; for the world is Mine, and all it contains."

6.D. Provision

Psalms 50:14–15
¹⁴**"Offer to God a sacrifice of thanksgiving,** and **pay your vows to the Most High;** ¹⁵and call upon Me in the day of trouble; I shall rescue you, and you will honor Me."

1.K. Paying Vows
6.A. God's Promises

Psalms 52:7
"Behold, the man who would not make God his refuge, **but trusted in the abundance of his riches,** and was strong in his evil desire."

2.L. Futility of Riches

Psalms 62:10
Do not trust in oppression, and do not vainly hope in robbery; if **riches increase, do not set your heart upon them.**

2.L. Futility of Riches

Psalms 62:11–12
¹¹Once God has spoken; twice I have heard this: that power belongs to God; ¹²and lovingkindness is Thine, O LORD, for **Thou dost recompense a man according to his work.**

6.D. Provision

---

*Sometimes the wicked prosper in this life. But their wealth stops at death while the believer's lasts for eternity. (See Psalm 73:17–18.)

Psalms 66:18
If I regard wickedness in my heart, the LORD **will not hear.**

2.I. Disobedient

Psalms 68:6
God makes a home for the lonely; He leads out the prisoners into prosperity, only the rebellious dwell in a parched land.

4.H. Helping Needy

Psalms 68:10
Thy creatures settled in it; **Thou didst provide in Thy goodness for the poor, O God.**

4.H. Helping Needy

Psalms 69:33
For the LORD **hears the needy,** and does not despise His who are prisoners.

4.H. Helping Needy

Psalms 72:4
May he vindicate the afflicted of the people, **save the children of the needy, and crush the oppressor.**

4.H. Helping Needy

Psalms 72:12–14
¹²For **he will deliver the needy when he cries for help,** the afflicted also, and him who has no helper. ¹³He will have compassion on the poor and needy, and the lives of the needy he will save. ¹⁴He will rescue their life from oppression and violence; and their blood will be precious in his sight.

4.H. Helping Needy

Psalms 73:2–3
²But as for me, my feet came close to stumbling; my steps had almost slipped. ³For I was **envious of the arrogant,** as I saw the prosperity of the wicked.

2.G. Envy*

Psalms 73:12
Behold, **these are the wicked;** and always at ease, they have increased in wealth.

2.L. Futility of Riches

Psalms 73:17–18
¹⁷Until I came into the sanctuary of God; then I perceived their end. ¹⁸**Surely Thou dost set them in slippery places;** Thou dost cast them down to destruction.

6.F. Justice

Psalms 75:4
"I said to the boastful, '**Do not boast,**' and to the wicked, 'Do not lift up the horn.'"

2.C. Pride

Psalms 82:2–4
²**How long will you judge unjustly, and show partiality to the wicked?** ³Vindicate the weak and fatherless; do justice to the afflicted and destitute. ⁴Rescue the weak and needy; deliver them out of the hand of the wicked.

2.H. Partiality
2.J. Injustice

---

*It's easy to get caught up in envy of the wicked. Read all of Psalm 73 to get a better perspective.

Scripture:	Subtopic:

Psalms 101:6
My eyes shall be upon the faithful of the land, that they may dwell with me; he who walks in a blameless way is the one who will minister to me.

1.F. Obedience

Psalms 101:7
He who practices deceit shall not dwell within my house; he who speaks falsehood shall not maintain his position before me.

2.F. Dishonesty

Psalms 105:37
Then **He brought them out with silver and gold;** and among His tribes there was not one who stumbled.

6.A. God's Promises

Psalms 106:5
That I may see the prosperity of Thy chosen ones, that I may rejoice in the gladness of Thy nation, that I may glory with Thine inheritance.

6.D. Provision

Psalms 107:40–41
[40]He pours contempt upon princes, and makes them wander in a pathless waste. [41]But **He sets the needy securely on high** away from affliction, and makes his families like a flock.

4.H. Helping Needy

Psalms 109:11
Let the creditor seize all that he has; and let strangers plunder the product of his labor.

3.E. Surety

Psalms 109:16
Because he did not remember to show lovingkindness, but **persecuted the afflicted and needy man,** and the despondent in heart, to put them to death.

2.J. Injustice

Psalms 109:31
For He stands at the right hand of the needy, to save him from those who judge his soul.

4.H. Helping Needy

Psalms 112:1
Praise the LORD! **How blessed is the man who fears the LORD,** who greatly delights in His commandments.

1.H. Trust

Psalms 112:3
Wealth and riches are in his house, and his righteousness endures forever.

6.D. Provision

Psalms 112:5
It is well with the man who is gracious and lends; he will maintain his cause in judgment.

3.B. Lending

Psalms 112:9
He has given freely to the poor; His righteousness endures forever; His horn will be exalted in honor.

4.H. Helping Needy

Scripture:	Subtopic:

Psalms 113:7–8
⁷He raises the poor from the dust, and lifts the needy from the ash heap, ⁸to make them sit with princes, with the princes of His people.

4.H. Helping Needy
6.A. God's Promises

Psalms 115:14
May the LORD give you increase, you and your children.

6.A. God's Promises

Psalms 118:25
O LORD, do save, we beseech Thee; O LORD, we beseech Thee, do send prosperity!

6.D. Provision

Psalms 119:14
I have rejoiced in the way of Thy testimonies, as much as in all riches.

1.E. Thankfulness

Psalms 119:36
Incline my heart to Thy testimonies, and not to dishonest gain.

2.F. Dishonesty

Psalms 119:57
The LORD is my portion; I have promised to keep Thy words.

1.G. Contentment

Psalms 119:72
The law of Thy mouth is better to me than thousands of gold and silver pieces.

1.E. Thankfulness

Psalms 119:113
I hate those who are double-minded, but I love Thy law.

2.F. Dishonesty*

Psalms 119:127
Therefore, I love Thy commandments above gold, yes, above fine gold.

1.E. Thankfulness

Psalms 119:162
I rejoice at Thy word, as one who finds great spoil.

1.E. Thankfulness

Psalms 120:2
Deliver my soul, O LORD, from lying lips, from a deceitful tongue.

2.F. Dishonesty

Psalms 122:7
"May peace be within your walls, and prosperity within your palaces."

6.A. God's Promises

Psalms 124:1–3
¹"Had it not been the LORD who was on our side," Let Israel now say, ²"Had it not been the LORD who was on our side, when men rose up against us; ³then they would have swallowed us alive, when their anger was kindled against us."

6.D. Provision

---

*James 1:8 says that a double-minded man in unstable. In Matthew 6:24 the Lord says that the conflict is between God and money.

Scripture:	Subtopic:

Psalms 127:2
It is vain for you to rise up early, to retire late, to eat the bread of painful labors; for He gives to His beloved even in his sleep.
2.K. Ego

Psalms 127:3
Behold, **children are a gift of the LORD;** the fruit of the womb is a reward.
6.C. Blessings

Psalms 128:5
The LORD bless you from Zion, and **may you see the prosperity of Jerusalem** all the days of your life.
6.A. God's Promises

Psalms 131:1–2
¹O LORD, **my heart is not proud,** nor my eyes haughty; nor do I involve myself in great matters, or in things too difficult for me. ²Surely I have composed and quieted my soul; like a weaned child rests against his mother, my soul is like a weaned child within me.
1.C. Humility

Psalms 132:15
"I will abundantly bless her provision; **I will satisfy her needy with bread."**
6.D. Provision

Psalms 138:6
For though the LORD is exalted, yet **He regards the lowly;** but the haughty He knows from afar.
4.H. Helping Needy

Psalms 140:12
I know that **the LORD will maintain the cause of the afflicted,** and justice for the poor.
1.I. Fairness
4.H. Helping Needy

Psalms 146:9
The LORD protects the strangers; **he supports the fatherless and the widow;** but He thwarts the way of the wicked.
1.I. Fairness
7.A. To Wicked

Proverbs

Scripture:	Subtopic:

Proverbs 1:5
A wise man will hear and increase in learning, and **a man of understanding will acquire wise counsel.**

1.J. Counsel of Men

Proverbs 1:7
The fear of the LORD **is the beginning of knowledge;** fools despise wisdom and instruction.

1.L. Wisdom

Proverbs 1:8
Hear, my son, your father's instruction, and do not forsake your mother's teaching.

5.B. Counsel and Discipline

Proverbs 1:10
My son, **if sinners entice you, do not consent.**

1.F. Obedience

Proverbs 1:13–14
[13]**"We shall find all kinds of precious wealth,** we shall fill our houses with spoil; [14]throw in your lot with us, we shall all have one purse."

2.J. Injustice

Proverbs 1:19
So are the ways of everyone who gains by violence; it takes away the life of its possessors.

2.J. Injustice

Proverbs 1:29–33
[29]"Because they hated knowledge, and did not choose the fear of the LORD. [30]They would not accept my counsel, they spurned all my reproof. [31]So they shall eat of the fruit of their own way, and be satiated with their own devices. [32]**For the waywardness of the naive shall kill them,** and the complacency of fools shall destroy them. [33]But he who listens to me shall live securely, and shall be at ease from the dread of evil."

6.B. Counsel of God

Proverbs 2:6
For the LORD **gives wisdom;** from His mouth come knowledge and understanding.

6.A. God's Promises*

Proverbs 2:9
Then you will discern righteousness and justice and equity and every good course.

1.I. Fairness

Proverbs 2:12
To **deliver you from the way of evil,** from the man who speaks perverse things.

2.F. Dishonesty

---

*Clearly the only true source of wisdom comes from God, including how to handle finances.

Scripture:	Subtopic:

Proverbs 2:15
Whose paths are crooked, and who are devious in their ways.

2.F. Dishonesty

Proverbs 3:2–4
²For length of days and years of life, and peace they will add to you.   ³**Do not let kindness and truth leave you;** bind them around your neck, write them on the tablet of your heart.   ⁴So you will find favor and good repute in the sight of God and man.

1.B. Honesty
6.A. God's Promises

Proverbs 3:5–6
⁵**Trust in the LORD with all your heart,** and do not lean on your own understanding.   ⁶In all your ways acknowledge Him, and He will make your paths straight.

1.H. Trust

Proverbs 3:9–10
⁹**Honor the LORD from your wealth,** and from the first of all your produce;   ¹⁰So your barns will be filled with plenty, and your vats will overflow with new wine.

4.E. First Fruits*

Proverbs 3:13–19
¹³**How blessed is the man who finds wisdom,** and the man who gains understanding.   ¹⁴**For its profit is better than the profit of silver,** and its gain than fine gold.   ¹⁵She is more precious than jewels; and nothing you desire compares with her.   ¹⁶Long life is in her right hand; in her left hand are riches and honor.   ¹⁷Her ways are pleasant ways, and all her paths are peace.   ¹⁸She is a tree of life to those who take hold of her, and happy are all who hold her fast.   ¹⁹The LORD by wisdom founded the earth; by understanding He established the heavens.

1.L. Wisdom

Proverbs 3:27–28
²⁷**Do not withhold good from those to whom it is due,** when it is in your power to do it.   ²⁸Do not say to your neighbor, "Go, and come back, and tomorrow I will give it," when you have it with you.

3.F. Paying Debts†

Proverbs 3:32
For the crooked man is an abomination to the LORD; but He is intimate with the upright.

2.F. Dishonesty

Proverbs 4:14
Do not enter the path of the wicked, and do not proceed in the way of evil men.

7.A. To Wicked

Proverbs 4:24
Put away from you a deceitful mouth, and put devious lips far from you.

2.F. Dishonesty

---

*God desires a voluntary contribution of our labor as a testimony to His ownership.
†God requires that all debts (including financial) must be paid.

Proverbs 5:10
Lest strangers be filled with your strength, and **your hard earned goods go to the house of an alien.**

6.B. Counsel of God

Proverbs 6:1–5
[1]**My son, if you have become surety for your neighbor,** have given a pledge for a stranger, [2]if you have been snared with the words of your mouth, have been caught with the words of your mouth, [3]**do this then, my son, and deliver yourself;** since you have come into the hand of your neighbor, go, humble yourself, and importune your neighbor. [4]Do not give sleep to your eyes, nor slumber to your eyelids; [5]deliver yourself like a gazelle from the hunter's hand, and like a bird from the hand of the fowler.

3.E. Surety*

Proverbs 6:6–8
[6]**Go to the ant, O sluggard, observe her ways and be wise,** [7]which, having no chief, officer or ruler, [8]prepares her food in the summer, and gathers her provision in the harvest.

9.B. Savings[†]

Proverbs 6:9–11
[9]**How long will you lie down, O sluggard?** When will you arise from your sleep? [10]"A little sleep, a little slumber, a little folding of the hands to rest"— [11]and your poverty will come in like a vagabond, and your need like an armed man.

12.E. Slothful

Proverbs 6:12–13
[12]**A worthless person,** a wicked man, **is the one who walks with a false mouth,** [13]who winks with his eyes, who signals with his feet, who points with his fingers.

2.F. Dishonesty

Proverbs 6:16–19
[16]**There are six things which the LORD hates,** yes, seven which are an abomination to Him: [17]haughty eyes, a lying tongue, and hands that shed innocent blood, [18]a heart that devises wicked plans, feet that run rapidly to evil, [19]a false witness who utters lies, and one who spreads strife among brothers.

2.F. Dishonesty

Proverbs 6:20
My son, observe the commandment of your father, and do not forsake the teaching of your mother.

5.B. Counsel and Discipline

Proverbs 7:20
"He has taken a bag of money with him, at full moon he will come home."

2.L. Futility of Riches

---

*Surety means taking on an uncertain obligation. Any personal endorsement of a debt creates surety.
[†]A principle of saving during productive periods (or years) for lean periods.

Scripture:	Subtopic:

Proverbs 8:10–12

[10]"Take my instruction, and not silver, and knowledge rather than choicest gold. [11]For wisdom is better than jewels; and all desirable things can not compare with her. [12]I, wisdom, dwell with prudence, and I find knowledge and discretion."

6.A. God's Promises
6.B. Counsel of God

Proverbs 8:18–21

[18]"Riches and honor are with me, enduring wealth and righteousness. [19]My fruit is better than gold, even pure gold, and my yield than choicest silver. [20]I walk in the way of righteousness, in the midst of the paths of justice, [21]to endow those who love me with wealth, that I may fill their treasuries."

6.D. Provision

Proverbs 8:35

"For he who finds me finds life, and obtains favor from the LORD."

6.A. God's Promises

Proverbs 9:9

Give instruction to a wise man, and he will be still wiser, teach a righteous man, and he will increase his learning.

1.J. Counsel of Men

Proverbs 10:1

The proverbs of Solomon. A wise son makes a father glad, but a foolish son is a grief to his mother.

5.B. Counsel and Discipline

Proverbs 10:2

Ill-gotten gains do not profit, but righteousness delivers from death.

2.F. Dishonesty

Proverbs 10:3

The LORD will not allow the righteous to hunger, but He will thrust aside the craving of the wicked.

7.A. To Wicked

Proverbs 10:4

Poor is he who works with a negligent hand, but the hand of the diligent makes rich.

12.E. Slothful

Proverbs 10:5

He who gathers in summer is a son who acts wisely, but he who sleeps in harvest is a son who acts shamefully.

12.F. Diligent

Proverbs 10:9

He who walks in integrity walks securely, but he who perverts his ways will be found out.

1.B. Honesty

Proverbs 10:10

He who winks the eye causes trouble, and a babbling fool will be thrown down.

2.F. Dishonesty

Proverbs 10:15

The rich man's wealth is his fortress, the ruin of the poor is their poverty.

2.L. Futility of Riches

Scripture:	Subtopic:
Proverbs 10:16 **The wages of the righteous is life,** the income of the wicked, punishment.	6.A. God's Promises 12.B. Wages
Proverbs 10:22 **It is the blessing of the LORD that makes rich,** and He adds no sorrow to it.	6.A. God's Promises* 6.D. Provision
Proverbs 10:27 **The fear of the LORD prolongs life,** but the years of the wicked will be shortened.	1.H. Trust 7.A. To Wicked
Proverbs 10:31 **The mouth of the righteous flows with wisdom,** but the perverted tongue will be cut out.	1.B. Honesty 2.F. Dishonesty
Proverbs 10:32 **The lips of the righteous bring forth what is acceptable,** but the mouth of the wicked, what is perverted.	1.B. Honesty
Proverbs 11:1 **A false balance is an abomination to the LORD,** but a just weight is His delight.	2.F. Dishonesty†
Proverbs 11:2 **When pride comes, then comes dishonor,** but with the humble is wisdom.	2.C. Pride
Proverbs 11:3 **The integrity of the upright will guide them,** but the falseness of the treacherous will destroy them.	1.B. Honesty
Proverbs 11:4 **Riches do not profit in the day of wrath,** but righteousness delivers from death.	2.L. Futility of Riches
Proverbs 11:6 **The righteousness of the upright will deliver them,** but the treacherous will be caught by their own greed.	2.E. Greed
Proverbs 11:14 **Where there is no guidance, the people fall,** but in abundance of counselors there is victory.	1.J. Counsel of Men

*God provides what is needed without worry, anxiety, fear, etc.

†A false balance (weight) was carried by a dishonest peddler to cheat buyers. Often it was the poor who were victimized because they lacked the resources to purchase their own weights to verify the sellers.

Scripture:	Subtopic:

Proverbs 11:15
He who is surety for a stranger will surely suffer for it, but **he who hates going surety is safe.**

3.E. Surety*

Proverbs 11:16
A gracious woman attains honor, and violent men attain riches.

2.E. Greed
6.A. God's Promises

Proverbs 11:18
The wicked earns deceptive wages, but he who sows righteousness gets a true reward.

7.A. To Wicked

Proverbs 11:20
The perverse in heart are an abomination to the LORD, but the blameless in their walk are His delight.

2.F. Dishonesty

Proverbs 11:24
There is one who scatters, yet increases all the more, and there is one who withholds what is justly due, but it results only in want.

4.F. Gifts†

Proverbs 11:25
The generous man will be prosperous, and he who waters will himself be watered.

4.F. Gifts

Proverbs 11:26
He who withholds grain, the people will curse him, but blessing will be on the head of him who sells it.

9.D. Selling†

Proverbs 11:28
He who trusts in his riches will fall, but the righteous will flourish like the green leaf.

2.L. Futility of Riches

Proverbs 12:1
Whoever loves discipline loves knowledge, but he who hates reproof is stupid.

1.J. Counsel of Men

Proverbs 12:5
The thoughts of the righteous are just, but the counsels of the wicked are deceitful.

1.B. Honesty

Proverbs 12:9
Better is he who is lightly esteemed and has a servant, than he who honors himself and lacks bread.

1.C. Humility
2.C. Pride§

Proverbs 12:11
He who tills his land will have plenty of bread, but **he who pursues vain things lacks sense.**

12.F. Diligent

---

*Surety in this Proverb refers to co-signing for the debt of another.
†Scatters. The context is as a farmer scatters seed in his fields.
‡Withholds. He holds out for a higher price.
§It's better to look poor and be rich, than look rich and be poor.

Proverbs 12:12
The wicked desires the booty of evil men, but the root of the righteous yields fruit.

2.E. Greed

Proverbs 12:15
The way of a fool is right in his own eyes, but a wise man is he who listens to counsel.

1.J. Counsel of Men

Proverbs 12:17
He who speaks the truth tells what is right, but a false witness, deceit.

1.B. Honesty
1.J. Counsel of Men

Proverbs 12:22
Lying lips are an abomination to the LORD, but those who deal faithfully are His delight.

2.F. Dishonesty

Proverbs 12:24
The hand of the diligent will rule, but the slack hand will be put to forced labor.

12.F. Diligent*

Proverbs 12:25
Anxiety in the heart of a man weighs it down, but a good word makes it glad.

1.J. Counsel of Men
2.M. Fear

Proverbs 12:27
A slothful man does not roast his prey, but the precious possession of a man is diligence.

12.E. Slothful†

Proverbs 13:1
A wise son accepts his father's discipline, but a scoffer does not listen to rebuke.

5.B. Counsel and Discipline‡
6.E. Discipline

Proverbs 13:4
The soul of the sluggard craves and gets nothing, but the soul of the diligent is made fat.

12.E. Slothful

Proverbs 13:10
Through presumption comes nothing but strife, but with **those who receive counsel is wisdom.**

1.J. Counsel of Men

Proverbs 13:11
Wealth obtained by fraud dwindles, but the one who gathers by labor increases it.

2.F. Dishonesty§

Proverbs 13:18
Poverty and shame will come to him who neglects discipline, but he who regards reproof will be honored.

1.J. Counsel of Men

---

*Diligent. Trustworthy to complete a task.
†Slothful. Lacking in self-discipline, lazy.
‡Scoffer. One who ignores or mocks the truth.
§This is where the old adage "easy come, easy go" originated.

Scripture:	Subtopic:

Proverbs 13:20
He who walks with wise men will be wise, but the companion of fools will suffer harm.

1.J. Counsel of Men*
2.N. Bad Counsel

Proverbs 13:21
Adversity pursues sinners, but the righteous will be rewarded with prosperity.

7.A. To Wicked

Proverbs 13:22
A good man leaves an inheritance to his children's children, and the wealth of the sinner is stored up for the righteous.

5.A. Inheritance

Proverbs 13:23
Abundant food is in the fallow ground of the poor, but it is swept away by injustice.

2.J. Injustice†

Proverbs 13:25
The righteous has enough to satisfy his appetite, but **the stomach of the wicked is in want.**

7.A. To Wicked

Proverbs 14:2
He who walks in his uprightness fears the LORD, but he who is crooked in his ways despises Him.

1.B. Honesty‡

Proverbs 14:4
Where no oxen are, the manger is clean, but much increase comes by the strength of the ox.

12.E. Slothful

Proverbs 14:7
Leave the presence of a fool, or you will not discern words of knowledge.

2.N. Bad Counsel

Proverbs 14:12
There is a way which seems right to a man, but its end is the way of death.

2.L. Futility of Riches§

Proverbs 14:15
The naive believes everything, but the prudent man considers his steps.

1.J. Consel of Men**

Proverbs 14:18
The naive inherit folly, but the prudent are crowned with knowledge.

1.L. Wisdom

---

*Also see Psalm 1:1.
†Often even the little the poor have is taken away by legal injustice, i.e. usury, taxes, etc.
‡A godly man will always be honest. The dishonest despise God.
§Don't trust human "instincts"; they're often wrong.
**Listen to counsel but always check it with God's Word.

Scripture:	Subtopic:

Proverbs 14:20
The poor is hated even by his neighbor, but those who love the rich are many.

2.H. Partiality*
2.J. Injustice

Proverbs 14:21
He who despises his neighbor sins, but happy is he who is gracious to the poor.

4.H. Helping Needy

Proverbs 14:31
He who oppresses the poor reproaches his Maker, but he who is gracious to the needy honors Him.

4.H. Helping Needy†

Proverbs 14:34
Righteousness exalts a nation, but sin is a disgrace to any people.

1.F. Obedience

Proverbs 14:35
The king's favor is toward a servant who acts wisely, but his anger is toward him who acts shamefully.

1.L. Wisdom

Proverbs 15:5
A fool rejects his father's discipline, but he who regards reproof is prudent.

5.B. Counsel and Discipline
6.E. Discipline

Proverbs 15:6
Much wealth is in the house of the righteous, but trouble is in the income of the wicked.

7.A. To Wicked

Proverbs 15:10
Stern discipline is for him who forsakes the way; he **who hates reproof will die.**

2.I. Disobedient

Proverbs 15:16
Better is a little with the fear of the LORD, than great treasure and turmoil with it.

1.G. Contentment

Proverbs 15:19
The way of the sluggard is as a hedge of thorns, but the path of the upright is a highway.

12.E. Slothful

Proverbs 15:20
A wise son makes a father glad, but a foolish man despises his mother.

1.L. Wisdom

Proverbs 15:22
Without consultation, plans are frustrated, but with many counselors they succeed.

1.J. Counsel of Men†

---

*People covet the favor of the wealthy.
†See Matthew 25:42–45.
†Contrast this with Proverbs 14:15, i.e. don't follow counsel blindly.

Proverbs 15:25
The LORD will tear down the house of the proud, but He will establish the boundary of the widow.

2.C. Pride

Proverbs 15:27
He who profits illicitly troubles his own house, but he who hates bribes will live.

2.F. Dishonesty

Proverbs 15:33
The fear of the LORD is the instruction for wisdom, and **before honor comes humility.**

1.C. Humility

Proverbs 16:1
The plans of the heart belong to man, but the answer of the tongue is from the LORD.

10. Planning

Proverbs 16:2
All the ways of a man are clean in his own sight, but **the LORD weighs the motives.**

1.A. Positive Attitudes
6.E. Discipline

Proverbs 16:3
Commit your works to the LORD, and your plans will be established.

10. Planning

Proverbs 16:5
Everyone who is proud in heart is an abomination to the LORD; assuredly, he will not be unpunished.

2.C. Pride

Proverbs 16:8
Better is a little with righteousness than great income with injustice.

1.C. Humility
2.J. Injustice

Proverbs 16:9
The mind of man plans his way, but the LORD directs his steps.

10. Planning*

Proverbs 16:11
A just balance and scales belong to the LORD; all the weights of the bag are His concern.

1.B. Honesty

Proverbs 16:16
How much **better it is to get wisdom than gold!** And to get understanding is to be chosen above silver.

1.L. Wisdom

Proverbs 16:18
Pride goes before destruction, and a haughty spirit before stumbling.

2.C. Pride†

---

*We are to be participants in God's plan, not observers.
†Pride is perhaps man's greatest sin.

Scripture:	Subtopic:

Proverbs 16:19
It is better to be of a humble spirit with the lowly, than to divide the spoil with the proud.

2.C. Pride*

Proverbs 16:26
A worker's appetite works for him, for his hunger urges him on.

12.A. Work

Proverbs 16:30
He who winks his eyes does so to devise perverse things; he who compresses his lips brings evil to pass.

2.F. Dishonesty

Proverbs 17:5
He who mocks the poor reproaches his Maker; he who rejoices at calamity will not go unpunished.

2.J. Injustice

Proverbs 17:8
A bribe is a charm in the sight of its owner; wherever he turns, he prospers.

2.B. Bribe

Proverbs 17:18
A man lacking in sense pledges, and becomes surety in the presence of his neighbor.

3.E. Surety

Proverbs 17:23
A wicked man receives a bribe from the bosom to pervert the ways of justice.

2.B. Bribe

Proverbs 17:25
A foolish son is a grief to his father, and bitterness to her who bore him.

5.B. Counsel and Discipline

Proverbs 18:8
The words of a whisperer are like dainty morsels, and they go down into the innermost parts of the body.

2.F. Dishonesty

Proverbs 18:9
He also who is slack in his work is brother to him who destroys.

12.E. Slothful

Proverbs 18:11
A rich man's wealth is his strong city, and like a high wall in his own imagination.

2.L. Futility of Riches

Proverbs 18:12
Before destruction **the heart of man is haughty,** but humility goes before honor.

2.C. Pride

Proverbs 18:15
The mind of the **prudent acquires knowledge,** and the ear of the wise seeks knowledge.

1.L. Wisdom

---

*See Matthew 16:26.

Proverbs 18:16
A man's gift makes room for him, and **brings him before great men.**

4.B. Giving to Men

Proverbs 18:23
The poor man utters supplications, but the rich man answers roughly.

1.E. Thankfulness
2.C. Pride

Proverbs 19:1
Better is a poor man who walks in his integrity than he who is perverse in speech and is a fool.

1.B. Honesty

Proverbs 19:4
Wealth adds many friends, but a poor man is separated from his friend.

2.H. Partiality

Proverbs 19:6
Many will entreat the favor of a generous man, and **every man is a friend to him who gives gifts.**

4.F. Gifts

Proverbs 19:7
All the brothers of a poor man hate him; how much more do his friends go far from him! He pursues them with words, but they are gone.

2.H. Partiality
2.J. Injustice

Proverbs 19:9
A false witness will not go unpunished, and he who tells lies will perish.

2.F. Dishonesty

Proverbs 19:14
House and wealth are an inheritance from fathers, but **a prudent wife is from the LORD.**

5.A. Inheritance*

Proverbs 19:15
Laziness casts into a deep sleep, and an idle man will suffer hunger.

12.E. Slothful

Proverbs 19:17
He who is gracious to a poor man lends to the LORD, and He will repay him for his good deed.

4.H. Helping Needy

Proverbs 19:18
Discipline your son while there is hope, and do not desire his death.

5.B. Counsel and Discipline
6.E. Discipline

Proverbs 19:19
A man of great anger shall bear the penalty, for if you rescue him, you will only have to do it again.

9.C. Get Rich

Proverbs 19:20
Listen to counsel and accept discipline, that you may be wise the rest of your days.

1.J. Counsel of Men

---

*A prudent wife is one who manages well. See Proverbs 31.

Proverbs 19:21
Many are the plans in a man's heart, but the counsel of the LORD, it will stand.

6.B. Counsel of God
10. Planning

Proverbs 19:22
What is desirable in a man is his kindness, and it is better to be a poor man than a liar.

1.I. Fairness

Proverbs 19:24
The sluggard buries his hand in the dish, and will not even bring it back to his mouth.

12.E. Slothful

Proverbs 20:4
The **sluggard** does not plow after the autumn, so he begs during the harvest and has nothing.

12.E. Slothful

Proverbs 20:5
A plan in the heart of a man is like deep water, but a man of understanding draws it out.

10. Planning

Proverbs 20:10
Differing weights and differing measures, both of them are abominable to the LORD.

2.F. Dishonesty

Proverbs 20:13
Do not love sleep, lest you become poor; open your eyes and you will be satisfied with food.

12.E. Slothful

Proverbs 20:14
"Bad, bad," says the buyer; but when he goes his way, then he boasts.

2.F. Dishonesty

Proverbs 20:15
There is gold, and an abundance of jewels; but the lips of **knowledge** are **a more precious thing.**

1.L. Wisdom

Proverbs 20:16
Take his garment **when he becomes surety** for a stranger; and for foreigners, hold him in pledge.

3.E. Surety

Proverbs 20:17
Bread obtained by falsehood is sweet to a man, but afterward his mouth will be filled with gravel.

2.F. Dishonesty

Proverbs 20:18
Prepare plans by consultation, and make war by wise guidance.

1.J. Counsel of Men

Proverbs 20:21
An inheritance gained hurriedly at the beginning, will not be blessed in the end.

5.A. Inheritance

Scripture:	Subtopic:

Proverbs 20:22
Do not say, "I will repay evil;" wait for the Lord, and He will save
you.

6.A. God's Prom-
ises

Proverbs 20:23
Differing weights are an abomination to the Lord, and a false scale
is not good.

2.F. Dishonesty*

Proverbs 21:3
To **do righteousness and justice** is desired by the Lord rather than
sacrifice.

1.A. Positive Atti-
tudes

Proverbs 21:5
The plans of the diligent lead surely to advantage, but everyone
who is hasty comes surely to poverty.

10. Planning†

Proverbs 21:6
The getting of treasures by a lying tongue is a fleeting vapor, the
pursuit of death.

2.F. Dishonesty

Proverbs 21:13
He who shuts his ear to the cry of the poor will also cry himself and
not be answered.

4.H. Helping
Needy

Proverbs 21:14
A gift in secret subdues anger, and a bribe in the bosom, strong
wrath.

2.B. Bribe

Proverbs 21:17
He who loves pleasure will become a poor man; he who loves wine
and oil will not become rich.

2.O. Indulgence†

Proverbs 21:20
There is precious treasure and oil in the dwelling of the wise, but **a
foolish man swallows it up.**

9.B. Savings§

Proverbs 21:25–26
[25]**The desire of the sluggard puts him to death,** for his hands refuse
to work; [26]all day long he is craving, while the righteous gives and
does not hold back.

12.E. Slothful

Proverbs 21:27
The sacrifice of the wicked is an abomination, how much more
when he brings it with evil intent!

3.E. Surety
7.A. To Wicked

---

*Dishonesty turns into bitterness later.
†God expects us to plan and avoid "get-rich-quick."
‡A "truism," you can always spend more than you can make.
§Also see Proverbs 6:6.

Scripture:	Subtopic:

Proverbs 21:29
A wicked man shows a bold face, but as for the upright, he makes
his way sure.

1.B. Honesty
2.F. Dishonesty

Proverbs 22:1
A good name is to be more desired than great riches, favor is better
than silver and gold.

1.B. Honesty

Proverbs 22:2
The rich and the poor have a common bond, the Lord is the maker
of them all.

6.A. God's Prom-
ises

Proverbs 22:3
The prudent sees the evil and hides himself, but the naive go on,
and are punished for it.

10. Planning*
12.F. Diligent

Proverbs 22:4
The reward of humility and the fear of the Lord **are riches,** honor
and life.

1.C. Humility

Proverbs 22:6
Train up a child in the way he should go, even when he is old he
will not depart from it.

5.B. Counsel and
Discipline
6.E. Discipline

Proverbs 22:7
The rich rules over the poor, and the borrower becomes the lender's
slave.

3.A. Borrowing†

Proverbs 22:9
He who is generous will be blessed, for he gives some of his food to
the poor.

4.F. Gifts

Proverbs 22:13
The sluggard says, "There is a lion outside; I shall be slain in the
streets."

12.E. Slothful

Proverbs 22:16
He who oppresses the poor to make much for himself or who gives
to the rich, will only come to poverty.

2.J. Injustice

Proverbs 22:22–23
²²**Do not rob the poor** because he is poor, or crush the afflicted at the
gate;   ²³for the Lord will plead their case, and take the life of those
who rob them.

2.J. Injustice

Proverbs 22:24–25
²⁴**Do not associate with a man given to anger;** or go with a hot-
tempered man,   ²⁵lest you learn his ways, and find a snare for
yourself.

2.N. Bad Counsel

---

*In other words, avoid the obvious problems that others create for themselves.
†The lender is in "authority" over the borrower.

Proverbs 22:26-27
²⁶Do not be among those who give pledges, among those who become sureties for debts. ²⁷If you have nothing with which to pay, why should he take your bed from under you?

3.E. Surety
3.C. Interest

Proverbs 22:28
Do not move the ancient boundary which your fathers have set.

2.F. Dishonesty

Proverbs 22:29
Do you see a man skilled in his work? He will stand before kings; he will not stand before obscure men.

12.D. Quality*

Proverbs 23:4-5
⁴Do not weary yourself to gain wealth, cease from your consideration of it. ⁵When you set your eyes on it, it is gone. For wealth certainly makes itself wings, like an eagle that flies toward the heavens.

9.C. Get Rich

Proverbs 23:10-11
¹⁰Do not move the ancient boundary, or go into the fields of the fatherless; ¹¹for their Redeemer is strong; he will plead their case against you.

2.J. Injustice

Proverbs 23:13-14
¹³Do not hold back discipline from the child, although you beat him with the rod, he will not die. ¹⁴You shall beat him with the rod, and deliver his soul from Sheol.

5.B. Counsel and Discipline
6.E. Discipline

Proverbs 23:17
Do not let your heart envy sinners, but live in the fear of the Lord always.

2.E. Greed
2.G. Envy

Proverbs 23:21
For the heavy drinker and the glutton will come to poverty . . .

12.E. Slothful

Proverbs 23:22
Listen to your father who begot you, and do not despise your mother when she is old.

5.B. Counsel and Discipline

Proverbs 24:1
Do not be envious of evil men, nor desire to be with them;

2.G. Envy

Proverbs 24:3-4
³By wisdom a house is built, and by understanding it is established; ⁴and by knowledge the rooms are filled with all precious and pleasant riches.

1.L. Wisdom

Proverbs 24:6
For by wise guidance you will wage war, and in abundance of counselors there is victory.

1.J. Counsel of Men

---

*Good workmanship will build a far-reaching reputation.

Proverbs 24:8
He who plans to do evil, men will call him a schemer.

2.F. Dishonesty

Proverbs 24:10
If you are slack in the day of distress, your strength is limited.

12.E. Slothful

Proverbs 24:17–18
[17]Do not rejoice when your enemy falls, and do not let your heart be glad when he stumbles; [18]lest the Lord see it and be displeased, and He turn away His anger from him.

1.D. Forgiveness
2.C. Pride

Proverbs 24:19–20
[19]Do not fret because of evildoers, or be envious of the wicked; [20]for there will be no future for the evil man; the lamp of the wicked will be put out.

2.G. Envy

Proverbs 24:23
These also are sayings of the wise. To show partiality in judgment is not good.

2.H. Partiality

Proverbs 24:27
Prepare your work outside, and make it ready for yourself in the field; afterwards, then, build your house.

10. Planning*

Proverbs 24:30–34
[30]I passed by the field of the sluggard, and by the vineyard of the man lacking sense; [31]and behold, it was completely overgrown with thistles, its surface was covered with nettles, and its stone wall was broken down. [32]When I saw, I reflected upon it; I looked, and received instruction. [33]"A little sleep, a little slumber, a little folding of the hands to rest," [34]then your poverty will come as a robber, and your want like an armed man.

12.E. Slothful

Proverbs 25:16
Have you found honey? Eat only what you need, lest you have it in excess and vomit it.

2.E. Greed[†]

Proverbs 25:21–22
[21]If your enemy is hungry, give him food to eat; and if he is thirsty, give him water to drink; [22]for you will heap burning coals on his head, and the Lord will reward you.

1.D. Forgiveness

Proverbs 25:28
Like a city that is broken into and without walls is a man who has no control over his spirit.

2.O. Indulgence

---

*An excellent principle for young couples.
†Develop a moderate lifestyle, regardless of income ability.

Scripture:	Subtopic:

Proverbs 26:13–16
[13]**The sluggard says,** "There is a lion in the road! A lion is in the open square!"   [14]As the door turns on its hinges, **so does the sluggard** on his bed.   [15]**The sluggard buries his hand** in the dish; he is weary of bringing it to his mouth again.   [16]**The sluggard is wiser in his own eyes** than seven men who can give a discreet answer.

12.E. Slothful

Proverbs 26:18–19
[18]Like a madman who throws firebrands, arrows and death,   [19]so is the man **who deceives his neighbor,** and says, "Was I not joking?"

2.F. Dishonesty

Proverbs 26:28
A lying tongue hates those it crushes, and a flattering mouth works ruin.

2.F. Dishonesty

Proverbs 27:1
Do not boast about tomorrow, for you do not know what a day may bring forth.

2.K. Ego*

Proverbs 27:7
A sated man loathes honey, but to a famished man any bitter thing is sweet.

1.G. Contentment
2.O. Indulgence

Proverbs 27:9
Oil and perfume make the heart glad, so **a man's counsel is sweet** to his friend.

1.J. Counsel of Men

Proverbs 27:10
Do not forsake your own friend or your father's friend, and do not go to your brother's house in the day of your calamity; better is a neighbor who is near than a brother far away.

1.J. Counsel of Men

Proverbs 27:12
A prudent man sees evil and hides himself, the naive proceed and pay the penalty.

10. Planning

Proverbs 27:13
Take his garment when he becomes surety for a stranger; and for an adulterous woman hold him in pledge.

3.E. Surety

Proverbs 27:18
He who tends the fig tree will eat its fruit; and he who cares for his master will be honored.

12.F. Diligent

Proverbs 27:23–24
[23]**Know well the condition of your flocks,** and pay attention to your herds;   [24]for riches are not forever, nor does a crown endure to all generations.

10. Planning†

---

*Also see James 4:13–14.
†A principle of planning.

Scripture:	Subtopic:

Proverbs 28:3
A poor man who oppresses the lowly is like a driving rain which leaves no food.

2.J. Injustice

Proverbs 28:6
Better is the poor who walks in his integrity, than he who is crooked though he be rich.

1.B. Honesty
2.F. Dishonesty

Proverbs 28:8
He who increases his wealth by interest and usury, gathers it for him who is gracious to the poor.

3.C. Interest
3.D. Usury

Proverbs 28:9
He who turns away his ear from listening to the law, even his prayer is an abomination.

2.F. Dishonesty

Proverbs 28:11
The rich man is wise in his own eyes, but the poor who has understanding sees through him.

2.K. Ego

Proverbs 28:12
When the righteous triumph, there is great glory, but **when the wicked rise, men hide themselves.**

1.B. Honesty
2.F. Dishonesty

Proverbs 28:13
He who conceals his transgressions will not prosper, but he who confesses and forsakes them will find compassion.

1.B. Honesty
2.F. Dishonesty

Proverbs 28:16
A leader who is a great oppressor lacks understanding, but he who hates unjust gain will prolong his days.

2.J. Injustice

Proverbs 28:19
He who tills his land will have plenty of food, but he who follows empty pursuits will have poverty in plenty.

12.F. Diligent

Proverbs 28:20
A faithful man will abound with blessings, but he who makes haste to be rich will not go unpunished.

9.C. Get Rich

Proverbs 28:21
To show partiality is not good, because for a piece of bread a man will transgress.

2.H. Partiality

Proverbs 28:22
A man with an evil eye hastens after wealth, and does not know that want will come upon him.

9.C. Get Rich

Proverbs 28:25
An arrogant man stirs up strife, but he who trusts in the Lord will prosper.

1.H. Trust
2.K. Ego

Scripture:	Subtopic:

Proverbs 28:27
He who gives to the poor will never want, but he who shuts his eyes will have many curses.

4.F. Gifts
4.H. Helping Needy

Proverbs 29:2
When the righteous increase, the people rejoice, but when a wicked man rules, people groan.

7.A To Wicked

Proverbs 29:3
A man who loves wisdom makes his father glad, but he who keeps company with harlots wastes his wealth.

1.L. Wisdom

Proverbs 29:4
The king gives stability to the land by justice, but a man who takes bribes overthrows it.

2.B. Bribe

Proverbs 29:7
The righteous is concerned for the rights of the poor, the wicked does not understand such concern.

4.H. Helping Needy

Proverbs 29:13
The poor man and the oppressor have this in common: **the Lord gives light to the eyes of both.**

6.D. Provision

Proverbs 29:15
The rod and reproof give wisdom, but a child who gets his own way brings shame to his mother.

6.E. Discipline
5.B. Counsel and Discipline

Proverbs 29:17
Correct your son, and he will give you comfort; he will also delight your soul.

6.E. Discipline
5.B. Counsel and Discipline

Proverbs 29:23
A man's pride will bring him low, but a humble spirit will obtain honor.

1.C. Humility
2.C. Pride

Proverbs 30:7–9
[7]Two things I asked of Thee, do not refuse me before I die: [8]keep deception and lies far from me, **give me neither poverty nor riches;** feed me with the food that is my portion, [9]lest I be full and deny Thee and say, "Who is the Lord?" Or lest I be in want and steal, and profane the name of my God.

1.G. Contentment
1.L. Wisdom

Proverbs 30:25
The ants are not a strong folk, but they prepare their food in the summer.

10. Planning

Proverbs 31:7
Let him drink and forget his poverty, and remember his trouble no more.

2.J. Injustice

Proverbs 31:9
Open your mouth, **judge righteously,** and defend the rights of the afflicted and needy.

4.H. Helping Needy

Proverbs 31:10
An excellent wife, who can find? For her worth is far above jewels.

5.B. Counsel and Discipline
6.C. Blessings

Proverbs 31:11
The heart of her husband trusts in her, and he will have no lack of gain.

5.B. Counsel and Discipline

Proverbs 31:16
She considers a field and buys it; from her earnings she plants a vineyard.

9.F. Profit

Proverbs 31:20
She extends her hand to the poor; and she stretches out her hands to the needy.

4.H. Helping Needy

Proverbs 31:24
She makes linen garments and sells them, and supplies belts to the tradesmen.

9.D. Selling*

---

*A "working wife."

Ecclesiastes

Scripture:	Subtopic:

Ecclesiastes 1:14
I have seen all the works which have been done under the sun, and behold, **all is vanity** and striving after wind.

2.L. Futility of Riches

Ecclesiastes 2:1
I said to myself, "Come now, **I will test you with pleasure.** So enjoy yourself." And behold, it too was futility.

2.L. Futility of Riches

Ecclesiastes 2:8–11
⁸Also, **I collected for myself silver and gold,** and the treasure of kings and provinces. I provided for myself male and female singers and the pleasures of men—many concubines. ⁹Then I became great and increased more than all who preceded me in Jerusalem. My wisdom also stood by me. ¹⁰And **all that my eyes desired I did not refuse them.** I did not withhold my heart from any pleasure, for my heart was pleased because of all my labor and this was my reward for all my labor. ¹¹Thus I considered all my activities which my hands had done and the labor which I had exerted, and behold **all was vanity** and striving after wind and there was no profit under the sun.

2.L. Futility of Riches

Ecclesiastes 2:18
Thus I hated all the fruit of my labor for which I had labored under the sun, for I must leave it to the man who will come after me.

5.A. Inheritance

Ecclesiastes 2:20
Therefore **I completely despaired of all the fruit of my labor** for which I had labored under the sun.

2.L. Futility of Riches

Ecclesiastes 2:21
When there is a man who has labored with wisdom, knowledge and skill, **then he gives his legacy to one who has not labored with them.** This too is vanity and a great evil.

5.A. Inheritance*

Ecclesiastes 2:22
For **what does a man get in all his labor** and in his striving with which he labors under the sun?

2.L. Futility of Riches

Ecclesiastes 2:23
Because **all his days his task is painful** and grievous; even at night his mind does not rest. This too is vanity.

2.A. Love of Money

---

*The vanity of leaving an inheritance to untrained offspring.

Scripture:	Subtopic:

Ecclesiastes 2:26
For to a person who is good in His sight He has given wisdom and knowledge and joy, while to the sinner He has given the task of gathering and collecting so that he may give to one who is good in God's sight. This too is vanity and striving after wind.

7.A. To Wicked

Ecclesiastes 3:13
. . . moreover, that every man who eats and drinks sees good in all his labor—it is the gift of God.

12.A. Work

Ecclesiastes 4:4
And I have seen that every labor and every skill which is done is the result of rivalry between a man and his neighbor. This too is vanity and striving after wind.

2.G. Envy

Ecclesiastes 4:7–8
⁷Then I looked again at vanity under the sun. ⁸There was a certain man without a dependent, having neither a son nor a brother, yet there was no end to all his labor. Indeed, his eyes were not satisfied with riches and he never asked, "And for whom am I laboring and depriving myself of pleasure?" This too is vanity and it is a grievous task.

2.L. Futility of Riches*

Ecclesiastes 4:9
Two are better than one because they have a good return for their labor.

9.F. Profit†

Ecclesiastes 4:13
A poor, yet wise lad is better than an old and foolish king who no longer knows how to receive instruction.

1.J. Counsel of Men
1.L. Wisdom

Ecclesiastes 5:4
When you make a vow to God, do not be late in paying it, for He takes no delight in fools. Pay what you vow!

1.K. Paying Vows†

Ecclesiastes 5:5
It is better that you should not vow than that you should vow and not pay.

1.K. Paying Vows

Ecclesiastes 5:8
If you see oppression of the poor and denial of justice and righteousness in the province, do not be shocked at the sight, for one official watches over another official, and there are higher officials over them.

2.J. Injustice

---

*The vanity of hoarding riches for no logical purpose.
†A reference to a partnership.
†A vow. Literally a promise to do something.

Scripture:	Subtopic:

Ecclesiastes 5:10
He who loves money will not be satisfied with money, nor he who loves abundance with its income. This too is vanity.

2.A. Love of Money*

Ecclesiastes 5:12
The sleep of the working man is pleasant, whether he eats little or much. But the full stomach of the rich does not allow him to sleep.

1.G. Contentment

Ecclesiastes 5:13
There is a grievous evil which I have seen under the sun: **riches being hoarded** by their owner to his hurt.

2.E. Greed†

Ecclesiastes 5:14
When **those riches were lost** through a bad investment and he had fathered a son, then there was nothing to support him.

9.G. Loss

Ecclesiastes 5:15
As he had come naked from his mother's womb, so will he return as he came. He will take nothing from the fruit of his labor that he can carry in his hand.

2.L. Futility of Riches

Ecclesiastes 5:18–19
Here is what I have seen to be good and fitting: to eat, to drink and **enjoy oneself in all one's labor** in which he toils under the sun during the few years of his life which God has given him; for this is his reward. [19]Furthermore, as **for every man to whom God has given riches and wealth, He has also empowered him to eat from them** and receive his reward and rejoice in his labor; this is the gift of God.

12.A. Work

Ecclesiastes 6:1–2
[1]**There is an evil which I have seen** under the sun and it is prevalent among men— [2]**a man to whom God has given riches** and wealth and honor so that his soul lacks nothing of all that he desires, but **God has not empowered him to eat from them,** for a foreigner enjoys them. This is a vanity and a severe affliction.

2.L. Futility of Riches†

Ecclesiastes 6:3–4
[3]If a man fathers a hundred children and lives many years, however many they be, but his soul is not satisfied with good things, and **he does not even have a proper burial,** then I say, "Better the miscarriage than he," [4]for it comes in futility and goes into obscurity; and its name is covered in obscurity.

5.A. Inheritance§

Ecclesiastes 6:7
All a man's labor is for his mouth and yet the appetite is not satisfied.

2.L. Futility of Riches

---

*Money itself never satisfies.
†Also see Luke 12:16–21.
‡A rich man who agonizes over his wealth.
§Fails to provide for his family. Also see I Timothy 5:8.

Ecclesiastes 6:8
For **what advantage does the wise man have** over the fool? What advantage does the poor man have, knowing how to walk before the living?

1.L. Wisdom

Ecclesiastes 7:7
For oppression makes a wise man mad, and a bribe corrupts the heart.

2.B. Bribe
2.J. Injustice

Ecclesiastes 7:12
For wisdom is protection just as money is protection. But the advantage of knowledge is that wisdom preserves the lives of its possessors.

1.L. Wisdom

Ecclesiastes 7:14
In the day of prosperity be happy, but **in the day of adversity consider—God has made the one as well as the other** so that man may not discover anything that will be after him.

2.L. Futility of Riches*

Ecclesiastes 8:10
So then, I have seen the wicked buried, those who used to go in and out from the holy place, and **they are soon forgotten** in the city where they did thus. This too is futility.

2.L. Futility of Riches

Ecclesiastes 8:12
. . . still I know that **it will be well for those who fear God,** who fear Him openly.

1.H. Trust

Ecclesiastes 9:10
Whatever your hand finds to do, verily, do it with all your might; for there is no activity or planning or wisdom in Sheol where you are going.

12.F. Diligent

Ecclesiastes 9:15
But there was found in it **a poor wise man and he delivered the city by his wisdom.** Yet no one remembered that poor man.

1.L. Wisdom

Ecclesiastes 9:16
So I said, "**Wisdom is better than strength.**" But the wisdom of the poor man is despised and his words are not heeded.

1.L. Wisdom
12.A. Work

Ecclesiastes 10:6
Folly is set in many exalted places while rich men sit in humble places.

2.J. Injustice

Ecclesiastes 10:19
Men prepare a meal for enjoyment, and wine makes life merry, and **money is the answer to everything.**

2.L. Futility of Riches

---

*Accepting God given circumstances. Also see Philippians 4:11–14.

Scripture:	Subtopic:

Ecclesiastes 11:1
Cast your bread on the surface of the waters, for you will find it
after many days.

9.A. Multiplication

Ecclesiastes 11:2
Divide your portion to seven, or even to eight, for you do not know
what misfortune may occur on the earth.

9.B. Savings*

Ecclesiastes 11:6
Sow your seed in the morning, and do not be idle in the evening, for
you do not know whether morning or evening sowing will succeed,
or whether both of them alike will be good.

12.F. Diligence

Ecclesiastes 12:13
The conclusion when all has been heard is: **fear God and keep His
commandments,** because this applies to every person.

1.H. Trust†

Ecclesiastes 12:14
Because God will bring every act to judgement, everything which
is hidden, whether it is good or evil.

6.F. Justice
6.E. Discipline

---

*Diversify your investments.
†The summation of Solomon's lifetime.

The Song of Solomon

Scripture:	Subtopic:

Song of Solomon 8:7
"Many waters cannot quench love, nor will rivers overflow it; **if a man were to give all the riches of his house for love, it would utterly be despised.**"

6.A. God's Promises

Isaiah

Scripture:	Subtopic:

Isaiah 1:23
"**Your rulers are rebels, and companions of thieves;** everyone loves a bribe, and chases after rewards. They do not defend the orphan, nor does the widow's plea come before them."

    2.B. Bribe

Isaiah 2:7
Their land has also been filled with silver and gold, and there **is no end to their treasures.**

    2.L. Futility of Riches
    6.G. Wealth

Isaiah 3:15
"**What do you mean by crushing my people,** and grinding the face of the poor?" declares the Lord God of hosts.

    2.J. Injustice

Isaiah 5:23
Who justify the wicked for a bribe, and take away the rights of the ones who are in the right!

    2.B. Bribe

Isaiah 10:1–2
¹**Woe to those who enact evil statutes,** and to those who constantly record unjust decisions, ²so as to deprive the needy of justice, and rob the poor of My people of their rights, in order that widows may be their spoil, and that they may plunder the orphans.

    2.J. Injustice

Isaiah 10:14
"And **my hand reached to the riches of the peoples** like a nest, and as one gathers abandoned eggs, I gathered all the earth; and there was not one that flapped its wing or opened its beak or chirped."

    6.D. Provision

Isaiah 11:4
But **with righteousness He will judge the poor,** and decide with fairness for the afflicted of the earth; and He will strike the earth with the rod of His mouth, and with the breath of His lips He will slay the wicked.

    6.A. God's Promises

Isaiah 13:17
Behold, I am going to stir up the Medes against them, who will not value silver or take pleasure in gold.

    6.F. Justice

Isaiah 16:4
"Let the outcasts of Moab stay with you; be a hiding place to them from the destroyer. For the extortioner has come to an end, destruction has ceased, **oppressors** have completely disappeared from the land."

    6.F. Justice

Scripture:	Subtopic:

Isaiah 24:2
And the people will be like the priest, the servant like his master, the maid like her mistress, **the buyer like the seller,** the lender like the borrower, the creditor like the debtor.

3.A. Borrowing
3.B. Lending

Isaiah 25:4
For Thou hast been **a defense for the helpless,** a defense for the needy in his distress, a refuge from the storm, a shade from the heat; for the breath of the ruthless is like a rain storm against à wall.

4.H. Helping Needy

Isaiah 30:6
The oracle concerning the beasts of the Negev. Through a land of distress and anguish, from where come lioness and lion, viper and flying serpent, they carry their riches on the backs of young donkeys and their treasures on camels' humps, to a people who cannot profit them.

2.L. Futility of Riches

Isaiah 30:23
Then He will give you rain for the seed which you will sow in the ground, and bread from the yield of the ground, and **it will be rich and plenteous;** on that day your livestock will graze in a roomy pasture.

6.D. Provision

Isaiah 33:15
He who walks righteously, and speaks with sincerity, **he who rejects unjust gain,** and shakes his hands so that they hold no bribe; he who stops his ears from hearing about bloodshed, and shuts his eyes from looking upon evil.

1.B. Honesty

Isaiah 39:4
And he said, "What have they seen in your house?" So Hezekiah answered, "They have seen all that is in my house; **there is nothing among my treasures that I have not shown them.**"

2.K. Ego

Isaiah 39:6
"Behold, the days are coming when all that is in your house, and **all that your fathers have laid up in store** to this day shall be carried to Babylon; **nothing shall be left,**" says the Lord.

6.E. Discipline

Isaiah 41:17
"The afflicted and needy are seeking water, but there is none, and their tongue is parched with thirst; I, the LORD, will answer them Myself, as the God of Israel I will not forsake them."

4.H. Helping Needy

Isaiah 43:23–24
[23]**"You have not brought to me the sheep of your burnt offerings;** nor have you honored Me with your sacrifices. I have not burdened you with offerings, nor wearied you with incense. [24]You have bought Me no sweet cane with money, neither have you filled Me with the fat of your sacrifices; rather you have burdened Me with your sins, you have wearied Me with your iniquities."

2.I. Disobedient

Isaiah 45:3
"And I will give you the treasures of darkness, and **hidden wealth of secret places,** in order that you may know that it is I, The LORD, the God of Israel, who calls you by your name."

6.D. Provision

Isaiah 45:13
"I have aroused him in righteousness, and I will make all his ways smooth; he will build My city, and will **let my exiles go free, without any payment of reward,**" says the LORD of hosts.

6.D. Provision

Isaiah 55:1–2
¹"Ho! Every one who thirsts, come to the waters; and **you who have no money come, buy and eat.** Come, buy wine and milk without money and without cost.   ²Why do you spend money for what is not bread, and your wages for what does not satisfy? Listen carefully to Me, and eat what is good, and delight yourself in abundance."

2.L. Futility of Riches

Isaiah 56:11
"And **the dogs are greedy,** they are not satisfied. And they are shepherds who have no understanding; they have all turned to their own way, each one to his unjust gain, to the last one."

2.E. Greed

Isaiah 57:17
"**Because of the iniquity of his unjust gain I was angry** and struck him; I hid My face and was angry, and he went on turning away, in the way of his heart."

2.J. Injustice

Isaiah 58:7
"**Is it not to divide your bread with the hungry,** and bring the homeless poor into the house; when you see the naked, to cover him; and not to hide yourself from your own flesh?"

4.H. Helping Needy

Isaiah 59:4
"**No one sues righteously and no one pleads honestly.** They trust in confusion, and speak lies; they conceive mischief, and bring forth iniquity."

2.F. Dishonesty

Isaiah 60:5
"Then you will see and be radiant, and your heart will thrill and rejoice; **because the abundance of the sea will be turned to you,** the wealth of the nations will come to you."

6.A. God's Promises

Isaiah 60:17
"**Instead of bronze I will bring gold,** and instead of iron I will bring silver, and instead of wood, bronze, and instead of stones, iron. And I will make peace your administrators, and righteousness your overseers."

6.A. God's Promises

Isaiah 61:6
". . . and **in their riches you will boast.**"

6.D. Provision

Jeremiah

Scripture:	Subtopic:

Jeremiah 5:28
"They are fat, they are sleek, they also excel in deeds of wickedness; **they do not plead the cause,** the cause of the orphan, that they may prosper; and they do not defend the rights of the poor."

2.J. Injustice

Jeremiah 6:13
"For from the least of them even to the greatest of them, **everyone is greedy for gain,** and from the prophet even to the priest everyone deals falsely."

2.E. Greed

Jeremiah 8:10
"Therefore I will give their wives to others, their fields to new owners; because from the least even to the greatest **everyone is greedy for gain;** from the prophet even to the priest everyone practices deceit."

2.E. Greed
2.F. Dishonesty

Jeremiah 9:4
"Let everyone be on guard against his neighbor, and do not trust any brother; because **every brother deals craftily,** and every neighbor goes about as a slanderer."

2.F. Dishonesty

Jeremiah 9:23
Thus says the Lord, "Let not a wise man boast of his wisdom, and let not the mighty man of his might, **let not a rich man boast of his riches.**"

2.K. Ego

Jeremiah 10:21
"For **the shepherds** have become stupid and **have not sought the Lord; therefore they have not prospered,** and all their flock is scattered."

6.E. Discipline

Jeremiah 15:10
"Woe to me, my mother, that you have borne me as a man of strife and a man of contention to all the land! **I have neither lent, nor have men lent money to me,** yet every one curses me."

3.B. Lending

Jeremiah 15:13
"**Your wealth and your treasures I will give for booty** without cost, even for all your sins and within all your borders."

6.E. Discipline

Jeremiah 17:3
"O mountain of Mine in the countryside, **I will give over your wealth and all your treasures for booty,** your high places for sin throughout your borders."

6.E. Discipline

Scripture:	Subtopic:

Jeremiah 17:5–6
⁵Thus says the LORD, "**Cursed is the man who trusts in mankind** and makes flesh his strength, and whose heart turns away from the LORD. ⁶For he will be like a bush in the desert and will not see when prosperity comes, but will live in stony wastes in the wilderness, a land of salt without inhabitant."

2.L. Futility of Riches

Jeremiah 17:9
"**The heart is more deceitful** than all else and is desperately sick; who can understand it?"

2.F. Dishonesty

Jeremiah 17:11
"As a partridge that hatches eggs which it has not laid, so is **he who makes a fortune, but unjustly;** in the midst of his days it will forsake him, and in the end he will be a fool."

2.J. Injustice

Jeremiah 20:5
"**I shall also give over all the wealth of this city,** all its produce, and all its costly things; even all the treasures of the kings of Judah I shall give over to the hand of their enemies, and they will plunder them, take them away, and bring them to Babylon."

6.F. Justice

Jeremiah 22:3
". . . Also **do not mistreat** or do violence to the stranger, **the orphan, or the widow;** and do not shed innocent blood in this place."

1.I. Fairness

Jeremiah 22:13
"**Woe to him who builds his house without righteousness** and his upper rooms without justice, who uses his neighbor's services without pay and does not give him his wages."

12.B. Wages

Jeremiah 22:16
"He **pled the cause of the afflicted and needy;** then it was well. Is not that what it means to know Me?" declares the LORD.

4.H. Helping Needy

Jeremiah 22:17
"But your eyes and your heart are **intent only upon your own dishonest gain,** and on shedding innocent blood and on practicing oppression and extortion."

2.F. Dishonesty

Jeremiah 22:21
"**I spoke to you in your prosperity;** but you said, 'I will not listen!' This has been your practice from your youth, that you have not obeyed My voice."

2.I. Disobedient

Jeremiah 32:7–14
⁷Behold, Hanamel the son of Shallum your uncle is coming to you, saying, "**Buy for yourself my field which is at Anathoth**, for you have the right of redemption to buy it." ⁸Then Hanamel my uncle's son came to me in the court of the guard according to the word of the LORD, and said to me, "Buy my field, please, that is at Anathoth, which is in the land of Benjamin; for you have the right of possession and the redemption is yours; buy it for yourself." Then I knew that this was the word of the LORD. ⁹**And I bought the field which was at Anathoth** from Hanamel my uncle's son, and I weighed out the silver for him, seventeen shekels of silver. ¹⁰And I signed and sealed the deed, and called in witnesses, and weighed out the silver on the scales. ¹¹Then I took the deeds of purchase, both the sealed copy containing the terms and conditions, and the open copy; ¹²and I gave the deed of purchase to Baruch the son of Neriah, the son of Mahseiah, in the sight of Hanamel my uncle's son, and in the sight of the witnesses who signed the deed of purchase, before all the Jews who were sitting in the court of the guard. ¹³And I commanded Baruch in their presence, saying, ¹⁴"Thus says the LORD of hosts, the God of Israel, 'Take these deeds, this sealed deed of purchase, and this open deed, and put them in an earthenware jar, that they may last a long time.'"

9.E. Buying

Jeremiah 32:25
"And Thou hast said to me, O LORD God, '**Buy for yourself the field with money,** and call in witnesses—although the city is given into the hand of the Chaldeans.'"

9.E. Buying

Jeremiah 32:44
"**Men shall buy fields for money,** sign and seal deeds, and call in witnesses in the land of Benjamin, in the environs of Jerusalem, in the cities of Judah, in the cities of the hill country, in the cities of the lowland, and in the cities of the Negev; for I will restore their fortunes," declares the LORD.

6.D. Provision
9.E. Buying

Jeremiah 39:10
But some of the **poorest people** who had nothing, Nebuzaradan the captain of the bodyguard **left behind in the land of Judah,** and gave them vineyards and fields at that time.

4.H. Helping Needy

Jeremiah 51:13
"O you who dwell by many waters, **abundant in treasures, your end has come,** the measure of your end."

6.E. Discipline
6.F. Justice

Jeremiah 52:34
And for his allowance, **a regular allowance was given him** by the king of Babylon, a daily portion all the days of his life until the day of his death.

12.B. Wages

Lamentations

Scripture:	Subtopic:

Lamentations 1:5
Her adversaries have become her masters, **her enemies prosper;** for the LORD has caused grief **because of the multitude of her transgressions;** her little ones have gone away as captives before the adversary.

7.A. To Wicked

Lamentations 1:7
In the days of her affliction and homelessness Jerusalem **remembers all her precious things** that were from the days of old when her people fell into the hand of the adversary, and no one helped her, they mocked at her ruin.

2.L. Futility of Riches

Lamentations 3:24
"The LORD **is my portion,**" says my soul, "Therefore I have hope in Him."

1.H. Trust

Lamentations 3:35–36
[35]To deprive a man of justice in the presence of the Most High, [36]to **defraud a man in his lawsuit**—of these things the LORD does not approve.

2.J. Injustice

Lamentations 4:1
How dark the gold has become, **how the pure gold has changed!** The sacred stones are poured out at the corner of every street.

2.L. Futility of Riches

Lamentations 4:2
The precious sons of Zion, **weighed against fine gold,** how they are regarded as earthen jars, the work of a potter's hands!

2.E. Greed

Lamentations 4:5
Those who ate delicacies are desolate in the streets; those reared in purple **embrace ash pits.**

2.L. Futility of Riches

Lamentations 5:2
Our inheritance has been turned over to strangers, our houses to aliens.

5.A. Inheritance

Ezekiel

Scripture:	Subtopic:

Ezekiel 7:11
"**Violence has grown into a rod of wickedness.** None of them shall remain, none of their multitude, none of their wealth, nor anything eminent among them."

6.F. Justice

Ezekiel 7:12–13
¹²"The time has come, the day has arrived. **Let not the buyer rejoice nor the seller mourn;** for wrath is against all their multitude. ¹³Indeed, the seller will not regain what he sold as long as they both live, for the vision regarding all their multitude will not be averted; nor will any of them maintain his life by his iniquity."

9.D. Selling
9.E. Buying

Ezekiel 7:19
"**They shall fling their silver into the streets,** and their gold shall become an abhorrent thing; their silver and their gold shall not be able to deliver them in the day of the wrath of the LORD. They cannot satisfy their appetite, nor can they fill their stomachs, for their iniquity has become an occasion of stumbling."

6.F. Justice

Ezekiel 16:10–13
¹⁰"I also clothed you with embroidered cloth, and put sandals of porpoise skin on your feet; **and I wrapped you with fine linen and covered you with silk. And I adorned you with ornaments,** put bracelets on your hands, and a necklace around your neck. ¹²I also put a ring in your nostril, earrings in your ears, and a beautiful crown on your head. ¹³Thus you were adorned with gold and silver, and your dress was of fine linen, silk, and embroidered cloth. You ate fine flour, honey, and oil; so you were exceedingly beautiful and advanced to royalty."

6.D. Provision

Ezekiel 16:17
"You also took your beautiful jewels made of My gold and of My silver, which I had given you, and **made for yourself male images** that you might play the harlot with them."

2.L. Futility of Riches

Ezekiel 16:33–34
³³"Men give gifts to all harlots, but **you give your gifts to all your lovers to bribe them** to come to you from every direction for your harlotries. ³⁴Thus you are different from those women in your harlotries, in that no one plays the harlot as you do, because you give money and no money is given you; thus you are different."

2.B. Bribe

Ezekiel 16:41
"And they will burn your houses with fire and execute judgments on you in the sight of many women. Then I shall stop you from playing the harlot, and you will also no longer pay your lovers."

7.A. To Wicked

Scripture:	Subtopic:

Ezekiel 16:49
"Behold, this was the guilt of your sister Sodom: she and her daughters had arrogance, abundant food, and careless ease, but **she did not help the poor and needy.**"

4.H. Helping Needy

Ezekiel 18:7–8
[7]"**If a man does not oppress any one,** but restores to the debtor his pledge, does not commit robbery, but gives his bread to the hungry, and covers the naked with clothing,   [8]if he does not lend money on interest or take increase, if he keeps his hand from iniquity, and executes true justice between man and man."

3.B. Lending
3.C. Interest

Ezekiel 18:12–13
[12]"**Oppresses the poor and needy,** commits robbery, does not restore a pledge, but lifts up his eyes to the idols, and commits abomination,   [13]he lends money on interest and takes increase; will he live? He will not live! He has committed all these abominations, he will surely be put to death; his blood will be on his own head."

3.B. Lending
3.C. Interest
6.E. Discipline

Ezekiel 18:16–18
[16]". . . or oppress anyone, or retain a pledge, or commit robbery, but he gives his bread to the hungry, and covers the naked with clothing,   [17]**he keeps his hand from the poor, does not take interest or increase,** but executes My ordinances, and walks in My statutes; he will not die for his father's iniquity, he will surely live.   [18]As for his father, because he practiced extortion, robbed his brother, and did what was not good among his people, behold, he will die for his iniquity."

3.B. Lending
3.C. Interest
6.E. Discipline
6.F. Justice

Ezekiel 20:28
"When I had brought them into the land which I swore to give to them, then they saw every high hill and every leafy tree, and they presented the provocation of their offering. There also they made their soothing aroma, and there they poured out their libations."

4.D. Offerings

Ezekiel 20:39–40
[39]"As for you, O house of Israel, thus says the Lord GOD, 'Go, serve every one his idols; but later, you will surely listen to Me, and My holy name you will profane no longer with your gifts and with your idols.   [40]For on My holy mountain, on the high mountain of Israel,' declares the Lord GOD, 'there the whole house of Israel, all of them, will serve Me in the land; there I shall accept them, and there **I shall seek your contributions** and the choicest of your gifts, with all your holy things.'"

4.D. Offerings

Ezekiel 22:12–13
[12]"In you **they have taken bribes to shed blood;** you have taken **interest and profits,** and you have injured your neighbors for gain by oppression, and you have forgotten Me," declares the Lord GOD.   [13]"Behold, then, I smite My hand at your dishonest gain which you have acquired and at the bloodshed which is among you."

2.B. Bribe

Ezekiel 22:18–20

[18]"Son of man, the house of Israel has become dross to Me; all of them are bronze and tin and iron and lead in the furnace; they are the dross of silver. [19]Therefore, thus says the Lord GOD, 'Because all of you have become dross, therefore, behold, I am going to gather you into the midst of Jerusalem. [20]As they gather silver and bronze and iron and lead and tin into the furnace to blow fire on it in order to melt it, so I shall gather you in My anger and in My wrath, and I shall lay you there and melt you.'"

7.A. To Wicked

Ezekiel 22:25

"There is a conspiracy of **her prophets** in her midst, like a roaring lion tearing the prey. They have devoured lives; **they have taken treasure and precious things;** they have made many widows in the midst of her."

2.J. Injustice

Ezekiel 22:29

"The **people of the land have practiced oppression** and committed robbery, and they have wronged the poor and needy and have oppressed the sojourner without justice."

2.J. Injustice

Ezekiel 26:12

"Also **they will make a spoil of your riches** and a prey of your merchandise, break down your walls and destroy your pleasant houses, and throw your stones and your timbers and your debris into the water."

6.E. Discipline

Ezekiel 27:12–34

[12]"Tarshish was your customer because of the abundance of all kinds of wealth; with silver, iron, tin, and lead, they paid for your wares. [13]Javan, Tubal, and Meshech, they were your traders; with the lives of men and vessels of bronze they paid for your merchandise. [14]Those from Beth-togarmah gave horses and war horses and mules for your wares. [15]The sons of Dedan were your traders. Many coastlands were your market; ivory tusks and ebony they brought as your payment. [16]Aram was your customer because of the abundance of your goods; they paid for your wares with emeralds, purple, embroidered work, fine linen, coral, and rubies. [17]Judah and the land of Israel, they were traders; with the wheat of Minnith, cakes, honey, oil, and balm they paid for your merchandise. [18]Damascus was your customer because of the abundance of your goods, because of the abundance of all kinds of wealth, because of the wine of Helbon and white wool. [19]Vedan and Javan paid for your wares from Uzal; wrought iron, cassia, and sweet cane were among your merchandise. [20]Dedan traded with you in saddlecloths for riding. [21]Arabia and all the princes of Kedar, they were your customers for lambs, rams, and goats; for these they were your customers. [22]The traders of Sheba and Raamah, they traded with you; they paid for your wares with the best of all kinds of spices, and with all kinds of precious stones, and gold. [23]Haran, Canneh, Eden, the traders of Sheba, Asshur, and Chilmad traded with you. [24]They traded with you in choice garments, in clothes of blue and embroidered work, and in carpets of many colors, and tightly wound cords, which were among your merchandise. [25]The ships of Tarshish were the carriers for your merchandise. And you were filled and were very glorious in the heart of the seas. [26]Your rowers have brought you into great waters; the east wind has broken you in the heart of the seas. [27]Your wealth, your wares, your merchandise, your sailors, and your pilots, your repairers of seams, your dealers in merchandise, and all your men of war who are in you, with all your company that is in your midst, will fall into the heart of the seas on the day of your overthrow. [28]At the sound of the cry of your pilots the pasture lands will shake. [29]And all who handle the oar, the sailors, and all the pilots of the sea, will come down from their ships; they will stand on the land, [30]and they will make their voice heard over you and will cry bitterly. They will cast dust on their heads, they will wallow in ashes. [31]Also they will make themselves bald for you and gird themselves with sackcloth; and they will weep for you in bitterness of soul with bitter mourning. [32]Moreover, in their wailing they will take up a lamentation for you and lament over you: 'Who is like Tyre, like her who is silent in the midst of the sea? [33]When your wares went out from the seas, you satisfied many peoples; with the abundance of your wealth and your merchandise, you enriched the kings of earth. [34]Now that you are broken by the seas in the depths of the waters, your merchandise and all your company have fallen in the midst of you.'"

Ezekiel 27:35–36
[35]"All the inhabitants of the coastlands are appalled at you, and their kings are horribly afraid; they are troubled in countenance. [36]The merchants among the peoples hiss at you; and you will be no more."

7.A. To Wicked

Ezekiel 28:4–5
[4]"By your wisdom and understanding you have acquired riches for yourself, and have acquired gold and silver for your treasuries. [5]By your great wisdom, by your trade you have increased your riches, and **your heart is lifted up because of your riches.**"

2.C. Pride

Ezekiel 28:13
"**You were in Eden,** the garden of God; every precious stone was your covering: the ruby, the topaz, and the diamond; the beryl, the onyx, and the jasper; the lapis lazuli, the turquoise, and the emerald; and the gold, the workmanship of your settings and sockets, was in you. On the day that you were created they were prepared."

6.D. Provision

Ezekiel 28:16
"**By the abundance of your trade you were internally filled with violence,** and you sinned; therefore I have cast you as profane from the mountain of God. And I have destroyed you, O covering cherub, from the midst of the stones of fire."

6.E. Discipline
9.E. Buying

Ezekiel 28:18
"By the multitude of your iniquities, in **the unrighteousness of your trade,** you profaned your sanctuaries. Therefore I have brought fire from the midst of you; it has consumed you, and I have turned you to ashes on the earth in the eyes of all who see you."

2.F. Dishonesty
6.E. Discipline

Ezekiel 29:14
"And **I shall turn the fortunes of Egypt** and shall make them return to the land of Pathros, to the land of their origin; and there they will be a lowly kingdom."

6.E. Discipline

Ezekiel 29:18–19
[18]Son of man, Nebuchadnezzar king of Babylon made his army labor hard against Tyre; every head was made bald, and every shoulder was rubbed bare. But he and his army had no wages from Tyre for the labor that he had performed against it. [19]Therefore, thus says the Lord GOD, "Behold, **I shall give the land of Egypt to Nebuchadnezzar** king of Babylon. And **he will carry off her wealth,** and capture her spoil and seize her plunder; and it will be wages for his army."

12.B. Wages

Ezekiel 30:4
"And a sword will come upon Egypt, and anguish will be in Ethiopia, when the slain fall in Egypt, **they take away her wealth,** and her foundations are torn down."

7.A. To Wicked

Scripture:	Subtopic:

Ezekiel 33:31
"And they come to you as people come, and they sit before you as My people, but they do the lustful desires expressed by their mouth, and **their heart goes after their gain.**"

2.E. Greed

Ezekiel 38:13
"Sheba, and Dedan, and the merchants of Tarshish, with all its villages, will say to you, 'Have you come to capture spoil? Have you assembled your company to seize plunder, to carry away silver and gold, to take away cattle and goods, to capture great spoil?'"

2.E. Greed

Ezekiel 39:25
Therefore thus says the Lord GOD, "Now **I shall restore the fortunes of Jacob,** and have mercy on the whole house of Israel; and I shall be jealous for My holy name."

6.A. God's Promises

Ezekiel 42:13
Then he said to me, "The north chambers and the south chambers, which are opposite the separate area, they are the holy chambers where the priests who are near to the LORD shall eat the most holy things. There they shall lay the most holy things, the grain offering, the sin offering, and the guilt offering; for the place is holy."

4.D. Offerings

Ezekiel 44:13
"And they shall not come near to Me to serve as priest to Me, nor come near to any of My holy things, to the things that are most holy; but they shall bear their shame and their abominations which they have committed."

7.A. To Wicked

Ezekiel 44:30
"And **the first of all the first fruits of every kind** and every contribution of every kind, from all your contributions, shall be for the priests; you shall also give to the priest the first of your dough to cause a blessing to rest on your house."

4.E. First Fruits

Ezekiel 45:10–12
[10]"**You shall have just balances,** a just ephah, and a just bath. [11]The ephah and the bath shall be the same quantity, so that the bath may contain a tenth of a homer, and the ephah a tenth of a homer; their standard shall be according to the homer. [12]And the shekel shall be twenty gerahs; twenty shekels, twenty-five shekels, and fifteen shekels shall be your maneh."

1.B. Honesty

Daniel

Scripture:	Subtopic:

Daniel 1:2
And the LORD gave Jehoiakim king of Judah into his hand, along with some of the vessels of the house of God; and he brought them to the land of Shinar, to the house of his god and he brought the vessels into the treasury of his god.

7.B. False Gods

Daniel 2:6
"But if you declare the dream and its interpretation, **you will receive from me gifts** and a reward and great honor; therefore declare to me the dream and its interpretation."

4.B. Giving to Men

Daniel 4:27
"Therefore, O king, may my advice be pleasing to you: **break away now from your sins** by doing righteousness, and from your iniquities by **showing mercy to the poor,** in case there may be a prolonging of your prosperity."

1.I. Fairness

Daniel 5:3–4
³Then they brought the gold vessels that had been taken out of the temple, the house of God which was in Jerusalem; and the king and his nobles, his wives, and his concubines drank from them. ⁴They drank the wine and praised the gods of gold and silver, of bronze, iron, wood, and stone.

7.B. False Gods

Daniel 5:17
Then **Daniel** answered and said before the king, **"Keep your gifts for yourself,** or give your rewards to someone else; however, I will read the inscription to the king and make the interpretation known to him."

4.B. Giving to Men

Daniel 5:23
" . . . but you have exalted yourself against the LORD of heaven; and they have brought the vessels of His house before you, and you and your nobles, your wives and your concubines have been drinking wine from them; and **you have praised the gods of silver and gold,** of bronze, iron, wood and stone, which do not see, hear or understand. But the God in whose hand are your life-breath and your ways, you have not glorified."

2.C. Pride
7.B. False Gods

Daniel 5:29
Then Belshazzar gave orders, and they clothed Daniel with purple and put a necklace of gold around his neck, and issued a proclamation concerning him that he **now** had authority as the third **ruler** in the kingdom.

4.B. Giving to Men

Daniel 6:1-3
¹It seemed good to Darius to appoint 120 satraps over the kingdom, that they should be in charge of the whole kingdom, ²and over them three commissioners (of whom Daniel was one), that these satraps might be accountable to them, and that the king might not suffer loss. ³Then this Daniel began distinguishing himself among the commissioners and satraps because he possessed an extraordinary spirit, and the king planned to appoint him over the entire kingdom.

12.F. Diligent

Daniel 10:5-6
⁵I lifted my eyes and looked, and behold, there was a certain man dressed in linen, whose waist was girded with a belt of pure gold of Uphaz. ⁶His body also was like beryl, his face and the appearance of lightning, his eyes were like flaming torches, his arms and feet like the gleam of polished bronze, and the sound of his words like the sound of a tumult.

6.F. Justice

Daniel 11:2
"And now I will tell you the truth. Behold, **three more kings are going to arise in Persia.** Then a fourth will gain far more riches than all of them; as soon as he becomes strong through his riches, he will arouse the whole empire against the realm of Greece."

7.B. False Gods

Daniel 11:8
"And also their gods with their metal images and their precious vessels of silver and gold he will take into captivity to Egypt, and he on his part will refrain from attacking the king of the North for some years."

7.B. False Gods

Daniel 11:20
"Then in his place one will arise who will send an oppressor through the Jewel of his kingdom; yet within a few days he will be shattered, though neither in anger nor in battle."

2.J. Injustice
7.B. False Gods

Daniel 11:24
"In a time of tranquility he will enter the richest parts of the realm, and he will accomplish what his fathers never did, nor his ancestors; he will distribute plunder, booty, and possessions among them, and he will devise his schemes against strongholds, but only for a time."

2.F. Dishonesty

Daniel 11:28
"Then he will return to his land with much plunder; but his heart will be set against the holy covenant, and he will take action and then return to his own land."

2.F. Dishonesty

Daniel 11:38
"But instead he will honor a god of fortresses, a god whom his fathers did not know; **he will honor him with gold,** silver, costly stones, and treasures."

7.B. False Gods

Daniel 11:43
"But he will gain control over the hidden treasures of gold and silver, and over all the precious things of Egypt; and Libyans and Ethiopians will follow at his heels."

2.L. Futility of Riches

Hosea

Scripture:	Subtopic:

Hosea 2:8
"For she does not know that it was I who gave her the grain, the new wine, and the oil, and lavished on her silver and gold, which they used for Baal."

6.A. God's Promises

Hosea 3:2
"So I bought her for myself for fifteen shekels of silver and a homer and a half of barley."

9.E. Buying

Hosea 8:4
They have set up kings, but not by Me; they have appointed princes, but I did not know it. With their silver and gold they have made idols for themselves, that they might be cut off.

7.B. False Gods

Hosea 9:6
"For behold, they will go because of destruction; Egypt will gather them up, Memphis will bury them. Weeds will take over their treasures of silver; thorns will be in their tents."

6.F. Justice

Hosea 12:7–8
⁷A merchant, in whose hands are false balances, he loves to oppress. ⁸And Ephraim said, "Surely I have become rich, I have found wealth for myself; in all my labors they will find in me no iniquity, which would be sin."

2.F. Dishonesty

Hosea 13:2
And now they sin more and more, and make for themselves molten images, idols skillfully made from their silver, all of them the work of craftsmen. They say of them, "Let the men who sacrifice kiss the calves!"

7.B. False Gods

Hosea 13:15
"Though he flourishes among the reeds, an east wind will come, the wind of the LORD coming up from the wilderness; and his foundation will become dry, and his spring will be dried up; it will plunder his treasury of every precious article."

6.F. Justice
7.B. False Gods

Joel

Scripture:	Subtopic:

Joel 1:17
"The seeds shrivel under their clods; **the storehouses are desolate,**
the barns are torn down, for the grain is dried up."

6.F. Justice

Joel 2:17
Let the priests, the LORD's ministers, weep between the porch and
the altar, and let them say, "Spare Thy people, O LORD, and **do not
make thine inheritance a reproach,** a byword among the nations.
Why should they among the peoples say, 'Where is their God?'"

5.A. Inheritance

Joel 3:5–8
⁵"Since you have taken My silver and My gold, brought My precious
treasures to your temples,   ⁶and sold the sons of Judah and Jerusalem to the Greeks in order to remove them far from their territory,   ⁷behold, I am going to arouse them from the place where
you have sold them, and return your recompense on your head.
⁸Also **I will sell your sons and your daughters into the hand of the
sons of Judah,** and they will sell them to the Sabeans, to a distant
nation," for the Lord has spoken.

6.F. Justice
9.D. Selling

Amos

Scripture:	Subtopic:

Amos 2:6–7
⁶Thus says the LORD, "For three transgressions of Israel and for four I will not revoke its punishment, **because they sell the righteous for money** and the needy for a pair of sandals. ⁷These who pant after the very dust of the earth on the head of the helpless also turn aside the way of the humble; and a man and his father resort to the same girl in order to profane My holy name."
    2.J. Injustice

Amos 3:11
Therefore, thus says the Lord GOD, "An enemy, even one surrounding the land, will pull down your strength from you and **your citadels will be looted.**"
    6.F. Justice

Amos 3:15
"I will smite the winter house together with the summer house; the houses of ivory will also perish and the great houses will come to an end," declares the LORD.
    7.A. To Wicked

Amos 4:1
Hear this word, you cows of Bashan who are on the mountain of Samaria, who oppress the poor, **who crush the needy**, who say to your husbands, "Bring now, that we may drink!"
    2.J. Injustice

Amos 4:4
"Enter Bethel and transgress; in Gilgal multiply transgression! **Bring your sacrifices every morning**, your tithes every three days."
    4.C. Tithe

Amos 4:5
"Offer **a thank offering** also from that which is leavened, and proclaim freewill offerings, make them known. For so you love to do, you sons of Israel," declares the Lord GOD.
    4.D. Offerings

Amos 5:11
"Therefore, because **you impose heavy rent on the poor** and exact a tribute of grain from them, though you have built houses of well-hewn stone, yet you will not live in them; you have planted pleasant vineyards, yet you will not drink their wine."
    2.J. Injustice

Amos 5:12
"For I know your transgressions are many and your sins are great, **you who distress the righteous and accept bribes**, and turn aside the poor in the gate."
    2.B. Bribe

Amos 6:1–7

[1]**Woe to those who are at ease** in Zion, and to **those who feel secure** in the mountain of Samaria, the distinguished men of the foremost of nations, to whom the house of Israel comes.   [2]Go over to Calneh and look, and go from there to Hamath the great, then go down to Gath of the Philistines. Are they better than these kingdoms, or is their territory greater than yours?   [3]Do you put off the day of calamity, and would you bring near the seat of violence?   [4]Those who recline on beds of ivory and sprawl on their couches, and eat lambs from the flock and calves from the midst of the stall,   [5]who improvise to the sound of the harp, and like David have composed songs for themselves,   [6]who drink wine from sacrificial bowls while they anoint themselves with the finest of oils, yet they have not grieved over the ruin of Joseph.   [7]Therefore, they will now go into exile at the head of the exiles, and the sprawlers' banqueting will pass away.

2.L. Futility of Riches

7.A. To Wicked

Amos 8:5–6

[5]. . . saying, "When will the new moon be over, so that we may buy grain, and the sabbath, that we may open the wheat market, to make the bushel smaller and the shekel bigger, and to **cheat with dishonest scales,** [6]so as to **buy the helpless for money** and the needy for a pair of sandals, and that we may sell the refuse of the wheat?"

2.F. Dishonesty

Obadiah

Scripture:	Subtopic:

Obadiah 1:5
"If thieves came to you, if robbers by night—O how you will be ruined!—**would they not steal only until they had enough?** If grape gatherers came to you, would they not leave some gleanings?"

2.F. Dishonesty

Obadiah 1:13
"Do not enter the gate of My people in the day of their disaster. Yes, you, do not gloat over their calamity in the day of their disaster. And **do not loot their wealth** in the day of their disaster."

2.J. Injustice

Obadiah 1:16
"Because just as you drank on My holy mountain, all the nations will drink continually. They will drink and swallow, and become as if they had never existed."

2.F. Dishonesty

Jonah

Scripture:	Subtopic:

Jonah 1:3
But **Jonah** rose up to flee the Tarshish from the presence of the LORD. So he went down to Joppa, found a ship which was going to Tarshish, **paid the fare**, and went down into it to go with them to Tarshish from the presence of the LORD.

9.E. Buying

Micah

Scripture:	Subtopic:

Micah 1:7
"All of her idols will be smashed, **all of her earnings will be burned with fire,** and all of her images I will make desolate, for she collected them from a harlot's earnings, and to the earnings of a harlot they will return."

6.F. Justice

Micah 2:2
"**They covet fields and then seize them,** and houses, and take them away. They rob a man and his house, a man and his inheritance."

2.E. Greed
2.J. Injustice

Micah 2:9
"**The women of my people you evict,** each one from her pleasant house. From her children you take My splendor forever."

2.E. Greed
2.F. Dishonesty

Micah 3:11
"Her **leaders pronounce judgment for a bribe,** her priests instruct for a price, and her prophets divine for money. Yet they lean on the LORD saying, 'Is not the LORD in our midst? Calamity will not come upon us.'"

2.B. Bribe

Micah 4:13
"Arise and thresh, daughter of Zion, for your horn I will make iron and your hoofs I will make bronze, that you may pulverize many peoples, that **you may devote to the LORD their unjust gain** and their wealth to the LORD of all the earth."

6.F. Justice

Micah 6:8
"He had told you, O man, what is good; and **what does the LORD require of you but to do justice,** to love kindness, and to walk humbly with your God?"

1.H. Trust

Micah 6:10-12
[10]"Is there yet a man in the wicked house, along with treasures of wickedness, and a short measure that is cursed? [11]**Can I justify wicked scales** and a bag of deceptive weights? [12]For the rich men of the city are full of violence, her residents speak lies, and their tongue is deceitful in their mouth."

2.F. Dishonesty

Micah 7:3
"Concerning evil, both hands do it well. The prince asks, also **the judge, for a bribe,** and a great man speaks the desire of his soul; so they weave it together."

2.B. Bribe

Nahum

Scripture:	Subtopic:

Nahum 2:9
"**Plunder the silver!** Plunder the gold! For there is no limit to the treasure—wealth from every kind of desirable object."

6.F. Justice

Nahum 3:16
"**You have increased your traders** more than the stars of heaven— the creeping locust strips and flies away."

2.L. Futility of Riches

Habakkuk

Scripture:	Subtopic:

Habakkuk 2:6–7
⁶"Will not all of these take up a taunt-song against him, even mockery and insinuations against him, and say, '**Woe to him who increases what is not his**—for how long—and **makes himself rich with loans?**' ⁷Will not your creditors rise up suddenly, and those who collect from you awaken? Indeed, you will become plunder for them."

3.B. Lending

Habakkuk 2:9
"**Woe to him who gets evil gain for his house** to put his nest on high to be delivered from the hand of calamity!"

2.F. Dishonesty

Habakkuk 2:19
"Woe to him who says to a piece of wood, 'Awake!' To a dumb stone, 'Arise!' and that is your teacher? Behold, it is overlaid with gold and silver."

2.F. Dishonesty

Habakkuk 3:14
"Thou didst pierce with his own spears the head of his throngs. They stormed in to scatter us; their exultation was like those **who devour the oppressed in secret.**"

2.J. Injustice

Zephaniah

Scripture:	Subtopic:

Zephaniah 1:12–13
[12]"And it will come about at that time that I will search Jerusalem with lamps, and I will punish the men who are stagnant in spirit, who say in their hearts, 'The LORD will not do good or evil!' [13]Moreover, their wealth will become plunder, and their houses desolate; yes, they will build houses but not inhabit them, and plant vineyards but not drink their wine."

6.E. Discipline

Zephaniah 1:18
Neither their silver nor their gold will be able to deliver them on the day of the LORD's wrath; and all the earth will be devoured in the fire of His jealousy, for He will make a complete end, indeed a terrifying one, of all the inhabitants of the earth.

6.F. Justice

Zephaniah 2:7
"And the coast will be for the remnant of the house of Judah, they will pasture on it. In the houses of Ashkelon they will lie down at evening; for the LORD their God will care for them and restore their fortune."

6.A. God's Promise

Haggai

Scripture:	Subtopic:

Haggai 1:4
"Is it time for you yourselves to dwell in your paneled houses while **this house lies desolate?**"

2.A. Love of Money

Haggai 1:6
"You have sown much, but harvest little; you eat, but there is not enough to be satisfied; you drink, but there is not enough to become drunk; you put on clothing, but no one is warm enough; and **he who earns, earns wages to put into a purse with holes.**"

7.A. To Wicked

Haggai 1:9
"You look for much, but behold, it comes to little; when you bring it home, I blow it away. Why?" declares the LORD of hosts, "Because My house lies desolate, while each of you run to your own house."

2.A. Love of Money
6.E. Discipline

Haggai 2:7–8
⁷"And I will shake all the nations; and they will come with the wealth of all nations; and I will fill this house with glory," says the LORD of hosts.   ⁸**"The silver is Mine, and the gold is Mine,"** declares the LORD of hosts.

6.A. God's Promises
6.D. Provision

Zechariah

Scripture:	Subtopic:

Zechariah 1:17
Again, proclaim, saying, "Thus says the LORD of hosts, 'My cities will again overflow with prosperity, and the LORD will again comfort Zion and again choose Jerusalem.' "

6.A. God's Promises

Zechariah 2:12
And the LORD will possess Judah as His portion in the holy land, and will again choose Jerusalem.

6.A. God's Promises

Zechariah 5:3–4
³Then he said to me, "This is the curse that is going forth over the face of the whole land; surely everyone who steals will be purged away according to the writing on one side, and everyone who swears will be purged away according to the writing on the other side. ⁴I will make it go forth," declares the LORD of hosts, "and it will enter the house of the thief and the house of the one who swears falsely by My name; and it will spend the night within that house and consume it with its timber and stones."

6.F. Justice

Zechariah 6:11
"And take silver and gold, make an ornate crown, and set it on the head of Joshua the son of Jehozadak, the high priest."

4.B. Giving to Men

Zechariah 7:9–10
⁹Thus has the LORD of hosts said, "Dispense true justice, and practice kindness and compassion each to his brother; ¹⁰and do not oppress the widow or the orphan, the stranger or the poor; and do not devise evil in your hearts against one another."

1.I. Fairness

Zechariah 8:17
"Also let none of you devise evil in your heart against another, and do not love perjury; for all these are what I hate," declares the LORD.

2.J. Injustice

Zechariah 9:3–4
³For Tyre built herself a fortress and piled up silver like dust, and gold like the mire of the streets. ⁴Behold, the Lord will dispossess her and cast her wealth into the sea; and she will be consumed with fire.

6.F. Justice
7.A. To Wicked

Zechariah 11:5
"Those who buy them slay them and go unpunished, and each of those who sell them says, 'Blessed be the LORD, for I have become rich!' And their own shepherds have no pity on them."

9.D. Selling
9.E. Buying

Scripture:	Subtopic:

Zechariah 11:12–13

[12]And I said to them, "If it is good in your sight, give me my wages; but if not never mind!" So **they weighed out thirty shekels of silver as my wages.** [13]Then the LORD said to me, "Throw it to the potter, that magnificent price at which I was valued by them." So I took the thirty shekels of silver and threw them to the potter in the house of the LORD.

12.B. Wages

Zechariah 13:9

"And I will bring the third part through the fire, refine them as silver is refined, and test them as gold is tested. They will call on My name, and I will answer them; I will say, 'There are My people,' and they will say, 'The LORD is my God.'"

6.A. God's Promises

Zechariah 14:14

And Judah also will fight at Jerusalem; and **the wealth of all the surrounding nations will be gathered,** gold and silver and garments in great abundance.

6.A. God's Promises

Malachi

Malachi 1:13
"You also say, 'My, how tiresome it is!' And you disdainfully sniff at it," says the LORD of hosts, "and you bring what was taken by robbery, and **what is lame or sick; so you bring the offering!** Should I receive that from your hand?" says the LORD.

4.G. Worthless Gifts

Malachi 2:12
"As for the man who does this, may the LORD cut off from the tents of Jacob everyone who awakes and answers, or who presents an offering to the LORD of hosts."

4.G. Worthless Gifts

Malachi 3:3
"And He will sit as a smelter and purifier of silver, and He will purify the sons of Levi and refine them like gold and silver, **so that they may present to the LORD offerings in righteousness.**"

4.D. Offerings

Malachi 3:5
"Then I will draw near to you for judgment; and I will be a swift witness against the sorcerers and against the adulterers and against those who swear falsely, and **against those who oppress the wage earner in his ways,** the widow and the orphan, and those who turn aside the alien, and do not fear Me," says the LORD of hosts.

6.E. Discipline
12.B. Wages

Malachi 3:7–11
[7]"From the days of your fathers you have turned aside from My statutes, and have not kept them. Return to Me, and I will return to you," says the LORD of hosts. "But you say, 'How shall we return?' [8]**Will a man rob God?** Yet you are robbing Me! But you say, 'How have we robbed Thee?' **In tithes and contributions.** [9]You are cursed with a curse, for you are robbing Me, the whole nation of you! [10]Bring the whole tithe into the storehouse, so that there may be food in My house, and test Me now in this," says the **LORD** of hosts, "if I will not open for you the windows of heaven, and pour out for you a blessing until it overflows. [11]Then I will rebuke the devourer for you, so that it may not destroy the fruits of the ground; nor will your vine in the field cast its grapes," says the **LORD** of hosts.

4.A. Storehouse
4.C. Tithe

Matthew

Scripture:	Subtopic:

Matthew 2:11
And they came into the house and saw the Child with Mary His mother; and they fell down and worshiped Him; and opening their treasures **they presented to Him gifts of gold and frankincense and myrrh.**

4.F. Gifts

Matthew 5:12
"Rejoice, and be glad, for your reward in heaven is great, for so they persecuted the prophets who were before you."

6.A. God's Promises

Matthew 5:16
"Let your light shine before men in such a way that they may see your good works, and glorify your Father who is in heaven."

12.A Work

Matthew 5:23–24
²³"If therefore you are presenting your offering at the altar, and there remember that your brother has something against you, ²⁴**leave your offering there before the altar,** and go your way; **first be reconciled** to your brother, and then come and present your offering."

11. Restitution*

Matthew 5:25–26
²⁵**"Make friends quickly with your opponent at law** while you are with him on the way, in order that your opponent may not deliver you to the judge, and the judge to the officer, and you be thrown into prison. ²⁶Truly I say to you, you shall not come out of there, until you have paid up the last cent."

1.C. Humility†
3.F. Paying Debts
11. Restitution

Matthew 5:38–40
³⁸"You have heard that it was said, 'An eye for an eye, and a tooth for a tooth.' ³⁹But I say to you, do not resist him who is evil; but whoever slaps you on your right cheek, turn to him the other also. ⁴⁰And **if anyone wants to sue you, and take your shirt, let him have your coat also.**"

1.C. Humility†

Matthew 5:42
"Give to him who asks of you, and do not turn away from him who wants to borrow from you."

4.F. Gifts

---

*God desires justice, not sacrifices. Also see Matthew 9:13.
†Obviously an admonition to those who are guilty.
†The Lord's position on retribution.

Matthew 5:43–46

[43]"You have heard that it was said, 'You shall love your neighbor, and hate your enemy.' [44]But I say to you, love your enemies, and pray for those who persecute you [45]in order that you may be sons of your Father who is in heaven; for He causes His sun to rise on the evil and the good, and sends rain on the righteous and the unrighteous. [46]**For if you love those who love you, what reward have you?** Do not even the tax-gatherers do the same?"

1.C. Humility

Matthew 6:1

"Beware of practicing your righteousness before men to be noticed by them; otherwise you have no reward with your Father who is in heaven."

1.C. Humility

Matthew 6:2–4

[2]"When therefore you give alms, do not sound a trumpet before you, as the hypocrites do in the synagogues and in the streets, that they may be honored by men. Truly I say to you, they have their reward in full. [3]But when you give alms, do not let your left hand know what your right hand is doing [4]that your alms may be in secret; and your Father who sees in secret will repay you."

2.K. Ego*

Matthew 6:19–21

[19]"**Do not lay up for yourselves treasures upon earth,** where moth and rust destroy, and where thieves break in and steal. [20]But lay up for yourselves treasures in heaven, where neither moth nor rust destroys, and where thieves do not break in or steal; [21]for where your treasure is, there will your heart be also."

2.L. Futility of Riches

Matthew 6:24

"**No one can serve two masters;** for either he will hate the one and love the other, or he will hold to one and despise the other. You cannot serve God and mammon."

1.F. Obedience[†]
2.A. Love of Money

Matthew 6:25–30

"For this reason I say to you, **do not be anxious for your life,** as to what you shall eat, or what you shall drink; nor for your body, as to what you shall put on. Is not life more than food, and the body than clothing? [26]Look at the birds of the air, that they do not sow, neither do they reap, nor gather into barns, and yet your heavenly Father feeds them. Are you not worth much more than they? [27]And which of you by being anxious can add a single cubit to his life's span? [28]And why are you anxious about clothing? Observe how the lilies of the field grow; they do not toil nor do they spin, [29]yet I say to you that even Solomon in all his glory did not clothe himself like one of these. [30]But if God so arrays the grass of the field, which is alive today and tomorrow is thrown into the furnace, will He not much more do for you, O men of little faith?"

1.H. Trust

---

*An admonition to those who give to gain recognition.
†Also see Proverbs 30:7–9. God desires our total allegiance.

Scripture:	Subtopic:

Matthew 6:31–34

³¹"**Do not be anxious then,** saying, 'What shall we eat?' or 'What shall we drink?' or 'With what shall we clothe ourselves?' ³²For all these things the Gentiles eagerly seek; for your heavenly Father knows that you need all these things. ³³**But seek first His kingdom and His righteousness;** and all these things shall be added to you. ³⁴Therefore do not be anxious for tomorrow; for tomorrow will care for itself. Each day has enough trouble of its own." — 1.H. Trust

Matthew 7:2

"**For in the way you judge, you will be judged;** and by your standard of measure, it will be measured to you." — 6.F. Justice

Matthew 7:9–11

⁹"Or what man is there among you, when his son shall ask him for a loaf, will give him a stone? ¹⁰Or if he shall ask for a fish, he will not give him a snake, will he? ¹¹If you then, being evil, know how to give good gifts to your children, how much more shall your Father who is in heaven give what is good to those who ask Him!" — 1.H. Trust*

Matthew 7:20

"So then, **you will know them by their fruits.**" — 1.F. Obedience

Matthew 8:20

And Jesus said to him, "**The foxes have holes,** and the birds of the air have nests; but the Son of Man has nowhere to lay His head." — 1.G. Contentment

Matthew 8:21–22

²¹And another of the disciples said to Him, "Lord, permit me first to go and bury my father." ²²But Jesus said to him, "Follow Me; and **allow the dead to bury their own dead.**" — 1.F. Obedience†

Matthew 10:9–10

⁹"Do not acquire gold, or silver, or copper for your money belts, ¹⁰or a bag for your journey, or even two tunics, or sandals, or a staff; for **the worker is worthy of his support.**" — 12.B. Wages‡

Matthew 10:17

"But **beware of men;** for they will deliver you up to the courts, and scourge you in their synagogues." — 2.J. Injustice

Matthew 10:29–30

²⁹"**Are not two sparrows sold for a cent?** And yet not one of them will fall to the ground apart from your Father. ³⁰But the very hairs of your head are all numbered." — 1.H. Trust

---

*Do you trust God or just **say** you trust?
†Also see Matthew 10:37.
‡Also see Luke 22:35–36.

Scripture:	Subtopic:

Matthew 10:37
"**He who loves father or mother more than Me is not worthy of Me;** and he who loves son or daughter more than Me is not worthy of Me."

1.H. Trust
2.E. Greed

Matthew 10:42
"And whoever in the name of a disciple gives to one of these little ones **even a cup of cold water to drink,** truly I say to you he shall not lose his reward."

4.H. Helping Needy

Matthew 11:5
". . . the blind receive sight and the lame walk, the lepers are cleansed and the deaf hear, and the dead are raised up, and **the poor have the gospel preached to them.**"

4.H. Helping Needy

Matthew 12:7
"But if you had known what this means, '**I desire compassion, and not a sacrifice,'** you would not have condemned the innocent."

2.H. Partiality

Matthew 12:11–12
¹¹And He said to them, "What man shall there be among you, who shall have one sheep, and if it falls into a pit on the Sabbath, will he not take hold of it, and lift it out? ¹²Of how much more value then is a man than a sheep! **So then, it is lawful to do good on the Sabbath.**"

1.A. Positive Attitudes*
12.A. Work

Matthew 12:35
"**The good man out of his good treasure brings forth what is good;** and the evil man out of his evil treasure brings forth what is evil."

1.B. Honesty
2.F. Dishonesty

Matthew 13:7
"And **others fell among the thorns,** and the thorns came up and choked them out."

2.L. Futility of Riches

Matthew 13:12
"For **whoever has, to him shall more be given,** and he shall have an abundance; but whoever does not have, even what he has shall be taken away from him."

6.E. Discipline†

Matthew 13:22
"And **the one on whom seed was sown among the thorns,** this is the man who hears the word, and the worry of the world, and the deceitfulness of riches choke the word, and it becomes unfruitful."

2.L. Futility of Riches

Matthew 13:24
He presented another parable to them, saying, "The kingdom of heaven may be compared to **a man who sowed good seed in his field.**"

1.F. Obedience

*Also see Colossians 2:16.
†Also see Matthew 25:29.

Matthew 13:44–46
44"**The kingdom of heaven is like a treasure hidden in the field,** which a man found and hid; and from joy over it he goes and sells all that he has, and buys that field.   45Again, **the kingdom of heaven is like a merchant seeking fine pearls,**   46and upon finding one pearl of great value, he went and sold all that he had, and bought it."

9.E. Buying

Matthew 13:52
And He said to them, "Therefore every scribe who has become a disciple of the kingdom of heaven is like a head of a household, **who brings forth out of his treasure things new and old.**"

5.C. Provision

Matthew 14:15
And when it was evening, the disciples came to Him, saying, "The place is desolate, and the time is already past; **so send the multitudes away,** that they may go into the villages and buy food for themselves."

9.E. Buying

Matthew 15:5–6
5"But you say, 'Whoever shall say to his father or mother, "**Anything of mine you might have been helped by has been given to God,**" 6he is not to honor his father or his mother.' And thus you invalidated the word of God for the sake of your tradition."

4.H. Helping Needy*

Matthew 15:19
"For out of the heart come evil thoughts, murders, adulteries, fornications, **thefts,** false witness, slanders."

2.F. Dishonesty

Matthew 16:24
Then Jesus said to His disciples, "If anyone wishes to come after Me, **let him deny himself, and take up his cross, and follow Me.**"

1.F. Obedience

Matthew 16:25
"For **whoever wishes to save his life shall lose it;** but whoever loses his life for My sake shall find it."

6.A. God's Promise

Matthew 16:26
"For **what will a man be profited, if he gains the whole world,** and forfeits his soul? Or what will a man give in exchange for his soul?"

2.L. Futility of Riches†

---

*Helping parents is not an option, it is a requirement.
†You can have but one master. Also see Matthew 6:24.

Matthew 17:24–27

And when they had come to Capernaum, those who collected the two-drachma tax came to Peter, and said, "Does your teacher not pay the two-drachma tax?" [25]He said, "Yes." And when he came into the house, Jesus spoke to him first, saying, "What do you think, Simon? From whom do the kings of the earth collect customers or poll-tax, from their sons or from strangers?" [26]And upon his saying, "From strangers," Jesus said to him, "Consequently the sons are exempt. [27]But, lest we give them offense, go to the sea, and throw in a hook, and take the first fish that comes up; and when you open its mouth, you will find a stater. Take that and give it to them for you and Me."

8.B. Administrative Tax

Matthew 18:15–17

[15]"And if your brother sins, go and reprove him in private; if he listens to you, you have won your brother. [16]But if he does not listen to you, take one or two more with you, so that by the mouth of two or three witnesses every fact may be confirmed. [17]And if he refuses to listen to them, tell it to the church; and if he refuses to listen even to the church, let him be to you as a Gentile and a tax-gatherer."

1.J. Counsel of Men*

Matthew 18:23–35

[23]"For this reason **the kingdom of heaven may be compared to a certain king who wished to settle accounts with his slaves.** [24]And when he had begun to settle them, there was brought to him one who owed him ten thousand talents. [25]But since he did not have the means to repay, his lord commanded him to be sold, along with his wife and children and all that he had, and repayment to be made. [26]The slave therefore falling down, prostrated himself before him, saying, 'Have patience with me, and I will repay you everything.' [27]And the lord of that slave felt compassion and released him and forgave him the debt. [28]But that slave went out and found one of his fellow slaves who owed him a hundred denarii; and he seized him and began to choke him, saying, 'Pay back what you owe.' [29]So his fellow slave fell down and began to entreat him, saying, 'Have patience with me and I will repay you.' [30]He was unwilling however, but went and threw him in prison until he should pay back what was owed. [31]So when his fellow slaves saw what had happened, they were deeply grieved and came and reported to their lord all that had happened. [32]Then summoning him, his lord said to him, 'You wicked slave, I forgave you all that debt because you entreated me. [33]Should you not also have had mercy on your fellow slave, even as I had mercy on you?' [34]And his lord, moved with anger, handed him over to the torturers until he should repay all that was owed him. [35]So shall My heavenly Father also do to you, if each of you does not forgive his brother from your heart."

1.D. Forgiveness
1.I. Fairness

---

*God's principle of confrontation. Also see I Corinthians 6:1.

Scripture:	Subtopic:

Matthew 19:21
Jesus said to him, "**If you wish to be complete, go and sell your possessions** and give to the poor, and you shall have treasure in heaven; and come, follow Me."

4.H. Helping Needy*
9.D. Selling

Matthew 19:23
And Jesus said to His disciples, "Truly I say to you, **it is hard for a rich man to enter the kingdom of heaven.**"

2.L. Futility of Riches†

Matthew 19:27
Then Peter answered and said to Him, "**Behold, we have left everything** and followed You; what then will there be for us?"

1.F. Obedience

Matthew 19:29
"And everyone who has left houses or brothers or sisters or father or mother or children or farms for My name's sake, shall receive many times as much, and shall inherit eternal life."

1.F. Obedience

Matthew 20:1–16
¹"For **the kingdom of heaven is like a landowner who went out early in the morning to hire laborers for his vineyard.** ²And when he had agreed with the laborers for a denarius for the day, he sent them into his vineyard. ³And he went out about the third hour and saw others standing idle in the market place; ⁴and to those he said, 'You too go into the vineyard, and whatever is right I will give you.' And so they went. ⁵Again he went out about the sixth and the ninth hour, and did the same thing. ⁶And about the eleventh hour he went out, and found others standing; and he said to them, 'Why have you been standing here idle all day long?' ⁷They said to him, 'Because no one hired us.' He said to them, 'You too go into the vineyard.' ⁸And when evening had come, the owner of the vineyard said to his foreman, 'Call the laborers and pay them their wages, beginning with the last group to the first.' ⁹And when those hired about the eleventh hour came, each one received a denarius. ¹⁰And when those hired first came, they thought that they would receive more; and they also received each one a denarius. ¹¹And when they received it, they grumbled at the landowner, ¹²saying, 'These last men have worked only one hour, and you have made them equal to us who have borne the burden and the scorching heat of the day.' ¹³But he answered and said to one of them, 'Friend, I am doing you no wrong; did you not agree with me for a denarius? ¹⁴Take what is yours and go your way, but I wish to give to this last man the same as to you. ¹⁵Is it not lawful for me to do what I wish with what is my own? Or is your eye envious because I am generous?' ¹⁶Thus the last shall be first, and the first last."

2.G. Envy
7.A. To Wicked

---

*Clearly Christ was dealing with his attitude. Also see Luke 22:36.
†Also see Matthew 19:30.

Scripture:	Subtopic:

Matthew 20:25–27

²⁵But Jesus called them to Himself, and said, "You know that the rulers of the Gentiles lord it over them, and their great men exercise authority over them. ²⁶It is not so among you, but whoever wishes to become great among you shall be your servant, ²⁷and whoever wishes to be first among you shall be your slave."

1.C. Humility

Matthew 21:12–13

¹²And **Jesus entered the temple and cast out all those who were buying and selling** in the temple, and overturned the tables of the moneychangers and the seats of those who were selling doves. ¹³And He said to them, "It is written, 'My house shall be called a house of prayer'; but you are making it a robbers' den."

9.D. Selling

Matthew 21:21

And Jesus answered and said to them, "Truly I say to you, **if you have faith, and do not doubt,** you shall not only do what was done to the fig tree, but even if you say to this mountain, 'Be taken up and cast into the sea,' it shall happen."

1.H. Trust

Matthew 21:22

"And all things you ask in prayer, believing, you shall receive."

1.H. Trust

Matthew 21:33–41

³³"Listen to another parable. **There was a landowner who planted a vineyard and put a wall around it and dug a wine press in it, and built a tower, and rented it out to vine-growers, and went on a journey. ³⁴And when the harvest time approached, he sent his slaves to the vine-growers to receive his produce. ³⁵And the vine-growers took his slaves and beat one, and killed another, and stoned a third. ³⁶Again he sent another group of slaves larger than the first; and they did the same thing to them. ³⁷But afterward he sent his son to them, saying, 'They will respect my son.' ³⁸But when the vine-growers saw the son, they said among themselves, 'This is the heir; come, let us kill him, and seize his inheritance.' ³⁹And they took him, and threw him out of the vineyard, and killed him. ⁴⁰Therefore when the owner of the vineyard comes, what will he do to those vine-growers?" ⁴¹They said to Him, "He will bring those wretches to a wretched end, and will rent out the vineyard to other vine-growers, who will pay him the proceeds at the proper season."**

2.E. Greed
5.A. Inheritance

Matthew 22:17–21

¹⁷"Tell us therefore, what do You think? **Is it lawful to give a poll-tax to Caesar, or not?"** ¹⁸But Jesus perceived their malice, and said, "Why are you testing Me, you hypocrites? ¹⁹Show Me the coin used for the poll-tax." And they brought Him a denarius. ²⁰And He said to them, "Whose likeness and inscription is this?" ²¹They said to Him, "Caesar's." Then He said to them, "Then render to Caesar the things that are Caesar's; and to God the things that are God's."

8.B. Administrative Tax

Scripture:	Subtopic:

Matthew 23:12
"And **whoever exalts himself shall be humbled; and whoever humbles himself shall be exalted.**"

1.C. Humility
2.K. Ego

Matthew 23:16–17
[16]"**Woe to you, blind guides,** who say, 'Whoever swears by the temple, that is nothing; but whoever swears by the gold of the temple, he is obligated.' [17]You fools and blind men; which is more important, the gold, or the temple that sanctified the gold?"

7.B. False Gods

Matthew 23:23
"Woe to you, scribes and Pharisees, hypocrites! **For you tithe mint and dill and cummin,** and have neglected the weightier provisions of the law: justice and mercy and faithfulness; but these are the things you should have done without neglecting the others."

4.C. Tithe*

Matthew 24:46–47
[46]"**Blessed is that slave whom his master finds so doing** when he comes. [47]Truly I say to you, that he will put him in charge of all his possessions."

1.F. Obedience

Matthew 25:9–10
[9]"But the prudent answered, saying, '**No, there will not be enough for us and you too;** go instead to the dealers and buy some for yourselves.' [10]And while they were going away to make the purchase, the bridegroom came, and those who were ready went in with him to the wedding feast; and the door was shut."

9.E. Buying

---

*God blesses the attitude, not the gift. Also see Matthew 12:7.

Matthew 25:14–30

[14]"For it is just like a man about to go on a journey, who called his   9.F. Profit
own slaves, and entrusted his possessions to them.   [15]And to one he
gave five talents, to another, two, and to another, one, each according to his own ability; and he went on his journey.   [16]Immediately
the one who had received the five talents went and traded with
them, and gained five more talents.   [17]In the same manner the one
who had received the two talents gained two more.   [18]But he who
received the one talent went away and dug in the ground, and hid
his master's money.   [19]Now after a long time the master of those
slaves came and settled accounts with them.   [20]And the one who
had received the five talents came up and brought five more talents, saying, 'Master, you entrusted five talents to me; see, I have
gained five more talents.'   [21]His master said to him, 'Well done,
good and faithful slave; you were faithful with a few things, I will
put you in charge of many things, enter into the joy of your master.'   [22]The one also who had received the two talents came up and
said, 'Master, you entrusted to me two talents; see, I have gained
two more talents.'   [23]His master said to him, 'Well done, good and
faithful slave; you were faithful with a few things, I will put you in
charge of many things; enter into the joy of your master.'   [24]And
the one also who had received the one talent came up and said,
'Master, I knew you to be a hard man, reaping where you did not
sow, and gathering where you scattered no seed.   [25]And I was
afraid, and went away and hid your talent in the ground; see, you
have what is yours.'   [26]But his master answered and said to him,
'You wicked, lazy slave, you knew that I reap where I did not sow,
and gather where I scattered no seed.   [27]Then you ought to have
put my money in the bank, and on my arrival I would have received my money back with interest.   [28]Therefore take away the
talent from him, and give it to the one who has the ten talents.'   [29]For to everyone who has shall more be given, and he shall
have an abundance; but from the one who does not have, even
what he does have shall be taken away.   [30]And cast out the worthless slave into the outer darkness; in that place there shall be weeping and gnashing of teeth.'"

Matthew 25:34

"Then the King will say to those on His right, 'Come, you who are   5.A. Inheritance
blessed of My Father, inherit the kingdom prepared for you from
the foundation of the world.' "

Matthew 25:35–45

³⁵" 'For I was hungry, and you gave Me something to eat; I was thirsty, and you gave Me drink; I was a stranger, and you invited Me in;   ³⁶naked, and you clothed Me; I was sick, and you visited Me; I was in prison, and you came to Me.'   ³⁷Then the righteous will answer Him, saying, 'Lord, when did we see You hungry, and feed You, or thirsty, and give You drink?   ³⁸And when did we see You a stranger, and invite You in, or naked, and clothe You? ³⁹And when did we see You sick, or in prison, and come to You?' ⁴⁰And the King will answer and say to them, 'Truly I say to you, to the extent that you did it to one of these brothers of Mine, even the least of them, you did it to me.'   ⁴¹Then He will also say to those on His left, 'Depart from Me, accursed ones, into the eternal fire which has been prepared for the devil and his angels;   ⁴²for I was hungry, and you gave Me nothing to eat; I was thirsty, and you gave Me nothing to drink;   ⁴³I was a stranger, and you did not invite Me in; naked, and you did not clothe Me; sick, and in prison, and you did not visit Me.'   ⁴⁴Then they themselves also will answer, saying, 'Lord, when did we see You hungry, or thirsty, or a stranger, or naked, or sick, or in prison, and did not take care of You?'   ⁴⁵Then He will answer them, saying, 'Truly I say to you, to the extent that you did not do it to one of the least of these, you did not do it to Me.' "

4.H. Helping Needy

Matthew 26:7–12

⁷. . . a woman came to him with an alabaster vial of very costly perfume, and she poured it upon His head as He reclined at the table.   ⁸But the disciples were indignant when they saw this, and said, "Why this waste?   ⁹For this perfume might have been sold for a high price and the money given to the poor."   ¹⁰But Jesus, aware of this, said to them, "Why do you bother the woman? For she has done a good deed to Me.   ¹¹For the poor you have with you always; but you do not always have Me.   ¹²For when she poured this perfume upon My body, she did it to prepare Me for burial."

4.H. Helping Needy
9.D. Selling

Matthew 26:15

"What are you willing to give me to deliver Him up to you?" And they weighed out to him thirty pieces of silver.

2.E. Greed

Matthew 27:3–10

[3]Then when Judas, who had betrayed Him, saw that He had been condemned, **he felt remorse and returned the thirty pieces of silver** to the chief priests and elders, [4]saying, "I have sinned by betraying innocent blood." But they said, "What is that to us? See to that yourself!" [5]And he threw the pieces of silver into the sanctuary and departed; and he went away and hanged himself. [6]And the chief priests took the pieces of silver and said, "It is not lawful to put them into the temple treasury, since it is the price of blood." [7]And they counseled together and with the money bought the Potter's Field as a burial place for strangers. [8]For this reason that field has been called the Field of Blood to this day. [9]Then that which was spoken through Jeremiah the prophet was fulfilled, saying, "And they took the thirty pieces of silver, the price of the One whose price had been set by the son of Israel; [10]and they gave them for the Potter's Field, as the Lord directed me."

2.E. Greed

Matthew 28:12–15

[12]And when they had assembled with the elders and counseled together, **they gave a large sum of money to the soldiers,** [13]and said, "You are to say, 'His disciples came by night and stole Him away while we were asleep.' [14]And if this should come to the governor's ears, we will win him over and keep you out of trouble." [15]And they took the money and did as they had been instructed; and this story was widely spread among the Jews, and is to this day.

2.B. Bribe

Mark

Scripture:	Subtopic:

Mark 3:27
"But **no one can enter the strong man's house** and plunder his property unless he first binds the strong man, and then he will plunder his house."

2.J. Injustice

Mark 4:18–19
[18]"And others are **the ones on whom seed was sown among the thorns;** these are the ones who have heard the word, [19]and the worries of the world, and the deceitfulness of riches, and the desires for other things enter in and choke the word, and it becomes unfruitful."

2.E. Greed

Mark 4:24
And He was saying to them, "Take care what you listen to. **By your standard of measure it shall be measured to you;** and more shall be given you besides."

1.I. Fairness

Mark 4:25
"**For whoever has, to him shall more be given;** and whoever does not have, even what he has shall be taken away from him."

6.A. God's Promises

Mark 6:8
. . . and He instructed them that **they should take nothing for their journey,** except a mere staff; no bread, no bag, no money in their belt.

1.H. Trust

Mark 6:37
But He answered and said to them, "**You give them something to eat!**" And they said to Him, "Shall we go and spend two hundred denarii on bread and give them something to eat?"

9.E. Buying

Mark 6:41
And **He took the five loaves and the two fish,** and looking up toward heaven, He blessed the food and broke the loaves and He kept giving them to the disciples to set before them; and He divided up the two fish among them all.

6.D. Provision

Mark 7:11–12
[11]". . . but you say, '**If a man says to his father or his mother, anything of mine you might have been helped by is Corban** (that is to say, given to God),' [12]you no longer permit him to do anything for his father or his mother."

4.H. Helping Needy

Mark 8:36–37
[36]"**For what does it profit a man to gain the whole world,** and forfeit his soul? [37]For what shall a man give in exchange for his soul?"

2.L. Futility of Riches

Mark 10:19
"You know the commandments, 'Do not murder, Do not commit adultry, Do not steal, Do not bear false witness, **Do not defraud,** Honor your father and mother.' "

1.B Honesty

Mark 10:21–26
²¹And looking at him, Jesus felt a love for him, and said to him, **"One thing you lack: go and sell all you possess,** and give to the poor, and you shall have treasure in heaven; and come, follow Me." ²²But at these words his face fell, and he went away grieved, for he was one who owned much property. ²³And Jesus, looking around, said to His disciples, "How hard it will be for those who are wealthy to enter the kingdom of God!" ²⁴And the disciples were amazed at His words. But Jesus answered again and said to them, "Children, how hard it is to enter the kingdom of God! ²⁵It is easier for a camel to go through the eye of a needle than for a rich man to enter the kingdom of God." ²⁶And they were even more astonished and said to Him, "Then who can be saved?"

2.A. Love of Money
4.H. Helping Needy

Mark 10:29–30
²⁹Jesus said, "Truly I say to you, **there is no one who has left house or brothers or sisters** or mother or father or children or farms, for My sake and for the gospel's sake, ³⁰but that he shall receive a hundred times as much now in the present age, houses and brothers and sisters and mothers and children and farms, along with persecutions; and in the age to come, eternal life."

6.A. God's Promises

Mark 11:15
And they came to Jerusalem. And He entered the temple and began **to cast out those who were buying and selling** in the temple, and overturned the tables of the moneychangers and the seats of those who were selling doves.

9.D. Selling

Mark 11:24
"Therefore I say to you, all things for which you pray and ask, **believe that you have received them,** and they shall be granted you."

1.H. Trust

Scripture:	Subtopic:

Mark 12:1–9

¹And He began to speak to them in parables: "**A man planted a vineyard, and put a wall around it,** and dug a vat under the wine press, and built a tower, and rented it out to vine-growers and went on a journey.   ²And at the harvest time he sent a slave to the vine-growers, in order to receive some of the produce of the vineyard from the vine-growers.   ³And they took him, and beat him, and sent him away empty-handed.   ⁴And again he sent them another slave, and they wounded him in the head, and treated him shamefully.   ⁵And he sent another, and that one they killed; and so with many others, beating some, and killing others.   ⁶He had one more to send, a beloved son; he sent him last of all to them, saying, 'They will respect my son.'   ⁷But those vine-growers said to one another, 'This is the heir; come, let us kill him, and the inheritance will be ours!'   ⁸And they took him, and killed him, and threw him out of the vineyard.   ⁹What will the owner of the vineyard do? He will come and destroy the vine-growers, and will give the vineyard to others."

2.E. Greed
5.A. Inheritance

Mark 12:14–17

¹⁴And they came and said to Him, "Teacher, we know that You are truthful, and defer to no one; for You are not partial to any, but teach the way of God in truth. **Is it lawful to pay a poll-tax to Caesar, or not?** ¹⁵Shall we pay, or shall we not pay?" But He, knowing their hypocrisy, said to them, "Why are you testing me? Bring Me a denarius to look at."   ¹⁶And they brought one. And He said to them, "Whose likeness and inscription is this?" And they said to Him, "Caesar's."   ¹⁷And Jesus said to them, "Render to Caesar the things that are Caesar's, and to God the things that are God's." And they were amazed at Him.

8.B. Administrative Tax

Mark 12:41

And He sat down opposite the treasury, and began observing how **the multitude were putting money into the treasury;** and many rich people were putting in large sums.

4.F. Gifts

Mark 12:42–44

⁴²**And a poor widow came** and put in two small copper coins, which amount to a cent.   ⁴³And calling His disciples to Him, He said to them, "Truly I say to you, this poor widow put in more than all the contributors to the treasury;   ⁴⁴for they all put in out of their surplus, but she, out of her poverty, put in all she owned, all she had to live on."

4.D. Offerings

Scripture:	Subtopic:

Mark 14:3–7

³And while He was in Bethany at the home of Simon the leper, and reclining at the table, **there came a woman with an alabaster vial of very costly perfume** of pure nard; and she broke the vial and poured it over His head.   ⁴But some were indignantly remarking to one another, "Why has this perfume been wasted?   ⁵For this perfume might have been sold for over three hundred denarii, and the money given to the poor." And they were scolding her.   ⁶But Jesus said, "Let her alone; why do you bother her? She has done a good deed to Me.   ⁷For the poor you always have with you, and whenever you wish, you can do them good; but you do not always have Me."

4.D. Offerings
4.H. Helping Needy
9.D. Selling

Mark 14:10–11

¹⁰And **Judas Iscariot,** who was one of the twelve, went off to the chief priests, in order to betray Him to them.   ¹¹And they were glad when **they heard this, and promised to give him money.** And he began seeking how to betray Him at an opportune time.

2.B. Bribe
2.E. Greed

Luke

Scripture:	Subtopic:

Luke 1:53
"**He has filled the hungry with good things;** and sent away the rich empty-handed."

6.F. Justice

Luke 3:11
And he would answer and say to them, "**Let the man who has two tunics share** with him who has none; and let him who has food do likewise."

4.H. Helping Needy

Luke 3:12–13
[12]And some tax-gatherers also came to be baptized, and they said to him, "Teacher, what shall we do?" [13]And he said to them, "**Collect no more than what you have been ordered to.**"

1.B. Honesty
8.B. Administrative Tax

Luke 3:14
And some soldiers were questioning him, saying, "And what about us, what shall we do?" And he said to them, "**Do not take money from anyone by force,** or accuse anyone falsely, and be content with your wages."

1.G. Contentment*
12.B. Wages

Luke 4:18
"The Spirit of the LORD is upon Me, because He anointed Me to **preach the gospel to the poor.** He has sent Me to proclaim release to the captives, and recovery of sight to the blind, to set free those who are downtrodden."

4.H. Helping Needy

Luke 5:11
And when they had brought their boats to land, they left everything and followed Him.

1.F. Obedience

Luke 5:27–28
[27]And after that He went out, and noticed **a tax-gatherer named Levi,** sitting in the tax office, and He said to him, "Follow Me." [28]And he left everything behind, and rose and began to follow Him.

1.F. Obedience
8.A. Church Tax

Luke 6:20
And turning His gaze on His disciples, He began to say, "**Blessed are you who are poor,** for yours is the kingdom of God."

4.H. Helping Needy

Luke 6:24
"**But woe to you who are rich,** for you are receiving your comfort in full."

2.L. Futility of Riches

---

*I believe the book of Luke contains the best references to financial principles of any of the gospels.

Scripture:	Subtopic:

Luke 6:29–30
[29]"Whoever hits you on the cheek, offer him the other also; and whoever takes away your coat, do not withhold your shirt from him either. [30]**Give to everyone who asks of you,** and whoever takes away what is yours, do not demand it back."

4.F. Gifts*

Luke 6:34–35
[34]"And **if you lend to those from whom you expect to receive,** what credit is that to you? Even sinners lend to sinners, in order to receive back the same amount. [35]But love your enemies, and do good, and lend, expecting nothing in return; and your reward will be great, and you will be sons of the Most High; for He Himself is kind to ungrateful and evil men."

3.B. Lending

Luke 6:38
"**Give, and it will be given to you;** good measure, pressed down, shaken together, running over, they will pour into your lap. For by your standard of measure it will be measured to you in return."

4.F. Gifts

Luke 6:41
"And why **do you look at the speck that is in your brother's eye,** but do not notice the log that is in your own eye?"

2.H. Partiality

Luke 7:22
And He answered and said to them, "Go and report to John what you have seen and heard: the blind receive sight, the lame walk, the lepers are cleansed, and the deaf hear, the dead are raised up, **the poor have the gospel preached to them.**"

4.H. Helping Needy

Luke 7:25
"But what did you go out to see? A man dressed in soft clothing? Behold, those who are splendidly clothed and live in luxury and found in royal palaces."

2.G. Envy
2.H. Partiality

Luke 7:41–42
[41]"A certain moneylender had two debtors: one owed five hundred denarii, and the other fifty. [42]When they were unable to repay, he graciously forgave them both. Which of them therefore will love him more?"

1.D. Forgiveness

Luke 8:14–15
[14]"**And the seed which fell among the thorns,** these are the ones who have heard, and as they go on their way they are choked with worries and riches and pleasures of this life, and bring no fruit to maturity. [15]And the seed in the good soil, these are the ones who have heard the word in an honest and good heart, and hold it fast, and bear fruit with perseverance."

2.L. Futility of Riches

---

*God's principle of humility demonstrated in attitudes about finances.

Scripture:	Subtopic:

Luke 8:18
"Therefore take care how you listen; **for whoever has, to him shall more be given;** and whoever does not have, even what he thinks he has shall be taken away from him."

1.F. Obedience

Luke 9:3
And He said to them, **"Take nothing for your journey, neither a staff, nor a bag, nor bread, nor money; and do not even have two tunics apiece."**

1.H. Trust*

Luke 9:13
But He said to them, **"You give them something to eat!"** And they said, "We have no more than five loaves and two fish, unless perhaps we go and buy food for all these people."

9.E. Buying

Luke 9:23
And He was saying to them all, "If anyone wishes to come after Me, let him deny himself, and **take up His cross daily,** and follow Me."

1.F. Obedience

Luke 9:25
"For **what is a man profited if he gains the whole world,** and loses or forfeits himself?"

2.A. Love of Money
2.L. Futility of Riches

Luke 9:26
"For whoever is ashamed of Me and My words, of him will the Son of Man be ashamed when He comes in His glory, and the glory of the Father and of the holy angels."

1.A. Positive Attitudes

Luke 9:48
And said to them, **"Whoever receives this child in My name receives Me;** and whoever receives Me receives Him who sent Me; for he who is least among you, this is the one who is great."

4.H. Helping Needy

Luke 9:59–60
[59]And He said to another, "Follow Me." But he said, **"Permit me first to go and bury my father."** [60]But He said to him, "Allow the dead to bury their own dead; but as for you, go and proclaim everywhere the kingdom of God."

2.A. Love of Money

Luke 9:61–62
[61]And another also said, "I will follow You, Lord; but first **permit me to say good-bye to those at home."** [62]But Jesus said to him, "No one, after putting his hand to the plow and looking back, is fit for the kingdom of God."

1.F. Obedience

Luke 10:4
"Carry no purse, no bag, no shoes; and greet no one on the way."

1.H. Trust

---

*Also see Luke 22:35 for balance.

Scripture:	Subtopic:

Luke 10:7
"And stay in that house, eating and drinking what they give you; for the laborer is worthy of his wages. Do not keep moving from house to house."

12.B. Wages

Luke 10:35
"And on the next day he took out two denarii and gave them to the innkeeper and said, 'Take care of him; and whatever more you spend, when I return, I will repay you.'"

4.H. Helping Needy

Luke 11:13
"If you then, being evil, know how to give good gifts to your children, how much more shall your heavenly Father give the Holy Spirit to those who ask Him?"

4.B. Giving to Men

Luke 11:42
"But woe to you Pharisees! For you pay tithe of mint and rue and every kind of garden herb, and yet disregard justice and the love of God; but these are the things you should have done without neglecting the others."

4.C. Tithe

Luke 12:6
"Are not five sparrows sold for two cents? And yet not one of them is forgotten before God."

9.D. Selling

Luke 12:15
And He said to them, "Beware, and be on your guard against every form of greed; for not even when one has an abundance does his life consist of his possessions."

2.E. Greed

Luke 12:16–21
[16]And He told them a parable, saying, "The land of a certain rich man was very productive. [17]And he began reasoning to himself, saying, 'What shall I do, since I have no place to store my crops?' [18]And he said, 'This is what I will do: I will tear down my barns and build larger ones, and there I will store all my grain and my goods. [19]And I will say to my soul, "Soul, you have many goods laid up for many years to come; take your ease, eat, drink and be merry."' [20]But God said to him, 'You fool! This very night your soul is required of you; and now who will own what you have prepared?' [21]So is the man who lays up treasure for himself, and is not rich toward God."

2.E. Greed*

Luke 12:25
"And which of you being anxious can add a single cubit to his life's span?"

1.H. Trust
2.L. Futility of Riches

---

*Affluence was not his problem, greed was.

Scripture:	Subtopic:

Luke 12:29–31
²⁹"And **do not seek what you shall eat**, and what you shall drink, and do not keep worrying. ³⁰For all these things the nations of the world eagerly seek; but your Father knows that you need these things. ³¹But **seek for His kingdom**, and these things shall be added to you."

1.H. Trust

Luke 12:33
"**Sell your possessions** and give to charity; make yourselves purses which do not wear out, an unfailing treasure in heaven, where no thief comes near, nor moth destroys."

4.H. Helping Needy

Luke 12:34
"For **where your treasure is**, there will your heart be also."

1.H. Trust

Luke 12:42
And the Lord said, "Who then is the faithful and sensible steward, whom his master will put in charge of his servants, to give them their rations at the proper time?"

6.A. God's Promises
12.F. Diligent

Luke 12:44
"Truly I say to you, that **he will put him in charge of all his possessions.**"

6.A. God's Promises
12.F. Diligent

Luke 12:48
". . . but the one who did not know it, and committed deeds worthy of a flogging, will receive but few. And **from everyone who has been given much shall much be required**; and to whom they entrusted much, of him they will ask all the more."

9.F. Profit

Luke 12:58–59
⁵⁸"For while you are going with your opponent to appear before the magistrate, on your way there **make an effort to settle with him**, in order that he may not drag you before the judge, and the judge turn you over to the constable, and the constable throw you into prison. ⁵⁹I say to you, you shall not get out of there until you have paid the very last cent."

3.F. Paying Debts

Luke 14:11
"**For everyone who exalts himself shall be humbled,** and he who humbles himself shall be exalted."

1.C. Humility
2.K. Ego

Luke 14:12–14
¹²And He also went on to say to the one who had invited Him, "When you give a luncheon or a dinner, do not invite your friends or your brothers or your relatives or rich neighbors, lest they also invite you in return, and repayment come to you. ¹³But **when you give a reception, invite the poor,** the crippled, the lame, the blind, ¹⁴and you will be blessed, since they do not have the means to repay you; for you will be repaid at the resurrection of the righteous."

4.H. Helping Needy

Luke 14:28–30
28"For which one of you, **when he wants to build a tower,** does not
first sit down and calculate the cost, to see if he has enough to complete it?   29Otherwise, when he has laid a foundation, and is not
able to finish, all who observe it begin to ridicule him,   30saying,
'This man began to build and was not able to finish.' "

10. Planning

Luke 14:33
"So therefore, no one of you can be My disciple who does not **give
up all his own possessions."**

1.H. Trust

Luke 15:8–9
8"Or what woman, **if she has ten silver coins and loses one coin,**
does not light a lamp and sweep the house and search carefully
until she finds it?   9And when she has found it, she calls together
her friends and neighbors, saying, 'Rejoice with me, for I have
found the coin which I had lost!' "

1.E. Thankfulness

Luke 15:11–24
11And He said, **"A certain man had two sons;**   12and the younger of
them said to his father, 'Father, give me the share of the estate that
falls to me.' And he divided his wealth between them.   13And not
many days later, the younger son gathered everything together and
went on a journey into a distant country, and there he squandered
his estate with loose living.   14Now when he had spent everything,
a severe famine occurred in that country, and he began to be in
need.   15And he went and attached himself to one of the citizens of
that country, and he sent him into his fields to feed swine.   16And
he was longing to fill his stomach with the pods that the swine were
eating, and no one was giving anything to him.   17But when he
came to his senses, he said, 'How many of my father's hired men
have more than enough bread, but I am dying here with
hunger!   18I will get up and go to my father, and will say to him,
"Father, I have sinned against heaven, and in your sight;   19I am no
longer worthy to be called your son; make me as one of your hired
men."'   20And he got up and came to his father. But while he was
still a long way off, his father saw him, and felt compassion for
him, and ran and embraced him, and kissed him.   21And the son
said to him, 'Father, I have sinned against heaven and in your sight;
I am no longer worthy to be called your son.'   22But the father said
to his slaves, 'Quickly bring out the best robe and put it on him,
and put a ring on his hand and sandals on his feet;   23and bring the
fattened calf, kill it, and let us eat and be merry;   24for this son of
mine was dead, and has come to life again; he was lost, and has
been found.' And they began to make merry."

5.A. Inheritance

Luke 16:1–9
¹Now He was also saying to the disciples, "**There was a certain rich man who had a steward,** and this steward was reported to him as squandering his possessions. ²And he called him and said to him, 'What is this I hear about you? Give an account of your stewardship, for you can no longer be steward.' ³And the steward said to himself, 'What shall I do, since my master is taking the stewardship away from me? I am not strong enough to dig; I am ashamed to beg. ⁴I know what I shall do, so that when I am removed from the stewardship, they will receive me into their homes.' ⁵And he summoned each one of his master's debtors, and he began saying to the first, 'How much do you owe my master?' ⁶And he said, 'A hundred measures of oil.' And he said to him, 'Take your bill, and sit down quickly and write fifty.' ⁷Then he said to another, 'And how much do you owe?' And he said, 'A hundred measures of wheat.' He said to him, 'Take your bill, and write eighty.' ⁸And his master praised the unrighteous steward because he had acted shrewdly; for the sons of this age are more shrewd in relation to their own kind than the sons of light. ⁹And I say to you, make friends for yourselves by means of the mammon of unrighteousness; that when it fails, they may receive you into the eternal dwellings."

2.B. Bribe
2.F. Dishonesty

Luke 16:10
"**He who is faithful in a very little thing** is faithful also in much; and he who is unrighteous in a very little thing is unrighteous also in much."

1.F. Obedience

Luke 16:11–12
¹¹"If therefore **you have not been faithful in the use of unrighteous mammon,** who will entrust the true riches to you? ¹²And if you have not been faithful in the use of that which is another's, who will give you that which is your own?"

2.I. Disobedient*

Luke 16:13
"**No servant can serve two masters;** for either he will hate the one, and love the other, or else he will hold to one, and despise the other. You cannot serve God and mammon."

2.A. Love of Money

Luke 16:14
Now **the Pharisees, who were lovers of money,** were listening to all these things, and they were scoffing at Him.

2.A. Love of Money
2.E. Greed

*Money is an outside indicator of the inside spiritual condition.

Luke 16:19–25

[19]"Now there was a certain rich man, and he habitually dressed in purple** and fine linen, gaily living in splendor every day.   [20]And a certain poor man named Lazarus was laid at his gate, covered with sores,   [21]and longing to be fed with the crumbs which were falling from the rich man's table; besides, even the dogs were coming and licking his sores.   [22]Now it came about that the poor man died and he was carried away by the angels to Abraham's bosom; and the rich man also died and was buried.   [23]And in Hades he lifted up his eyes, being in torment, and saw Abraham far away, and Lazarus in his bosom.   [24]And he cried out and said, 'Father Abraham, have mercy on me, and send Lazarus, that he may dip the tip of his finger in water and cool off my tongue; for I am in agony in this flame.'   [25]But Abraham said, 'Child, remember that during your life you received your good things, and likewise Lazarus bad things; but now he is being comforted here, and you are in agony.'"

2.L. Futility of Riches
6.F. Justice

Luke 17:3

"Be on your guard! If a brother sins, rebuke him; and **if he repents, forgive him.**"

1.D. Forgiveness

Luke 17:31

"On that day, let not the one who is on the housetop and whose goods are in the house go down to take them away; and likewise **let not the one who is in the field turn back.**"

1.F. Obedience

Luke; 18:10–14

[10]"Two men went up into the temple to pray,** one a Pharisee, and the other a tax-gatherer.   [11]The Pharisee stood and was praying thus to himself, 'God, I thank Thee that I am not like other people: swindlers, unjust, adulterers, or even like this tax-gatherer.   [12]I fast twice a week; I pay tithes of all that I get.'   [13]But the tax-gatherer, standing some distance away, was even unwilling to lift up his eyes to heaven, but was beating his breast, saying, 'God, be merciful to me, the sinner!'   [14]I tell you, this man went down to his house justified rather than the other; for every one who exalts himself shall be humbled, but he who humbles himself shall be exalted."

1.C. Humility
2.C. Pride

Luke 18:22–25

[22]And when Jesus heard this, He said to him, "One thing you still lack; **sell all that you possess, and distribute it to the poor,** and you shall have treasure in heaven; and come, follow Me."   [23]But when he heard these things, he became very sad; for he was extremely rich.   [24]And Jesus looked at him and said, "How hard it is for those who are wealthy to enter the kingdom of God!   [25]For it is easier for a camel to go through the eye of a needle, than for a rich man to enter the kingdom of God."

2.L. Futility of Riches
4.H Helping Needy

Scripture:	Subtopic:

Luke 18:28–30

²⁸And Peter said, "**Behold, we have left our own homes,** and followed You." ²⁹And He said to them, "Truly I say to you, there is no one who has left house or wife or brothers or parents or children, for the sake of the kingdom of God, ³⁰who shall not receive many times as much at this time and in the age to come, eternal life."

1.H. Trust

Luke 19:8–9

⁸And **Zaccheus** stopped and said to the Lord, "Behold, Lord, **half of my possessions I will give to the poor,** and if I have defrauded anyone of anything, I will give back four times as much." ⁹And Jesus said to him, "Today salvation has come to this house, because he, too, is a son of Abraham."

11. Restitution

Luke 19:13–26

¹³"And **he called ten of his slaves, and gave them ten minas,** and said to them, 'Do business with this until I come back.' ¹⁴But his citizens hated him, and sent a delegation after him, saying, 'We do not want this man to reign over us.' ¹⁵And it came about that when he returned, after receiving the kingdom, he ordered that these slaves, to whom he had given the money, be called to him in order that he might know what business they had done. ¹⁶And the first appeared, saying, 'Master, your mina has made ten minas more.' ¹⁷And he said to him, 'Well done, good slave, because you have been faithful in a very little thing, be in authority over ten cities.' ¹⁸And the second came, saying, 'Your mina, master, has made five minas.' ¹⁹And he said to him also, 'And you are to be over five cities.' ²⁰And another came, saying, 'Master, behold your mina, which I kept put away in a handkerchief; ²¹for I was afraid of you, because you are an exacting man; you take up what you did not lay down, and reap what you did not sow.' ²²He said to him, 'By your own words I will judge you, you worthless slave. Did you know that I am an exacting man, taking up what I did not lay down, and reaping what I did not sow? ²³Then why did you not put the money in the bank, and having come, I would have collected it with interest?' ²⁴And he said to the bystanders, 'Take the mina away from him, and give it to the one who has the ten minas.' ²⁵And they said to him, 'Master, he has ten minas already.' ²⁶I tell you, that to everyone who has shall more be given, but from the one who does not have, even what he does have shall be taken away."

9.F. Profit

Luke 19:45–46

⁴⁵And He entered the temple and **began to cast out those who were selling,** ⁴⁶saying to them, "It is written, '**And My house shall be a house of prayer,**' but you have made it a robbers' den."

9.D. Selling

Luke 20:9–16

[9]And He began to tell the people this parable: "**A man planted a vineyard and rented it out to vine-growers,** and went on a journey for a long time. [10]And at the harvest time he sent a slave to the vine-growers, in order that they might give him some of the produce of the vineyard; but the vine-growers beat him and sent him away empty-handed. [11]And he proceeded to send another slave; and they beat him also and treated him shamefully, and sent him away empty-handed. [12]And he proceeded to send a third; and this one also they wounded and cast out. [13]And the owner of the vineyard said, 'What shall I do? I will send my beloved son; perhaps they will respect him.' [14]But when the vine-growers saw him, they reasoned with one another, saying, 'This is the heir; let us kill him that the inheritance may be ours.' [15]And they threw him out of the vineyard and killed him. What, therefore, will the owner of the vineyard do to them? [16]He will come and destroy these vine-growers and will give the vineyard to others." And when they heard it, they said, "May it never be!"

5.A. Inheritance

Luke 20:22

"**Is it lawful for us to pay taxes** to Caesar, or not?"

8.B. Administrative Tax

Luke 20:25

And He said to them, "Then render to Caesar the things that are Caesar's, and to God the things that are God's."

8.B. Administrative Tax

Luke 20:46–47

[46]"**Beware of the scribes,** who like to walk around in long robes, and love respectful greetings in the market places, and chief seats in the synagogues, and places of honor at banquets, [47]**who devour widows' houses,** and for appearance's sake offer long prayers; these will receive greater condemnation."

2.J. Injustice

Luke 21:1–4

[1]And He looked up and saw the rich putting their gifts into the treasury. [2]And He saw **a certain poor widow putting in two small copper coins.** [3]And He said, "Truly I say to you, this poor widow put in more than all of them; [4]for they all out of their surplus put into the offering; but she out of her poverty put in all that she had to live on."

4.D. Offerings

Luke 22:4–5

[4]And he went away and discussed with the chief priests and officers how he might betray Him to them. [5]And **they were glad, and agreed to give him money.**

2.B. Bribe

Luke 22:35

And He said to them, "When I sent you out without purse and bag and sandals, **you did not lack anything, did you?**" And they said, "No, nothing."

1.H. Trust

Scripture:	Subtopic:

Luke 23:2
And they began to accuse Him, saying, "**We found this man** mis-
leading our nation and **forbidding to pay taxes to Caesar,** and saying that He Himself is Christ, a King."

8.B. Administrative
Tax

John

Scripture:	Subtopic:

John 1:1–3
[1]In the beginning was the Word, and the Word was with God, and the Word was God. [2]He was in the beginning with God. [3]**All things came into being through Him,** and apart from Him nothing came into being that has come into being.

6.G. Wealth

John 2:14–16
[14]And He found in the temple those who were selling oxen and sheep and doves, and the moneychangers seated. [15]And He made a scourge of cords, and **drove them all out of the temple,** with the sheep and the oxen; and He poured out the coins of the money-changers, and overturned their tables; [16]and to those who were selling the doves He said, "Take these things away; stop making My Father's house a house of merchandise."

9.D. Selling

John 6:5–7
[5]Jesus therefore lifting up His eyes, and seeing that a great multitude was coming to Him, said to Philip, **"Where are we to buy bread, that these may eat?"** [6]And this He was saying to test him; for He Himself knew what He was intending to do. [7]Philip answered Him, "Two hundred denarii worth of bread is not sufficient for them, for everyone to receive a little."

9.E. Buying

John 6:27
"Do not work for the food which perishes, but for the food which endures to eternal life, which the Son of Man shall give to you, for on Him the Father, even God, has set His seal."

1.H. Trust

John 12:3–7
[3]**Mary therefore took a pound of very costly perfume of pure nard,** and anointed the feet of Jesus, and wiped His feet with her hair; and the house was filled with the fragrance of the perfume. [4]But Judas Iscariot, one of His disciples, who was intending to betray Him, said, [5]"Why was this perfume not sold for three hundred denarii, and given to poor people?" [6]Now he said this, not because he was concerned about the poor, but because he was a thief, and as he had the money box, he used to pilfer what was put into it. [7]Jesus therefore said, "Let her alone, in order that she may keep it for the day of My burial."

4.F. Gifts

John 12:25
"He who loves his life loses it; and he who hates his life in this world shall keep it to life eternal."

1.H. Trust
2.L. Futility of Riches

Scripture:	Subtopic:

John 12:26
"If anyone serves Me, let him follow Me; and where I am, there shall My servant also be; if anyone serves Me, the Father will honor him."

1.H. Trust

John 13:29
For some were supposing, because **Judas has the money box,** that Jesus was saying to him, "Buy the things we have need of for the feast"; or else, that he should give something to the poor.

9.E. Buying

John 15:19
"If you were of the world, the world would love its own; but because you are not of the world, but I chose you out of the world, therefore the world hates you."

6.B. Counsel of God

John 16:26–27
²⁶"**In that day you will ask in My name,** and I do not say to you that I will request the Father on your behalf; ²⁷for the Father Himself loves you, because you have loved Me, and have believed that I came forth from the Father."

6.A. God's Promises

John 21:3
Simon Peter said to them, "I am going fishing." They said to him, "We will also come with you." They went out, and got into the boat; and that night they caught nothing.

12.A. Work

John 21:15–17
¹⁵So when they had finished breakfast, Jesus said to Simon Peter, "Simon, son of John, do you love Me more than these?" He said to Him, "Yes, Lord; You know that I love You." He said to him, "Tend My lambs." ¹⁶He said to him a second time, "Simon, son of John, do you love Me?" He said to him, "Yes, Lord; You know that I love You." He said to him, "Shepherd My sheep." ¹⁷He said to him the third time, "Simon, son of John, do you love Me?" Peter was grieved because He said to him the third time, "Do you love Me?" And he said to Him, "Lord, You know all things; You know that I love You." Jesus said to him, "Tend My sheep."

1.A. Positive
1.F. Obedience

Acts

Scripture:	Subtopic:

Acts 2:44–45

⁴⁴And all **those who had believed were together, and had all things in common;** ⁴⁵and they began selling their property and possessions, and were sharing them with all, as anyone might have need.

4.H. Helping
   Needy
9.F. Profit

Acts 3:2–6

²And a certain man who had been lame from his mother's womb was being carried along, whom they used to set down every day at the gate of the temple which is called Beautiful, in order to beg alms of those who were entering the temple. ³And when he saw Peter and John about to go into the temple, he began asking to receive alms. ⁴And Peter, along with John, fixed his gaze upon him and said, "Look at us!" ⁵And he began to give them his attention, expecting to receive something from them. ⁶But Peter said, **"I do not possess silver and gold, but what I do have I give to you:** In the name of Jesus Christ the Nazarene—walk!"

4.H. Helping
   Needy

Acts 4:32–35

³²And the congregation of those who believed were of one heart and soul; and **not one of them claimed that anything belonging to him was his own;** but all things were common property to them. ³³And with great power the apostles were giving witness to the resurrection of the Lord Jesus, and abundant grace was upon them all. ³⁴For there was not a needy person among them, for all who were owners of land or houses would sell them and bring the proceeds of the sales, ³⁵and lay them at the apostles feet; and they would be distributed to each, as any had need.

4.H. Helping
   Needy

Acts 4:36–37

³⁶And Joseph, a Levite of Cyprian birth, who was also called **Barnabas** by the apostles (which translated means, Son of Encouragement), ³⁷and **who owned a tract of land,** sold it and brought the money and laid it at the apostles' feet.

4.D. Offerings
4.H. Helping
   Needy
9.F. Profit

Scripture:	Subtopic:

Acts 5:1–10

[1]But a certain man named Ananias, with his wife Sapphira, sold a piece of property, [2]and kept back some of the price for himself, with his wife's full knowledge, and bringing a portion of it, he laid it at the apostles' feet. [3]But Peter said, "Ananias, why has Satan filled your heart to lie to the Holy Spirit, and to keep back some of the price of the land? [4]While it remained unsold, did it not remain your own? And after it was sold, was it not under your control? Why is it that you have conceived this deed in your heart? You have not lied to men, but to God." [5]And as he heard these words, Ananias fell down and breathed his last; and great fear came upon all who heard of it. [6]And the young men arose and covered him up, and after carrying him out, they buried him. [7]Now there elapsed an interval of about three hours, and his wife came in, not knowing what had happened. [8]And Peter responded to her, "Tell me whether you sold the land for such and such a price?" And she said, "Yes, that was the price." [9]Then Peter said to her, "Why is it that you have agreed together to put the Spirit of the Lord to the test? Behold, the feet of those who have buried your husband are at the door, and they shall carry you out as well." [10]And she fell immediately at his feet, and breathed her last; and the young men came in and found her dead, and they carried her out and buried her beside her husband.

2.F. Dishonesty
4.G. Worthless Gifts
6.D. Selling

Acts 5:29

But Peter and the apostles answered and said, "We must obey God rather than men."

1.F. Obedience

Acts 6:1–2

[1]Now at this time the disciples were increasing in number, a complaint arose on the part of the Hellenistic Jews against the native Hebrews, because their widows were being overlooked in the daily serving of food. [2]And the twelve summoned the congregation of the disciples and said, "It is not desirable for us to neglect the word of God in order to serve tables."

4.H. Helping Needy

Acts 7:9

"And the patriarchs became jealous of Joseph and sold him into Egypt. And yet God was with him."

2.G. Envy

Acts 8:18–21

[18]Now when Simon saw that the Spirit was bestowed through the laying on of the apostles' hands, he offered them money, [19]saying, "Give this authority to me as well, so that everyone on whom I lay my hands may receive the Holy Spirit." [20]But Peter said to him, "May your silver perish with you, because you thought you could obtain the gift of God with money! [21]You have no part or portion in this matter, for your heart is not right before God."

2.B. Bribe

Scripture:	Subtopic:

Acts 8:27
And he arose and went; and behold, there was an Ethiopian eunuch, a court official of Candace, queen of the Ethiopians, who was in charge of all her treasure; and he had come to Jerusalem to worship.
— 1.C. Humility

Acts 10:2
. . . **a devout man,** and one who feared God with all his household, and **gave many alms to the Jewish people,** and prayed to God continually.
— 4.H. Helping Needy

Acts 10:4
And fixing his gaze upon him and being much alarmed, he said, "What is it, Lord?" And he said to him, "**Your prayers and alms have ascended as a memorial before God.**"
— 4.H. Helping Needy

Acts 10:31
". . . and he said, 'Cornelius, your prayer has been heard and **your alms have been remembered** before God.' "
— 4.H. Helping Needy

Acts 11:29
And in the proportion that any of the disciples had means, **each of them determined to send a contribution** for the relief of the brethren living in Judea.
— 4.H. Helping Needy

Acts 13:19
"And when He had destroyed seven nations in the land of Canaan, **He distributed their land as an inheritance**—all of which took about four hundred and fifty years."
— 5.A. Inheritance

Acts 14:9–10
This man was listening to Paul as he spoke, who, when he had fixed his gaze upon him, and had seen that he had faith to be made well, [10]said with a loud voice, "Stand upright on your feet." And he leaped up and began to walk.
— 1.H. Trust

Acts 16:14
And a certain woman named Lydia, from the city of Thyatira, a seller of purple fabrics, a worshiper of God, was listening; and the Lord opened her heart to respond to things spoken by Paul.
— 12.A. Work

Acts 16:16
And it happened that as we were going to the place of prayer, a certain slave-girl having a spirit of divination met us, who was bringing her masters much profit by fortunetelling.
— 2.E. Greed

Acts 16:19
But **when her masters saw that their hope of profit was gone, they seized Paul** and Silas and dragged them into the market place before the authorities.
— 2.E. Greed

Acts 17:29
"Being then the offspring of God, we ought not to think that the Divine Nature is like gold or silver or stone, an image formed by the art and thought of man."
— 7.B. False Gods

Scripture:	Subtopic:

Acts 18:3
. . . and because he was of the same trade, he stayed with them and they were working; for by their trade they were tent-makers.

12.A. Work

Acts 19:19
And many of **those who practiced magic brought their books together and began burning them** in the sight of all; and they counted up the price of them and found it fifty thousand pieces of silver.

1.F. Obedience

Acts 19:24–26
²⁴For a certain man named **Demetrius**, a silversmith, who made silver shrines of Artemis, was bringing no little business to the craftsmen; ²⁵these he gathered together with the workmen of similar trades, and said, "Men, you know that **our prosperity depends upon this business.** ²⁶And you see and hear that not only in Ephesus, but in almost all of Asia, this Paul has persuaded and turned away a considerable number of people, saying that gods made with hands are no gods at all."

2.E. Greed

Acts 20:33–35
³³"**I have coveted no one's silver or gold or clothes.** ³⁴You yourselves know that these hands ministered to my own needs and to the men who were with me. ³⁵In everything I showed you that by working hard in this manner you must help the weak and remember the words of the Lord Jesus, that He Himself said, 'It is more blessed to give than to receive.'"

1.G. Contentment
12.F. Diligent

Acts 21:24
"Take them and purify yourself along with them, and **pay their expenses** in order that they may shave their heads; and all will know that there is nothing to the things which they have been told about you, but that you yourself also walk orderly, keeping the Law."

4.D. Offerings

Acts 22:28
And the commander answered, "**I acquired this citizenship with a large sum of money.**" And Paul said, "But I was actually born a citizen."

9.E. Buying

Acts 24:17
"Now after several years **I came to bring alms to my nation** and to present offerings."

4.D. Offerings
4.H. Helping Needy

Acts 24:26
At the same time too, **he was hoping that money would be given him by Paul;** therefore he also used to send for him quite often and converse with him.

2.B. Bribe

Acts 28:30
And **he stayed two full years in his own rented quarters,** and was welcoming all who came to him.

9.E. Buying

Romans

Scripture:	Subtopic:
Romans 1:29 . . . being filled with all unrighteousness, wickedness, **greed**, evil; full of envy, murder, strife, deceit, malice; they are gossips.	2.E. Greed
Romans 2:21 . . . you, therefore, who teach another, do you not teach yourself? You who preach that one should not steal, **do you steal?**	2.F. Dishonesty
Romans 2:22 You who say that one should not commit adultery, do you commit adultery? You who abhor idols, **do you rob temples?**	2.E. Greed
Romans 6:16 Do you not know that when you present yourselves to someone as slaves for obedience, you are slaves of the one whom you obey, either of sin resulting in death, or of obedience resulting in righteousness?	1.H. Trust
Romans 6:23 For the wages of sin is death, but the free gift of God is eternal life in Christ Jesus our Lord.	12.B. Wages
Romans 8:23 And not only this, but also we ourselves, having the first fruits of the Spirit, even we ourselves groan within ourselves, **waiting eagerly for our adoption as sons,** the redemption of our body.	4.E. First Fruits
Romans 10:11–12 [11]For the Scripture says, **"Whoever believes in Him will not be disappointed."** [12]For there is no distinction between Jew and Greek; **for the same Lord is Lord of all, abounding in riches** for all who call upon Him.	6.A. God's Promises
Romans 11:34–36 [34]**For who has known the mind of the Lord, or who became His counselor?** [35]**Or who has first given to him that it might be paid back to him again?** [36]For from Him and through Him and to Him are all things. To Him be the glory forever. Amen.	4.I. Giving to Get
Romans 12:8 . . . or he who exhorts, in his exhortation; **he who gives, with liberality;** he who leads, with diligence; he who shows mercy, with cheerfulness.	4.F. Gifts

Scripture:	Subtopic:

Romans 12:16–17
[16]Be of the same mind toward one another; **do not be haughty in mind, but associate with the lowly.** Do not be wise in your own estimation. [17]Never pay back evil for evil to anyone. Respect what is right in the sight of all men.

1.C. Humility

Romans 13:1
Let every person be in subjection to the governing authorities. For there is no authority except from God, and those which exist are established by God.

8.B. Administrative Tax

Romans 13:6–7
[6]For **because of this you also pay taxes,** for rulers are servants of God, devoting themselves to this very thing. [7]Render to all what is due them: tax to whom tax is due; custom to whom custom; fear to whom fear; honor to whom honor.

8.B. Administrative Tax

Romans 13:8
Owe nothing to anyone except to love one another; for he who loves his neighbor has fulfilled the law.

3.F. Paying Debts

Romans 13:9
For this, "**You shall not commit adultery, You shall not murder, You shall not steal, You shall not covet,**" and if there is any other commandment, it is summed up in this saying, "**You shall love your neighbor as yourself.**"

1.B. Honesty

Romans 14:12
So then each one of us shall give account of himself to God.

1.J. Counsel of Men

Romans 15:26–27
[26]**For Macedonia and Achaia have been pleased to make a contribution** for the poor among the saints in Jerusalem. [27]Yes, they were pleased to do so, and they are indebted to them. For if the Gentiles have shared in their spiritual things, they are indebted to minister to them also in material things.

4.H. Helping Needy

I Corinthians

Scripture:	Subtopic:

I Corinthians 3:21–23
²¹So then let no one boast in men. For all things belong to you, ²²whether Paul or Appollos or Cephas or the world or life or death or things present or things to come; **all things belong to you,** ²³**and you belong to Christ;** and Christ belongs to God.

6.D. Provision

I Corinthians 4:8
You are already filled, **you have already become rich,** you have become kings without us; and I would indeed that you had become kings so that we also might reign with you.

2.K. Ego

I Corinthians 5:11
But actually, I wrote to you **not to associate with any so-called brother** if he should be an immoral person, or **covetous,** or an idolater, or a reviler, or a drunkard, or a swindler—not even to eat with such a one.

2.D. Covetousness

I Corinthians 6:1
Does any one of you, when he has a case against his neighbor, **dare to go to law** before the unrighteous, and not before the saints?

2.P. Suing

I Corinthians 6:10
. . . nor thieves, **nor the covetous,** nor drunkards, nor revilers, nor swindlers, shall inherit the kingdom of God.

2.D. Coveteousness
2.F. Dishonesty

I Corinthians 6:20
For you have been bought with a price: therefore glorify God in your body.

9.E. Buying

I Corinthians 7:23
You were bought with a price; do not become slaves of men.

9.E. Buying

I Corinthians 9:7
Who at any time serves as a soldier at his own expense? Who plants a vineyard, and does not eat the fruit of it? Or who tends a flock and does not use the milk of the flock?

12.B. Wages

I Corinthians 9:9–11
⁹For it is written in the Law of Moses, "**You shall not muzzle the ox while he is threshing.**" God is not concerned about oxen, is He? ¹⁰Or is He speaking altogether for our sake? Yes, for our sake it was written, because the plowman ought to plow in hope, and the thresher to thresh in hope of sharing the crops. ¹¹If we sowed spiritual things in you, is it too much if we should reap material things from you?

12.B. Wages

I Corinthians 9:14
So also **the Lord directed those who proclaim the gospel to get their living from the gospel.**

12.B. Wages

I Corinthians 10:26
For the earth is the LORD's, **and all it contains.**

6.G. Wealth

I Corinthians 10:31
Whether, then, you eat or drink or whatever you do, **do all to the glory of God.**

12.F. Diligent

I Corinthians 13:3
And if **I give all my possessions** to feed the poor, and if I deliver my body to be burned, but do not have love, it profits me nothing.

4.I. Giving to Get

I Corinthians 15:20–23
[20]But now Christ has been raised from the dead, the first fruits of those who are asleep. [21]For since by a man came death, by a man also came the resurrection of the dead. [22]For as in Adam all die, so also in Christ all shall be made alive. [23]But each in his own order: **Christ the first fruits,** after that those who are Christ's at His coming.

6.G. Wealth

I Corinthians 15:32
If from human motives I fought with wild beasts at Ephesus, what does it profit me? **If the dead are not raised, let us eat and drink, for tomorrow we die.**

2.L. Futility of Riches

I Corinthians 15:33
Do not be deceived: **"Bad company corrupts good morals."**

2.N. Bad Counsel

I Corinthians 16:1–2
[1]**Now concerning the collection for the Saints,** as I directed the churches of Galatia, so do you also. [2]On the first day of every week let each one of you put aside and save, as he may prosper, that no collections be made when I come.

4.H. Helping Needy

II Corinthians

Scripture:	Subtopic:

II Corinthians 2:17
For we are not like many, peddling the word of God, but as from
sincerity, but as from God, we speak in Christ in the sight of God.

1.B. Honesty

II Corinthians 6:10
. . . as sorrowful yet always rejoicing, **as poor yet making many
rich,** as having nothing yet possessing all things.

1.E. Thankfulness
4.H. Helping
Needy

II Corinthians 6:14–15
¹⁴**Do not be bound together with unbelievers;** for what partnership
have righteousness and lawlessness, or what fellowship has light
with darkness? ¹⁵Or what harmony has Christ with Belial, or
what has a believer in common with an unbeliever?

12.G. Yoke

II Corinthians 8:2–5
. . . ²that in a great ordeal of affliction their abundance of joy and
their deep poverty overflowed in the wealth of their liberality. ³For I testify that according to their ability, and beyond their
ability **they gave of their own accord,** ⁴begging us with much en-
treaty for the favor of participation in the support of the saints,
⁵and this, not as we had expected, but they first gave themselves to
the Lord and to us by the will of God.

4.H. Helping
Needy

II Corinthians 8:9
For you know the grace of our Lord Jesus Christ, that **though He
was rich, yet for your sake He became poor,** that you through His
poverty might become rich.

4.H. Helping
Needy

II Corinthians 8:11–12
¹¹But now finish doing it also; that just as there was the readiness to
desire it, so there may be also the completion of it by your ability. ¹²For if the readiness is present, **it is acceptable according to
what a man has,** not according to what he does not have.

4.H. Helping
Needy

II Corinthians 8:13–15
¹³For this is not for the ease of others and for your affliction, but by
way of equality— ¹⁴at this present time your abundance being a
supply for their want, that their abundance also may become a
supply for your want, that there may be equality; ¹⁵as it is written, "He who gathered much did not have too much, and he who
gathered little had no lack."

4.H. Helping
Needy

II Corinthians 9:6
Now this I say, **he who sows sparingly shall also reap sparingly;** and
he who sows bountifully shall also reap bountifully.

4.D. Offerings

Scripture:	Subtopic:

II Corinthians 9:7
Let each one do just as he has purposed in his heart; not grudgingly
or under compulsion; for God loves a cheerful giver.

4.F. Gifts

II Corinthians 9:8–13
⁸And God is able to make all grace abound to you, that always
having all sufficiency in everything, **you may have an abundance
for every good deed;** ⁹as it is written, **"He scattered abroad, He
gave to the poor, His righteousness abides forever."** ¹⁰Now **He who
supplies seed to the sower and bread for food, will supply and multiply your seed** for sowing and increase the harvest of your
righteousness; ¹¹you will be enriched in everything for all liberality, which through us is producing thanksgiving to God. ¹²For the
ministry of this service is not only fully supplying the needs of the
saints, but is also overflowing through many thanksgivings to God.
¹³Because of the proof given by this ministry they will glorify God
for your obedience to your confession of the gospel of Christ, and
for the liberality of your contribution to them and to all.

4.H. Helping
Needy

II Corinthians 11:7–9
⁷Or did I commit a sin in humbling myself that you might be
exalted, because I preached the gospel of God to you without
charge? ⁸**I robbed other churches, taking wages from them to
serve you;** ⁹and when I was present with you and was in need, I
was not a burden to anyone; for when the brethren came from
Macedonia, they fully supplied my need, and in everything I kept
myself from being a burden to you, and will continue to do so.

12.B. Wages

II Corinthians 12:14
Here for this third time I am ready to come to you, and I will not be
a burden to you; for I do not seek what is yours, but you; for children are not responsible to save up for their parents, but parents for
their children.

5.A. Inheritance

Galatians

Scripture:	Subtopic:

Galatians 2:10
They only asked us **to remember the poor**— the very thing I also was eager to do.
4.H. Helping Needy

Galatians 4:1
Now I say, **as long as the heir is a child,** he does not differ at all from a slave although he is owner of everything,
5.A. Inheritance

Galatians 4:7
Therefore **you are no longer a slave,** but a son; and if a son, then an heir through God.
5.A. Inheritance

Galatians 6:6
And let the one who is taught the word share all good things with him who teaches.
4.B. Giving to Men

Galatians 6:9
And let us not lose heart in doing good, for in due time we shall reap if we do not grow weary.
12.F. Diligent

Ephesians

Scripture:	Subtopic:

Ephesians 4:14
As a result, **we are no longer to be children,** tossed here and there
by waves, and carried about by every wind of doctrine, by the
trickery of men, by craftiness in deceitful scheming.

2.F. Dishonesty

Ephesians 4:28
Let him who steals steal no longer; but rather let him labor, per-
forming with his own hands what is good, in order that he may
have something to share with him who has need.

2.F. Dishonesty
12.A. Work

Ephesians 5:3
But do not let immorality or any impurity or **greed even be named
among you,** as is proper among saints.

2.E. Greed

Ephesians 5:5
For this you know with certainty, that no immoral or impure person
or **covetous man,** who is an idolater, **has an inheritance** in the kingdom of Christ and God.

2.D. Covetousness

Ephesians 6:4
And, **fathers, do not provoke your children** to anger; but bring
them up in the discipline and instruction of the Lord.

5.B. Counsel and
Discipline

Philippians

Scripture:	Subtopic:

Philippians 2:3
Do nothing from selfishness or empty conceit, but with humility of mind let each of you regard one another as more important than himself.

1.C. Humility

Philippians 4:6
Be anxious for nothing, but in everything by prayer and supplication with thanksgiving let your requests be made known to God.

1.H. Trust

Philippians 4:11–14
[11]**Not that I speak from want;** for I have learned to be content in whatever circumstances I am. [12]I know how to get along with humble means, and I also know how to live in prosperity; in any and every circumstance I have learned the secret of being filled and going hungry, both of having abundance and suffering need. [13]I can do all things through Him who strengthens me. [14]Nevertheless, you have done well to share with me in my affliction.

1.G. Contentment

Philippians 4:15–18
[15]And you yourselves also know, Philippians, that at the first preaching of the gospel, after I departed from Macedonia, no church shared with me in the matter of giving and receiving but you alone; [16]for even in Thessalonica **you sent a gift more than once for my needs.** [17]Not that I seek the gift itself, but I seek for the profit which increases to your account. [18]But I have received everything in full, and have an abundance; I am amply supplied, having received from Epaphroditus what you have sent, a fragrant aroma, an acceptable sacrifice, well-pleasing to God.

4.H. Helping Needy

Philippians 4:19
And my God shall supply all your needs according to His riches in glory in Christ Jesus.

6.D. Provision

Colossians

Scripture:	Subtopic:

Colossians 2:14
. . . having canceled out the certificate of debt consisting of decrees against us and which was hostile to us; and He has taken it out of the way, having nailed it to the cross.

3.F. Paying Debts

Colossians 2:16
Therefore let no one act as your judge in regard to food or drink or in respect to a festival or a new moon or a Sabbath day.

2.H. Partiality

Colossians 2:23
These are matters which have, to be sure, the appearance of wisdom in self-made religion and self-abasement and severe treatment of the body, but are of no value against fleshly indulgence.

2.F. Dishonesty

Colossians 3:2–3
²**Set your mind on the things above,** not on the things that are on earth.   ³For you have died and your life is hidden with Christ in God.

1.H. Trust

Colossians 3:5
Therefore consider the members of your earthly body as dead to immorality, impurity, passion, evil desire, and greed, which amounts to idolatry.

7.B. False Gods

Colossians 3:17
And whatever you do in word or deed, **do all in the name of the Lord Jesus,** giving thanks through Him to God the Father.

12.F. Diligent

Colossians 3:23
Whatever you do, **do your work heartily,** as for the Lord rather than for men.

12.A. Work
12.F. Diligent

I Thessalonians

Scripture:	Subtopic:

I Thessalonians 2:5
For we never came with flattering speech, as you know, **nor with a pretext for greed**—God is witness.

2.E. Greed

I Thessalonians 4:12
. . . so that you may behave properly toward outsiders and **not be in any need.**

12.A. Work

I Thessalonians 5:18
In everything give thanks; for this is God's will for you in Christ Jesus.

1.E. Thankfulness

II Thessalonians

Scripture:	Subtopic:

II Thessalonians 3:6
Now we command you, brethren, in the name of the Lord Jesus Christ, that you keep aloof from every brother who leads an unruly life and not according to the tradition which you received from us.

2.N. Bad Counsel

II Thessalonians 3:8
. . . nor did we eat anyone's bread without paying for it, but with labor and hardship we kept working night and day so that we might not be a burden to any of you.

12.A. Work
12.F. Diligent

II Thessalonians 3:10
For even when we were with you, we used to give you this order: **if anyone will not work, neither let him eat.**

12.A. Work
12.E. Slothful

I Timothy

Scripture:	Subtopic:

I Timothy 3:3
. . . not addicted to wine or pugnacious, but gentle, uncontentious, **free from the love of money.**

1.G. Contentment

I Timothy 3:8
Deacons likewise must be **men of dignity, not** double-tongued, or addicted to much wine or **fond of sordid gain.**

1.B. Honesty
2.F. Dishonesty

I Timothy 5:3
Honor widows who are widows indeed.

4.D. Offerings
4.H. Helping
      Needy

I Timothy 5:5
Now **she who is a widow, indeed,** and who has been left alone has fixed her hope on God, and continues in entreaties and prayers night and day.

4.H. Helping
      Needy

I Timothy 5:8
But **if any one does not provide for his own,** and especially for those of his household, he has denied the faith, and is worse than an unbeliever.

5.C. Provision

I Timothy 5:16
If any woman who is a believer has dependent widows, let her assist them, and let not the church be burdened, so that it may assist those who are widows indeed.

4.H. Helping
      Needy

I Timothy 5:18
For the Scripture says, **"You shall not muzzle the ox while he is threshing,"** and "The laborer is worthy of his wages."

12.B. Wages

I Timothy 6:5–8
. . . [5]and constant friction between **men of depraved mind** and deprived of the truth, **who suppose that godliness is a means of gain.** [6]But godliness actually is a means of great gain, when accompanied by contentment. [7]For we have brought nothing into the world, so we cannot take anything out of it either. [8]And if we have food and covering, with these we shall be content.

1.E. Thankfulness
1.G. Contentment
2.E. Greed
5.C. Provision

I Timothy 6:9
But **those who want to get rich** fall into temptation and a snare and many foolish and harmful desires which plunge men into ruin and destruction.

2.A. Love of
      Money
2.L. Futility of
      Riches

Scripture:	Subtopic:

I Timothy 6:10
For **the love of money is a root of all sorts of evil,** and some by longing for it have wandered away from the faith, and pierced themselves with many a pang.

9.C. Get Rich
2.A. Love of Money

I Timothy 6:17
Instruct those who are rich in this present world not to be conceited or to fix their hope on the uncertainty of riches, but on God, who richly supplies us with all things to enjoy.

2.C. Pride
2.K. Ego
2.L. Futility of Riches

I Timothy 6:18–19
[18]Instruct them to do good, to be rich in good works, **to be generous and ready to share,** [19]storing up for themselves the treasure of a good foundation for the future, so that they may take hold of that which is life indeed.

4.H. Helping Needy

II Timothy

Scripture:	Subtopic:

II Timothy 2:4
No soldier in active service **entangles himself in the affairs of every-day life,** so that he may please the one who enlisted him as a soldier.

12.A. Work

II Timothy 2:6
The hard-working farmer ought to be the first to receive his share of the crops.

12.A. Work

II Timothy 3:1–2
[1]But realize this, that in the last days difficult times will come. [2]For **men will be lovers of self, lovers of money,** boastful, arrogant, revilers, disobedient to parents, ungrateful, unholy.

2.A. Love of Money

II Timothy 3:16–17
[16]**All Scripture is inspired** by God and profitable for teaching, for reproof, for correction, for training in righteousness; [17]that the man of God may be adequate, equipped for every good work.

1.H. Trust

Titus

Scripture:	Subtopic:

Titus 1:7
For **the overseer must be above** reproach as God's steward, not self-willed, not quick-tempered, not addicted to wine, not pugnacious, not fond of sordid gain.

1.B. Honesty

Titus 1:11
. . . who must be silenced because they are upsetting whole families, **teaching things they should not teach,** for the sake of sordid gain.

2.E. Greed

Titus 2:10
. . . **not pilfering**, but showing all good faith that they may adorn the doctrine of God our Savior in every respect.

1.B. Honesty

Philemon

Scripture:	Subtopic:

Philemon 18–19

[18]But if he has wronged you in any way, or owes you anything, **charge that to my account;** [19]I, Paul, am writing this with my own hand, I will repay it (lest I should mention to you that you owe to me even your own self as well).

3.F. Paying Debts

Hebrews

Scripture:	Subtopic:

Hebrews 7:1–9
¹**For this Melchizedek**, king of Salem, priest of the Most High God, who met Abraham as he was returning from the slaughter of the kings and blessed him, ²to whom also Abraham apportioned a tenth part of all the spoils, was first of all, by the translation of his name, king of righteousness, and then also king of Salem, which is king of peace. ³Without father, without mother, without geneal- ogy, having neither beginning of days nor end of life, but made like the Son of God, he abides a priest perpetually. ⁴Now observe how great this man was to whom Abraham, the patriarch, **gave a tenth of the choicest spoils.** ⁵And those indeed of the sons of Levi who receive the priest's office have commandment in the Law to collect a tenth from the people, that is, from their brethren, although these are descended from Abraham. ⁶But the one whose genealogy is not traced from them collected a tenth from Abraham, and blessed the one who had the promises. ⁷But without any dispute the lesser is blessed by the greater. ⁸And in this case mortal men receive tithes, but in that case one receives them, of whom it is witnessed that he lives on. ⁹And, so to speak, through **Abraham even Levi, who received tithes, paid tithes.**

4.C. Tithe

Hebrews 9:16–17
¹⁶For where a covenant is, there must of necessity be the death of the one who made it. ¹⁷For **a covenant is valid only when men are dead,** for it is never in force while the one who made it lives.

1.K. Paying Vows

Hebrews 10:34
For you showed sympathy to the prisoners, and **accepted joyfully the seizure of your property,** knowing that you have for yourselves a better possession and an abiding one.

4.H. Helping Needy

Hebrews 11:26
. . . considering **the reproach of Christ greater riches than the trea- sures of Egypt;** for he was looking to the reward.

1.F. Obedience

Hebrews 12:16–17
. . . ¹⁶that there be no immoral or godless person **like Esau, who sold his own birthright** for a single meal. ¹⁷For you know that even afterwards, when he desired to inherit the blessing, he was re- jected, for he found no place for repentance, though he sought for it with tears.

5.A. Inheritance

Hebrews 13:5
Let your character be free from the love of money, being content with what you have; for He Himself has said, "**I will never desert you, nor will I ever forsake you.**"

1.G. Contentment

James

Scripture:	Subtopic:

James 1:1–3
[1]James, a bond-servant of God and of the Lord Jesus Christ, to the twelve tribes who are dispersed abroad, greetings. [2]**Consider it all joy, my brethern,** when you encounter various trials, [3]knowing that the testing of your faith produces endurance.

1.E. Thankfulness

James 1:10–11
[10]And **let the rich man glory in his humiliation,** because like flowering grass he will pass away. [11]For the sun rises with a scorching wind, and withers the grass; and its flower falls off, and the beauty of its appearance is destroyed; so too the rich man in the midst of his pursuits will fade away.

2.L. Futility of Riches

James 1:18
In the exercise of His will He brought us forth by the word of truth, so that we might be, as it were, **the first fruits among His creatures.**

4.E. First Fruits

James 1:22
But prove yourselves doers of the word, and not merely hearers who delude themselves.

1.F. Obedience

James 1:27
This is pure and undefiled religion in the sight of our God and Father, to **visit orphans and widows in their distress,** and to keep oneself unstained by the world.

4.H. Helping Needy

James 2:1–16

¹My brethren, **do not hold your faith in our glorious Lord Jesus Christ with an attitude of personal favoritism.** ²For if a man comes into your assembly with a gold ring and dressed in fine clothes, and there also comes in a poor man in dirty clothes, ³and you pay special attention to the one who is wearing the fine clothes, and say, "You sit here in a good place," and you say to the poor man, "You stand over there, or sit down by my footstool," ⁴have you not made distinctions among yourselves, and become judges with evil motives? ⁵Listen, my beloved brethren: **did not God choose the poor of this world** to be rich in faith and heirs of the kingdom which He promised to those who love Him? ⁶But you have dishonored the poor man. Is it not the rich who oppress you and personally drag you into court? ⁷Do they not blaspheme the fair name by which you have been called? ⁸If, however, you are fulfilling the royal law, according to the Scripture, "**You shall love your neighbor as yourself,**" you are doing well. ⁹But if you show partiality, you are committing sin and are convicted by the law as transgressors. ¹⁰For whoever keeps the whole law and yet stumbles in one point, he has become guilty of all. ¹¹For He who said, "**Do not commit adultery,**" also said, "**Do not commit murder.**" Now if you do not commit adultery, but do commit murder, you have become a transgressor of the law. ¹²So speak and so act, as those who are to be judged by the law of liberty. ¹³For judgment will be merciless to one who has shown no mercy; mercy triumphs over judgment. ¹⁴What use is it, my brethren, if a man says he has **faith, but he has no works?** Can that faith save him? ¹⁵**If a brother or sister is without clothing and in need of daily food,** ¹⁶and one of you says to them, "Go in peace, be warmed and be filled," and yet you do not give them what is necessary for their body, what use is that?

2.J. Injustice
4.H. Helping Needy

James 4:1–3

¹What is your source of quarrels and conflicts among you? Is it not the source of your pleasures that wage war in your members? ²**You lust and do not have;** so you commit murder. And you are envious and cannot obtain; so you fight and quarrel. You do not have because you do not ask. ³**You ask and do not receive, because you ask with wrong motives,** so that you may spend it on your pleasures.

2.E. Greed
2.G. Envy

James 4:13–14

¹³**Come now, you who say, "Today or tomorrow, we shall go to such and such a city,** and spend a year there and engage in business and make a profit." ¹⁴Yet you do not know what your life will be like tomorrow. You are just a vapor that appears for a little while and then vanishes away.

9.F. Profit

Scripture: Subtopic:

James 5:1–5

¹Come now, you rich, weep and howl for your miseries which are coming upon you.   ²Your riches have rotted and your garments have become moth-eaten.   ³Your gold and your silver have rusted; and their rust will be a witness against you and will consume your flesh like fire. It is in the last days that you have stored up your treasure!   ⁴Behold, the pay of the laborers who mowed your fields, and which has been withheld by you, cries out against you; and the outcry of those who did the harvesting has reached the ears of the Lord of Sabaoth.   ⁵You have lived luxuriously on the earth and led a life of wanton pleasure; you have fattened your hearts in a day of slaughter.

2.L. Futility of Riches

12.B. Wages

I Peter

Scripture:	Subtopic:

I Peter 1:7
. . . that **the proof of your faith, being more precious than gold** which is perishable, even though tested by fire, may be found to result in praise and glory and honor at the revelation of Jesus Christ.

1.H. Trust

I Peter 1:18
. . . knowing that **you were not redeemed with perishable things** like silver or gold from your futile way of life inherited from your forefathers.

2.L. Futility of Riches

I Peter 2:1
Therefore, **putting aside all malice** and all guile and hypocrisy and envy and all slander.

2.G. Envy

I Peter 2:14
. . . or to **governors as sent by him for the punishment of evildoers** and the praise of those who do right.

7.A. To Wicked

I Peter 3:3–4
[3]And **let not your adornment be merely external**—braiding the hair, and wearing gold jewelry, and putting on dresses; [4]but let it be the hidden person of the heart, with the imperishable quality of a gentle and quiet spirit, which is precious in the sight of God.

2.C. Pride

I Peter 4:11
Whoever speaks, let him speak, as it were, the utterances of God; whoever serves, let him do so as by the strength which God supplies; **so that in all things God may be glorified** through Jesus Christ, to whom belongs the glory and dominion forever and ever. Amen.

12.F. Diligent

I Peter 4:15
By no means let any of you suffer as a murderer, or thief, or evil-doer, or a troublesome meddler.

2.F. Dishonesty

I Peter 5:2
Shepherd the flock of God among you, not under compulsion, but voluntarily, according to the will of God; and **not for sordid gain,** but with eagerness.

1.G. Contentment

II Peter

Scripture:	Subtopic:

II Peter 1:5–6
[5]Now for this very reason also, applying all diligence, in your faith supply moral excellence, and in your moral excellence, knowledge; [6]and **in your knowledge, self-control,** and in your self-control, perseverance, and in your perseverance, godliness.

1.G. Contentment

II Peter 2:3
. . . and **in their greed they will exploit** you with false words; their judgment from long ago is not idle, and their destruction is not asleep.

2.E. Greed

II Peter 2:14
. . . having eyes full of adultery and that never cease from sin; enticing unstable souls, **having a heart trained in greed,** accursed children.

2.E. Greed

II Peter 2:15
. . . forsaking the right way they have gone astray, **having followed the way of Balaam, the son of Beor,** who loved the wages of unrighteousness.

2.F. Dishonesty

I John

Scripture:	Subtopic:

I John 2:15–16

15Do not love the world, nor the things in the world. If anyone loves the world, the love of the Father is not in him. 16For all that is in the world, the lust of the flesh and the lust of the eyes and the boastful pride of life, is not from the Father, but is from the world.

1.A. Positive Attitudes
2.C. Pride

I John 3:17–18

17But whoever has the world's goods, and beholds his brother in need and closes his heart against him, how does the love of God abide in him? 18Little children, let us not love with word or with tongue, but in deed and truth.

4.H. Helping Needy

III John

Scripture:	Subtopic:

III John 6–7
⁶. . . and they bear witness to your love before the church; and you **will do well to send them on their way in a manner worthy of God.** ⁷For they went out for the sake of the Name, accepting nothing from the Gentiles.

4.H. Helping Needy
12.B. Wages

III John 8
Therefore **we ought to support such men,** that we may be fellow workers with the truth.

4.D. Offerings

Jude

Scripture:	Subtopic:

Jude 11
Woe to them! For they have gone the way of Cain, and for pay **they have rushed headlong into the error of Balaam**, and perished in the rebellion of Korah.

2.E. Greed

Revelation

Scripture:	Subtopic:

Revelation 2:9
"**I know your tribulation and your poverty** (but you are rich), and the blasphemy by those who say they are Jews and are not, but are a synagogue of Satan."

1.C. Humility

Revelation 2:19
"I know your deeds, and your love and faith and service and perseverance, and that your deeds of late are greater than the first."

12.F. Diligent

Revelation 3:17–18
[17]"**Because you say, 'I am rich**, and have become wealthy, and have need of nothing,' and you do not know that you are wretched and miserable and poor and blind and naked, [18]I advise you to buy from Me gold refined by fire, that you may become rich, and white garments, that you may clothe yourself; and that the shame of your nakedness may not be revealed; and eye salve to anoint your eyes, that you may see."

2.C. Pride

Revelation 5:12
. . . saying with a loud voice, "Worthy is the Lamb that was slain to receive power and riches and wisdom and might and honor and glory and blessing."

1.L. Wisdom

Revelation 6:6
And I heard as it were a voice in the center of the four living creatures saying, "**A quart of wheat for a denarius, and three quarts of barley for a denarius;** and do not harm the oil and the wine."

9.D. Selling

Revelation 6:15
And the kings of the earth and the great men and the commanders and **the rich and the strong and every slave and free man, hid** themselves in the caves and among the rocks of the mountains.

6.F. Justice

Revelation 7:16
"**They shall hunger no more,** neither thirst anymore; neither shall the sun beat down on them, nor any heat."

4.H. Helping Needy

Revelation 9:20
And **the rest of mankind,** who were not killed by these plagues, **did not repent of the works of their hands,** so as not to worship demons, and the idols of gold and of silver and of brass and of stone and of wood, which can neither see nor hear nor walk.

2.I. Disobedient
7.B. False Gods

Revelation 13:16
And he causes all, **the small and the great, and the rich and the poor,** and the free men and the slaves, **to be given a mark** on their right hand, or on their forehead.

7.B. False Gods

Scripture:	Subtopic:

Revelation 13:17
. . . and he provides that **no one should be able to buy or to sell,** except the one who has the mark, either the name of the beast or the number of his name.

9.E. Buying

Revelation 14:4
These are the ones who have not been defiled with women, for they have kept themselves chaste. These are the ones who follow the Lamb wherever He goes. These have been purchased **from among men as first fruits to God** and to the Lamb.

4.E. First Fruits

Revelation 17:4
And **the woman** was clothed in purple and scarlet, and **adorned with gold and precious stones** and pearls, having in her hand a gold cup full of abominations and of the unclean things of her immorality.

2.L. Futility of Riches

Revelation 18:3
"For all the nations have drunk of the wine of the passion of her immorality, and the kings of the earth have committed acts of immorality with her, and **the merchants of the earth have become rich by the wealth** of her sensuality."

2.E. Greed
7.B. False Gods

Revelation 18:11
"And the merchants of the earth weep and mourn over her, because **no one buys their cargoes any more."**

9.E. Buying

Revelation 18:12–13
[12] . . . **cargoes of gold and silver and precious stones** and pearls and fine linen and purple and silk and scarlet, and every kind of citron wood and every article of ivory and every article made from very costly wood and bronze and iron and marble, [13]and cinnamon and spice and incense and perfume and frankincense and wine and olive oil and fine flour and wheat and cattle and sheep, and cargoes of horses and chariots and slaves and human lives.

2.L. Futility of Riches

Revelation 18:14–19
[14]"And the fruit you long for has gone from you, and all things that were luxurious and splendid have passed away from you and men will no longer find them. [15]**The merchants of these things, who became rich from her,** will stand at a distance because of the fear of her torment, weeping and mourning, [16]saying, 'Woe, woe, the great city, she who was clothed in fine linen and purple and scarlet, and adorned with gold and precious stones and pearls; [17]for in one hour such great wealth has been laid waste!' And every shipmaster and every passenger and sailor, and as many as make their living by the sea, stood at a distance, [18]and were crying out as they saw the smoke of her burning, saying, 'What city is like the great city?' [19]And they threw dust on their heads and were crying out, weeping and mourning, saying, 'Woe, woe, the great city, in which all who had ships at sea became rich by her wealth, for in one hour she has been laid waste!'"

6.F. Justice
6.E. Discipline

Scripture:	Subtopic:

Revelation 21:6–7

[6]And He said to me, "It is done. I am the Alpha and Omega, the beginning and the end. I will give to the one who thirsts from the spring of the water of life without cost.   [7]He who overcomes shall inherit these things, and I will be his God and he will be My son."

4.F. Gifts
5.A. Inheritance

Revelation 22:17

And the Spirit and the bride say, "Come." And let the one who hears say, "Come." And let the one who is thirsty come; let the one who wishes to take the water of life without cost.

4.F. Gifts

About the Author

Larry Burkett is the founder and director of Christian Financial Concepts, a nonprofit, nondenominational ministry dedicated to teaching God's principles of handling money. He has written over 10 books and is heard daily on the five-minute radio program *How to Manage Your Money*, broadcast on almost 800 outlets in the U.S. and abroad. He also hosts a 30-minute, live call-in program, *Money Matters*, broadcast on more than 250 outlets. Burkett is the father of four children and resides in Dahlonega, Ga., with his wife, Judy.

Other works by Larry Burkett include:

- *Your Finances in Changing Times*
- *How to Manage Your Money*
- *The Financial Planning Workbook*
- *What Husbands Wish Their Wives Knew About Money*
- *Using Your Money Wisely*
- *God's Guide Through the Money Jungle*
- *Answers to Your Family's Financial Questions*
- *The Complete Financial Guide for Young Couples*
- *Debt-free Living*